Collected Poems
1958–2015

ALSO BY CLIVE JAMES

CLIVE JAMES

Collected Poems
1958–2015

PICADOR

First published 2016 by Picador
an imprint of Pan Macmillan
20 New Wharf Road, London N1 9RR
Associated companies throughout the world
www.panmacmillan.com

ISBN 978-1-5098-1240-0

To Prue

Or v'è sola una piuma, che all'invito
Del vento esita, palpita leggera:
Qual sogno antico in anima severa
Fuggente sempre e non ancor fuggito.

Pascoli

A single feather sought out by the wind
Hesitates and lightly trembles,
As an old desire remains in a strict soul:
Always about to fly but not yet flown.

Quod si inseris me lyricis vatibus,
feriam sidera sublimi vertici.

Horace

If you rank me with the lyric poets,
my exalted head shall strike the stars.

Each man starts with his very first breath
To devise shrewd means for outwitting death.

James Cagney

Acknowledgements

In past collections I was always careful to list the publications in which my poems first appeared, and to thank their editors. But here at the end of a long life the full list would go on for pages, and the names of the editors would look like a mechanically historicist notation, especially since some of them are by now deceased. Almost in that condition myself, I feel justified in providing a mere sketch. Some names, however, were crucial in those times when I was either only just emerging as a poet, or else threatening to destroy my incipient literary reputation in the gaudy fire of celebrity accruing to regular appearances on television. No matter how well-known I got in all the wrong ways, the London editors Karl Miller, Ian Hamilton and John Gross still printed my poems, as did Claire Tomalin and Anthony Thwaite, nowadays the only survivors of that brilliant crew. Young writers of today sometimes look back in envy on the bustling cockpit of the London Literary World in the 1960s and 1970s, but unless they realize the decisive importance of the editors they miss the real story. The editors could write; which meant that the poets could not bluff them, and had to graft hard for prominence. In the back of the limousine to the studio, I was very aware that I might not look as if I were starving for my art.

In more recent times, after I retired from the small screen at the turn of the millennium, my personal picture clarified; and after I fell ill ten years later I necessarily looked almost as serious as a writer can get. In cold fact I went on writing because there were still some subjects waiting for their proper expression, so really I was beginning again. To help make that latter-day ambition seem worthwhile, the judgment of editors continued to play a part. Though the structure of literary journalism went on dissolving towards a condition of universal click-bait, there were still, at key points, highly qualified people on the lookout for work that might last; and I would particularly like to acknowledge the scrupulous attentions of Alan Jenkins at the *TLS*, Paul Muldoon at the *New Yorker*, Christian Wiman at *Poetry* (Chicago), Daniel Johnson at *Standpoint*, Tom Gatti at the *New Statesman* and Hugo Williams at the *Spectator*. In Australia, Les Murray at *Quadrant* has continued with his kind willingness to bring some of my work home: our country's supreme poet would be an historically important editor and anthologist even if he had never written a poem of his own. Peter Rose at the *Australian Book Review* and Peter Craven at *Best Australian Poems* have also been generous with their hospitality. Sometimes a single editor, by taking a single initiative, can alter the geography of a poet's ambition: during her time at the *New Yorker*, Tina Brown published my poem 'What Happened to Auden', and suddenly I saw the possibility of ranging across the Atlantic. In later years, and also in New York, Robert Weil has been a great encouragement by offering me access to his publishing labels at Norton and Liveright. The poems that have come to me in the recent period of my ill health have benefited greatly from close reading by Stephen Edgar, David Free, Tom Stoppard and two members of my immediate family, Prue Shaw and Claerwen James. Finally and as always, I should bless my luck in having attracted the curatorial advice and courage of Don Paterson at Picador: courage because for the editor of a lifetime collection to suggest to the poet that some of his poems might be better left out is to court tears and petulance. But if it is not done, the volume dies of its own dimensions; and after all those years as a professional entertainer I would not like to lose the virtues of keeping things brief.

Contents

Introduction

For this collection I have chosen, from a lifetime's work in verse, only those poems and lyrics that I believe might stand alone. Previous selections – *Other Passports*, *The Book of My Enemy* and *Opal Sunset* – were already winnowings, and this volume makes even more of a point out of setting things aside that once cost many nights of labour. At the time, I thought that anything I wrote was indispensable, but eventually, sometimes after only a decade or so, a sense of proportion came to the rescue. With a few exceptions, my longer poems have been left out on the grounds that they were tied to their time; although one day *Peregrine Prykke's Pilgrimage* might return in a book of its own, because its picture of the London Literary World still strikes me as true even if most of its cast have by now been carried from the stage. The excitement of that clueless young man as he took his place among the poets and the critics was still with him as he met his doom.

Excitement and poetry ought never to be alien to one another, but there is always a tendency, in the homeland of poetry in English, to look on the fabulously rich literary heritage as an established church. The privilege of the American, Irish and Australian poets – not to mention poets from Canada, South Africa, New Zealand, India and the Caribbean, and there might be one from Belize – is to provide fresh reminders that the tradition is not a litany, but a permanent upheaval, not to say a carnival. As an Australian in England for more than half a century, I have never felt cause to stop setting some of my poems in my homeland. The British readership likes hearing about it, and nowadays even the Americans can make a fair stab at guessing where Australia is. As for the critics, guardians of the ramparts, eventually they have to listen to the readers: and anyway the jokes about Australian culture being a contradiction in terms are by now so out of date that only a politician would use them, out of his head on Australian wine as he does so. There are quite a few poems about Australia here, even more of them near the end than near the beginning; but really they are all about the English language, which is the powerhouse at the heart of the subject. Even a poem about nothing would have to be about that.

Poems about nothing can be useful to anyone who wants to combine cult status with academic respectability, but that combination always struck me as something dependent on an abstract concept of literature, instead of arising from the sung lyricism of the English lyric before Shakespeare – the same sung lyricism that my daughters heard when they bopped around with Abba's greatest hits blasting in their headphones, and that is heard today by my granddaughter, aged ten, as she contemplates on YouTube the enthralling intricacies of Taylor Swift singing 'We Are Never Ever Getting Back Together'. When the poem strays too far from the song it risks death by refinement. Luckily, from my Cambridge Footlights days onward, I was in a position to test this idea through my working partnership with Pete Atkin. Some of the lyrics I wrote for him are here. The music is on his albums, and shows what the form and its punctuation are meant to be like: but the lyric on the page still has the phrasing, which, for me, is the bedrock of the whole thing. If a poem or a lyric does not end up studded with turns of phrase that I had no idea were going to happen, I should not have begun it.

But it's easy to lay down the law now, when the light is fading. The trick is to follow your creative principles in the long years before you even know how to define them. I hope that younger readers, especially, will find this book to be a progression from one clarity to the next, even when it seems like one mystery after another. That's just how it was for me.

Cambridge 2016

Early Poems

As I See You

As I see you
Crystals grow
Leaves chime
Roses flow

As I touch you
Tables turn
Towers lean
Witches burn

As I leave you
Lenses shiver
Flags fall
Show's over

The Deep Six

Because the leaves relaxing on the water
Arrange themselves in attitudes of death
Like mannequins who practise languor
I know it must be autumn in the sea.

When the time comes for me to take you there
Through hanging gardens, and all colour trails away
To leave your eyes entirely my secret
And your hair like smoke rising

You will never learn from me about the winter
That will keep us locked at wrist and lips for ever
Like a broken clockwork model of a kiss
When everything is over, where we came from.

Berowra Waters, New South Wales

The seas of the moon are white on white towards evening
Kingfisher strikes head out on the deck for the trees
Veils of tulle are drawn by the dragonflies
The treetops shudder to silence like coins set spinning.

Fireships of cirrus assemble and ride in the west
Tracksuit trousers go on, and a second sweater
Baiting for low-level fish is like writing a letter
To someone whose last name you caught but whose first you missed.

The sun goes over the hill with a whole day's flames
The bottles fluoresce going down, like silver spiders
The old astronomers' animals graze the fields of stars
The guttering cirrus drops on the tide to the Sea of Dreams.

The Morning from Cremorne, Sydney Harbour

Someone sets it
Turning again,
Dumps of junk
Jewellery doing
Their slow burn:
Bonbons spill, and a
Rocket rips,
Pops, goes haywire
Inside the head
Of an emerald pit
Some con man sold
Who's dead, perhaps.

With each night showing
Your share less
You weep for the careless
Day's use:
A play of light
That folds each night
While the milkmen dress.

Con man, milkman,
Someone wires
The light traps,
Ice fires:
The hail-fall blazing
Trails to dawn
That will take the wraps
Of white glass wool
From the warships
Coming into their own
Cold steel.

The Lady in Mourning at Camelot

Before the tournament began
She walked abroad in sable sack:
Embattled knights rang hollow when
They tapped each other on the back
And pointed
(Get the one in black)

All plumage is but camouflage
To shapeliness, this lady knew,
And brilliants shame the lips and eyes:
Simplicity, not sadness, so
Became her
(Check. She stole the show)

Four Poems about Porpoises

I

Swallows in leotards
Burrowing holes
Submarine termites
Quicksilver moles

Dazzling galleries
Spiralling aisles
Daydreams in sunlight
Sinking for miles

Hurtling shuttles
Trip up and flee –
Porpoises, weaving
A shot-silk sea.

II

In Operation Silent Sails
For submarines at sea last night
The porpoises, on fire with fright
Blew every tube in Fylingdales.

III

I take one look and I know I'm dreaming –
Planing fins and the colour streaming
Boundary layers in the mind.

I take a breath and I'm sure I'm stalling –
Looping blades and the harvest falling:
Grain blown back like a bugle calling
Light brigades along the wind.

I take my ease and I'm scared I'm ageing –
Stunting jets and a war game raging;
Seas are riddled, undermined.

I take my leave and I know I'm crying
Tears I'll be a lifetime drying,
The tree house down and the peach tree dying
Home behind.

IV

Porpoises move
Through tunnels of love.

The Banishment

Ma fu' io solo, là dove sofferto
fu per ciascun di tòrre via Fiorenza,
colui che la difesi a viso aperto.

Blemishes age
The Arno tonight
The lamps on the bridges
Piledrive light

Kinky bright krisses
Bent new pin
Opal portcullises
Lychees in gin

Bean-rows of breakable
Stakes going in

Chinese brass burnishes.

Pearlshell caskets
Tumble plunder
Soft rose ledges
Give, go under

Bolts of lamé
Fray
Sunder.

If you open slowly
Eyes half crying
That whole flowing
Blurs like dying

Chi'en-Lung
Colours
Run.

Pinking scissors
Choke on velvet:
Cut-throat razors
Rust in claret.

The Crying Need for Snow

It's cold without the softness of a fall
Of snow to give these scenes a common bond
And though, besotted on a viewless rime,
The ducks can do their standing-on-the-pond
Routine that leaves you howling, all in all
We need some snow to hush the whole thing up.

The ducks can do their flatfoot-waterfool
Mad act that leaves you helpless, but in fine
We need their footprints in a higher field
Made pure powder, need their wig-wag line
Of little kites pressed in around the pool:
An afternoon of snow should cover that.

Some crystalline precipitate should throw
Its multifarious weightlessness around
For half a day and paint the whole place out,
Bring back a soft regime to bitter ground:
An instant plebiscite would vote for snow
So overwhelmingly if we could call it now.

An afternoon of snow should cover that
Milk-bottle neck bolt upright in the slime
Fast frozen at the pond's edge, brutal there:
We need to see junk muffled, whitewashed grime,
Lean brittle ice grown comfortably fat,
A world prepared to take our footprints in.

A world prepared to take our footprints in
Needs painting out, needs be a finer field:
So overwhelmingly, if we could call it now,
The fluffy stuff would prime it: it would yield
To lightest step, be webbed and toed and heeled,
Pushed flat, smoothed off, heaped high, pinched anyhow,
Yet be inviolable. Put like that,
Gently, the cold makes sense. Snow links things up.

The Glass Museum

In cabinets no longer clear, each master's exhibit
Of Murano-manufactured glass has the random look,
Chipped and dusty with eclectic descriptive cards,
Of the chemistry set the twelve-year-old abandons,
The test tubes cracked, the pipette choked solid with dirt:
A work-with-your-hands vocation that never took
And was boxed away near the bottom of the cupboard
Between the clockwork Hornby and the Coldstream Guards.

The supreme exemplars, Ferro, Bigaglia, Radi;
Their prize examples, goblet, bottle and dish;
These classical clearings overgrown in a lifetime
By a jungle of tabular triumphs and tendrilled fish,
Dummy ceramics tricked out with a hand-faked Guardi,
Tubular chandeliers like a mine of serpents:
Age in, age out, the demand was supplied for wonders,
And talent discovered bravura could pay like crime –
To the death of taste and the ruin of common sense.

So the few good things shine on in the junk museum –
A dish with a milk-white helix imprisoned inside,
Miniature polychrome craters and pocket amphoras
Flambeau-skinned like an oil slick slimmed by the tide –
While more global-minded than ever the buyers come
By the jet-load lot into Marco Polo to order
Solid glass sharks complete with sucking remoras
Or thigh-high vases certain to sell like a bomb
Whether north of Bering Strait or south of the Border,
As throughout the island the furnaces roar all day
And they crate the stuff in wood wool to barge it across

To Venice which flogs it direct or else ships it away
And must know by now these gains add up to a loss
But goes on steadily selling itself down the river.

In Sydney years ago when my eyes were wider
I would shuffle the midway sawdust at the Easter Show
As the wonder-boy from Murano rolled pipes of glass
In the furnace-glow underneath a sailcloth roof
And expelled his marvellous breath into gleaming spheres
Which abruptly assumed the shape of performing seals,
Silvered inside and no heavier than a moth –
Between the Hall of Mirrors and the Pygmy Princess
Across from the Ferris wheel and the Wall of Death.

The Young Australian Rider, P. G. Burman

Philip Burman bought an old five hundred
Side-valve BSA for twenty quid.
Unlicensed as they were, both it and him,
He poker-faced ecstatically rode home
In second gear, one of the two that worked,
And everything that subsequently could be done
To make 'her' powerful and bright, he did:
Inside a year she fled beneath the sun
Symphonically enamelled black and plated chrome.

At eighteen years of age he gave up food,
Beer and all but the casual cigarette
To lay his slim apprentice money out
On extra bits like a special needle jet
For a carb the makers never knew about.
Gradually the exhaust note waxed more lewd,
Compression soared, he fitted stiffer springs
To keep the valves from lagging at their duties.
The decibels edged up, the neighbours nearly sued,
Hand over fist that breathed-on bike grew wings
Until her peak lay in the naughty nineties.

Evenings after school I'd bolt my meal
And dive around to his place. In the back
Veranda where he slept and dressed he'd have
Her roaring with her back wheel off the floor
Apocalyptically – the noise killed flies –
Her uncased primary chain a singing blur.
His pet Alsatian hid behind a stack
Of extra wheels, and on the mantelpiece
A balsa Heinkel jiggled through imagined skies.

There was a weekend that we took her out
To Sutherland to sprint the flying mile
Against a mob of Tiger Hundreds. I
Sat wild-eyed and saw his style tell,
Streaming the corners like remembered trails.
They topped him, nearly all of them, but still
They stood around and got the story. 'What
It cost? No bull?' And when we thundered home
I sat the pillion, following his line
Through corners with the drag behind my back
Plucking and fluttering my shirt like sails,
Dreaming his dreams for him of AVUS Track,
Of Spa, the Ring, the Isle of Man TT,
The Monza Autodromo and the magic words, Grand Prix.

Two years later, on my spine at Ingleburn
Just after I came back from leave, I thought
Out piece by piece what must have happened.
He was older, and the bike was new: I'd seen
It briefly the year before and heard the things
He planned to do to it. Another BSA,
Still a push-rod job but OHV at least;
One-lung three-fifty. Home-made swinging arm
Both front and rear, a red-hot shaven head,
Light piston, special rings – the heavy stuff.
We lost contact. I kept hearing off and on
How broke he was from racing and improving her.

One Saturday while I practised the Present
With Bayonet Fixed, a thousand entities
In bullring splendour of precision blaze

To gladden hearts of all who'd guard our shores,
He banked through Dunlop Corner at Mount Druitt
Leading a pack of AJ7Rs –
All camshaft jobs, but not a patch on him.
A fork collapsed. The bike kicked up and paused,
Her throttle stuck wide open, as he sprawled
With helpless hours to watch her pitch and toss
Like some slow-motion diver on a screen
Before the chain came down across his throat.

I had leave the evening after. Halfway down
The street a neighbour told me at her gate,
And then another neighbour – they were all
Ready and willing, full of homilies
And clucking hindsight. And, I'll give them this,
Of grief, too. He was noisy, but they'd liked him –
'Phil killed himself at Druitt yesterday.'

It's not that I felt nothing. I felt nothingness
Pluck at the armpits of my loose KDs
And balsa models jiggled on their shelves
While soaring roadways hurtled, shoulder high.
I had one thought before I turned away:

The trouble is, with us, we overreach ourselves.

A Line and a Theme from Noam Chomsky[*]

Furiously sleep; ideas green; colourless
Sweet dreams just lately ain't been had.
Sweat smells like the colour of the jungle.
Things looked bad then. They go on looking bad.

No question Charlie asked for what he got
Below from us, from up there by the jets;
Else their I D-ola G'd've prevailed,
They'd've swum here and stole our TV sets.

We lined 'em up, we knocked 'em down; we smoked.
We finished off what we'd been told to do.
Back stateside I expected to forget
How heads look when an M16 gets through.

Green nightmares; pillow strangled; sheets mussed up
By day a 'Go' light stops me in my tracks.
Shades don't help: they make the whole *works* green.
A night's sleep is a string of heart attacks.

Furiously sleep; ideas green, colourless
Sweet dreams just lately ain't been had.
That time our gunships hit us by mistake,
I was mad then, I mean angry. But this is mad.

[*] Noam Chomsky gave *colourless green ideas sleep furiously* as an example of a random sequence of words which could have no meaning. It seemed possible that they could, if the context were wide enough, and that their meaning might relate to the Vietnam War, at that time Chomsky's main political concern.

The Outgoing Administration

The gods have eyes the colour of the sky.
They drink from crystal goblets full of cloud.
They laugh and sing a lot, but not aloud,
Since their appeal is mainly to the eye.

Their games become less hectic with the years,
Their wanton cries too feeble to deceive.
The very sight of them seems keen to leave:
It turns to powder like the salt of tears.

The vivid images are growing soft,
The purple robes are ceasing to wear well.
You see the azure through the muscatel
In all those grapes they've held so long aloft.

To think our children now will never know
How beautiful those creatures used to be,
How much more confident than you and me!
The reason why we had to let them go.

Neither One Thing Nor the Other

Sometimes I think perhaps I'm just obtuse.
Noon yesterday I took a turn through King's.
The crippled physicist came whirring by,
No doubt preoccupied with cosmic things.
I stepped aside. Above us in the sky
A burping biplane shook a glider loose
Whose pilot, swerving sunward, must have felt
As overwhelmingly at liberty
As this man felt pinned down. Was that right, though?
To lie still yet see all might feel more free
Than not to know quite why you're free to go.
The chair hummed off. The glider made no sound.
If I can't fly, why am I not profound?

Le Cirque Imaginaire at Riverside Studios

In 'The Phantom of the Clouds' Apollinaire
Pretended to have gone downstairs to see
The acrobats, and found that when he tried
To drink in what he saw them do, it all
Turned bitter on the tongue. Pink pantaloons
Looked like decaying lungs. The fun was spoiled,
The family act more destitute than when
Picasso painted it. The War was on.
Apollinaire was in it, hence the dudgeon.

Without belittling him, you still might say
He needed horror to dilute delight,
Since childish joy to grown men feels like loss,
If only of childhood. There was a time,
Quite early in *Le Cirque Imaginaire*,
When Vicky Chaplin walked on the tight wire
Inverted underneath it, that I thought
I'd just turned five. Her father in his film
The Circus did a stunt like that, but had
To fake it, though with good results. He died
The death in later life, became a bore
About his immortality, which was
No longer under his control. It lives again
When his thin daughter, blessed with Oona's looks,
Draped in sheet silver enters on all fours
High up on four tall stilts that look like six,
A basketballing insect from the depths
Of a benign nightmare.

                    Her husband makes
Surprises happen, just as, long ago,
With something of the same humility,
Her father could. A suitcase full of tricks
Yields up its secrets. Wherein lies the joke:
I mean the joke is that you *see* the way
It works. Except when the huge rabbit,
Which really *couldn't* be in that red box,
Emerges to remind you that this coy
Parade of diffidence is based on full
Mastery of white magic.

                    Now the stage
Is full of birds and bouncing animals,
Of which only a few do not excrete.
Silk-slippered on the bare boards pipped with mire,
The happy couple take their curtain calls
And we go back into the world, which has,
No doubt, produced, while we've been gone,
Plenty of stuff to cut this down to size –
Car bombs in day-care centres, *coups d'état*
In countries whose cash crop earns in a year
Less than *Evita* in a so-so week,
A torture farm in California
That takes all major credit cards.

                    Back in
Reality it needs Apollinaire
(Who went on being right about a war
That cost him half his head) to help retrieve
My reason from the most misleading evening
We spent at the imaginary circus –
Which children shouldn't see without a warning
Things might start looking different in the morning.

from The Book of My Enemy

POEMS

The Book of My Enemy Has Been Remaindered

The book of my enemy has been remaindered
And I am pleased.
In vast quantities it has been remaindered.
Like a van-load of counterfeit that has been seized
And sits in piles in a police warehouse,
My enemy's much-praised effort sits in piles
In the kind of bookshop where remaindering occurs.
Great, square stacks of rejected books and, between them, aisles
One passes down reflecting on life's vanities,
Pausing to remember all those thoughtful reviews
Lavished to no avail upon one's enemy's book –
For behold, here is that book
Among these ranks and banks of duds,
These ponderous and seemingly irreducible cairns
Of complete stiffs.

The book of my enemy has been remaindered
And I rejoice.
It has gone with bowed head like a defeated legion
Beneath the yoke.
What avail him now his awards and prizes,
The praise expended upon his meticulous technique,
His individual new voice?
Knocked into the middle of next week
His brainchild now consorts with the bad buys,
The sinkers, clinkers, dogs and dregs,

The Edsels of the world of movable type,
The bummers that no amount of hype could shift,
The unbudgeable turkeys.

Yea, his slim volume with its understated wrapper
Bathes in the glare of the brightly jacketed *Hitler's War Machine*,
His unmistakably individual new voice
Shares the same scrapyard with a forlorn skyscraper
Of *The Kung-Fu Cookbook*,
His honesty, proclaimed by himself and believed in by others,
His renowned abhorrence of all posturing and pretence,
Is there with *Pertwee's Promenades and Pierrots –*
One Hundred Years of Seaside Entertainment,
And (oh, this above all) his sensibility,
His sensibility and its hair-like filaments,
His delicate, quivering sensibility is now as one
With *Barbara Windsor's Book of Boobs*,
A volume graced by the descriptive rubric
'My boobs will give everyone hours of fun.'

Soon now a book of mine could be remaindered also,
Though not to the monumental extent
In which the chastisement of remaindering has been meted out
To the book of my enemy,
Since in the case of my own book it will be due
To a miscalculated print run, a marketing error –
Nothing to do with merit.
But just supposing that such an event should hold
Some slight element of sadness, it will be offset
By the memory of this sweet moment.
Chill the champagne and polish the crystal goblets!
The book of my enemy has been remaindered
And I am glad.

Sack Artist

Reeling between the redhead and the blonde
Don Juan caught the eye of the brunette.
He had no special mission like James Bond.
He didn't play the lute or read *Le Monde*.
Why was it he on whom their sights were set?

For let's make no mistake, the women pick
Which men go down in history as avid
Tail-chasers with the enviable trick
Of barely needing to chat up the chick –
From Warren Beatty back to ruddy David.

But why the broads latch on to the one bloke
Remains what it has always been, a riddle.
Byron though famous was both fat and broke
While Casanova was a standing joke,
His wig awry, forever on the fiddle.

Mozart made Juan warble but so what?
In *Don Giovanni* everybody sings.
The show would fall flat if the star did not
And clearly he's not meant to sound so hot:
His women praise him, but for other things.

They trill of his indifference and disdain
But might have liked his loyalty still more.
We can't, from how they lyrically complain,
Conclude that when he left they liked the pain
As much as they enjoyed the bliss before.

Bad treatment doesn't do it: not from him,
Still less from us, who find out when we try it
That far from looking tickled they turn grim,
Leaving us at a loss out on a limb,
Instructed to obtain a kite and fly it.

Which doesn't make the chap of whom we speak
Some gigolo devoted to their pleasure.
The fancy man turns no strong woman weak
But merely pumps out what was up the creek.
Plundering hulks he lays up little treasure.

Good looks don't hurt but rate low on their own.
The teenage girls who fall for Richard Gere
Admit his face is random flesh and bone
Beside Mel Gibson's, that his skin lacks tone
And when he smiles his pin eyes disappear.

They go bananas when he bares his chest
But torsos that outstrip his leave them cold.
One bit of you might well be the world's best
But women won't take that and leave the rest:
The man entire is what they would enfold.

The phallus fallacy thus shows its roots
Afloat in the pornographer's wet dream
By which a synecdochic puss in boots
Strides forward frantic to be in cahoots
With his shy mote grown into a great beam.

A shame to be without the wherewithal
But all the wherewith you might have down there
Won't get the ladies queuing in the hall –
Not if you let it loose at a masked ball,
Not if you advertise it on the air.

None of which means that lust takes a back seat.
Contrariwise, it is the main event.
The grandest *grandes dames* cease to be discreet.
Their souls shine through their bodies with the heat.
They dream of more to come as they lie spent.

The sort of women who don't do such things
Do them for him, wherein might lie the clue.
The smell of transcendental sanction clings
Like injured ozone to angelic wings –
An envoy, and he's only passing through.

In triumph's moment he must hit the trail.
However warm the welcome, he can't stay.
Lest those fine fingers read his back like braille
He has to pull out early without fail –
Preserve his mystery with a getaway.

He is the perfect stranger. Humbler grades
Of female don't get even a brief taste –
With Errol Flynn fenced in by flashing blades
And Steve McQueen in aviator shades
It always was a dream that they embraced.

Sheer fantasy makes drama from the drab,
Sweet reverie a slow blues from the bleak:
How Cary Grant would not pick up the tab,
Omar Sharif sent roses in a cab,
Those little lumps in Robert Redford's cheek.

Where Don's concerned the first glance is enough:
For certain he takes soon what we might late.
The rest of us may talk seductive guff
Unendingly and not come up to snuff,
Whereat we most obscenely fulminate.

We say of her that she can't pass a prick.
We call him cunt-struck, stick-man, power tool,
Muff-diver, stud, sack artist, motor dick,
Getting his end away, dipping his wick,
A stoat, a goat, a freak, a fucking fool.

So we stand mesmerized by our own fuss,
Aware that any woman, heaped with grief,
Will give herself to him instead of us
Because there is so little to discuss –
And cry *perfido mostro!* in relief.

Her true desires at long last understood,
She ponders, as she holds him locked above her,
The living definition of the good –
Her blind faith in mankind and womanhood
Restored by the dumb smile of the great lover.

The Supreme Farewell of Handkerchiefs

With acknowledgements to Arthur Gold and
Robert Fizdale, authors of Misia

'I've left that great page blank,' said Mallarmé
When asked why he'd not written of his boat.
There are such things as mean too much to say.
You have to let it drift, to let it float.

The man who did the asking was Manet,
Whose niece's journal treasures the reply.
There are such things as mean too much to say,
But little Julie Manet had a try.

To represent the young, Paul Valéry
Delivered half a speech and then broke down.
He missed his master's deep simplicity.
Then everybody started back to town.

Among those present were Rodin, Bonnard,
Lautrec, Mirbeau, Vallotton, Maeterlinck
And Misia's eternal slave Vuillard.
But Renoir, who had painted her in pink,

Knew ways to tame her when she got annoyed
At how they laughed instead of looking glum.
He thought such moments ought to be enjoyed.
Had not mortality been overcome?

Said Renoir, who had been the poet's friend:
'A Mallarmé does not die every day.'
A sly hint of his own approaching end?
There are such things as mean too much to say.
'I've left that great page blank,' said Mallarmé.

A Gesture towards James Joyce

My gesture towards *Finnegans Wake* is deliberate.
Ronald Bush, *T. S. Eliot: A Study in Character and Style*

The gesture towards *Finnegans Wake* was deliberate.
It was not accidental.
Years of training went into the gesture,
As W. C. Fields would practise a juggling routine
Until his eczema-prone hands bled in their kid gloves;
As Douglas Fairbanks Sr trimmed the legs of a table
Until, without apparent effort and from a standing start,
He could jump up on to it backwards;
Or as Gene Kelly danced an entire tracking shot over and over
Until the final knee-slide ended exactly in focus,
Loafers tucked pigeon-toed behind him,
Perfect smile exultant,
Hands thrown open saying 'How *about* that?'

The gesture towards *Finnegans Wake* was deliberate.
Something so elaborate could not have been otherwise.
Though an academic gesture, it partook in its final form
Of the balletic arabesque,
With one leg held out extended to the rear
And the equiponderant forefinger pointing demonstratively
Like the statue of Eros in Piccadilly Circus,
Or, more correctly, the Mercury of Giambologna,
Although fully, needless to say, clad.

The gesture towards *Finnegans Wake* was deliberate,
Its aim assisted by the position of the volume,
A 1957 printing in the yellow and orange wrapper
Propped on a sideboard and opened at page 164
So that the gesture might indicate a food-based conceit
About *pudding the carp before doeuvre hors* –
The Joycean amalgam in its ludic essence,
Accessible to students and yet also evincing
The virtue of requiring a good deal of commentary
Before what looked simple even if capricious
Emerged as precise even if complex
And ultimately unfathomable.

The gesture towards *Finnegans Wake* was deliberate,
Being preceded by an 'It is no accident, then',
An exuberant 'It is neither accidental nor surprising'
And at least two cases of 'It is not for nothing that',
These to adumbrate the eventual paroxysm
In the same way that a bouncer from Dennis Lillee
Has its overture of giant strides galumphing towards you
With the face both above and below the ridiculous moustache
Announcing by means of unmistakable grimaces
That what comes next is no mere spasm
But a premeditated attempt to knock your block off.

The gesture towards *Finnegans Wake* was deliberate
And so was my gesture with two fingers.
In America it would have been one finger only
But in Italy I might have employed both arms,
The left hand crossing to the tense right bicep
As my clenched fist jerked swiftly upwards –
The most deliberate of all gestures because most futile,
Defiantly conceding the lost battle.

The gesture towards *Finnegans Wake* was deliberate:
So much so that Joyce should have seen it coming.
Even through the eyepatch of his last years.
He wrote a book full of nothing except writing
For people who can't do anything but read,
And now their gestures clog the air around us.
He asked for it, and we got it.

Thoughts on Feeling Carbon-Dated

No moons are left to see the other side of.
Curved surfaces betray once secret centres.
Those plagues were measles the Egyptians died of.
A certain note of disillusion enters.

Were Empson starting now, no doubt exists
That now no doubt exists about space–time's
Impetuosity, his pithy gists
Would still stun, but no more so than his rhymes.

Physics has dished its prefix meta. Science,
First having put black shoes and a blue suit on,
Controls the world's supply of mental giants.
A Goethe now would lack words to loathe Newton.

It's forty years since James Joyce named the quark.
Now nobody's nonplussed to hear light rays
Get sucked down holes so fast they show up dark.
Nor would the converse of that news amaze.

It all gets out of reach as it grows clear.
What we once failed to grasp but still were thrilled with
Left us for someone else, from whom we hear
Assurances about the awe they're filled with.

One night in Cambridge Empson read to us.
He offered us some crisps and seemed delighted
So many young should still want to discuss
Why science once got laymen so excited.

Johnny Weissmuller Dead in Acapulco

Apart possibly from waving hello to the cliff-divers
Would the real Tarzan have ever touched Acapulco?
Not with a one-hundred-foot vine.
Jungle Jim maybe, but the Ape Man never.
They played a tape at his funeral
In the Valley of Light cemetery of how he had sounded
Almost fifty years back giving the pristine ape-call,
Which could only remind all present that in decline
He would wander distractedly in the garden
With his hands to his mouth and the unforgettable cry
Coming out like a croak –
This when he wasn't sitting in his swim-trunks
Beside the pool he couldn't enter without nurses.

Things had not been so bad before Mexico
But they were not great.
He was a greeter in Caesar's Palace like Joe Louis.
Sal, I want you should meet Johnny Weissmuller.
Johnny, Mr Sal Volatile is a friend of ours from Chicago.
With eighteen Tarzan movies behind him
Along with the five Olympic gold medals,
He had nothing in front except that irrepressible paunch
Which brought him down out of the tree house
To earth as Jungle Jim
So a safari suit could cover it up.
As Jungle Jim he wasn't just on salary,
He had a piece of the action,
But coming so late in the day it was not enough
And in Vegas only the smile was still intact.

As once it had all been intact, the Greek classic body
Unleashing the new-style front-up crawl like a baby
Lifting itself for the first time,
Going over the water almost as much as through it,
Curing itself of childhood polio
By making an aquaplane of its deep chest,
Each arm relaxing out of the water and stiffening into it,
The long legs kicking a trench that did not fill up
Until he came back on the next lap,
Invincible, easily breathing
The air in the spit-smooth, headlong, creek-around-a-rock trough
Carved by his features.

He had six wives like Henry VIII but don't laugh,
Because Henry VIII couldn't swim a stroke
And if you ever want to see a true king you should watch Weissmuller
In *Tarzan Escapes* cavorting underwater with Boy
In the clear river with networks of light on the shelving sand
Over which they fly weightless to hide from each other behind the log
While Jane wonders where they are.
You will wonder where you are too and be shy of the answer
Because it is Paradise.

When the crocodile made its inevitable entry into the clear river
Tarzan could always settle its hash with his bare hands
Or a knife at most,
But Jungle Jim usually had to shoot it
And later on he just never got to meet it face to face –
It was working for the Internal Revenue Service.

There was a chimpanzee at his funeral,
Which must have been someone's idea of a smart promotion,
And you might say dignity had fled,
But when Tarzan dropped from the tall tree and swam out of the splash
Like an otter with an outboard to save Boy from the waterfall
It looked like poetry to me,
And at home in the bath I would surface giving the ape-call.

Reflections on a Cardboard Box

Hostathion contains Triazophos,
Controls seed weevil, pea moth, carrot fly.
Of pesticides Hostathion is the boss.
Pests take one sip, kick up their heels and die.

They never find out what Hostathion is.
Triazophos remains the merest word,
Though partly echoed by the acrid fizz
Which suddenly grows too loud to be heard.

Hostathion was once Achilles' friend,
Staunch at his elbow before Ilios,
But now that name brings pea moth a quick end
Assisted by the cruel Triazophos.

Heroic words are too brave for the deeds
They do, yet maybe now they do less evil –
Ferocious but in service to our needs,
Venting our wrath for us on the seed weevil.

Forests of swords on the Homeric plain
Are momentarily invoked. Well, then,
It says much for this age where we complain
Men die like flies, that flies should die like men.

Triazophos sailed with Hostathion
Through centuries as if this were their goal:
Infinite enemies to fall upon,
Killing so common it is called control.

But all the old insanity is gone.
Where are the funeral pyres, the shrieks of loss?
You need to watch only Hostathion.
Hostathion contains Triazophos,

Who once reaped heads by night in no-man's-land
Obeying no man's orders but his own.
Look at him now, Hostathion's right hand –
Cleaning their guns beside the telephone.

The Philosophical Phallus

Female desire aims to subdue, overcome and pacify
the unbridled ambition of the phallus.

Roger Scruton

The unbridled phallus of the philosopher
Was seen last week galloping across the South Downs,
Flame spurting from its flared nostril.

The phallus being a horse in which
Both mane and tail are bunched together at the back end,
This unharnessed piece of horseflesh was of necessity unable
To accompany with a display of shaken neck-hair
The tossing of its head,
But the tossing of its head was tremendous nevertheless,
Like that of Bucephalus, the steed of Alexander.

Where the lush grass curves up to the rim of the chalk cliffs
So that they drop away where you cannot see them
When looking from inland,
Such was the cyclorama against which ran rampant
The unbridled phallus of the philosopher,
Pulling lawn like an emerald treadmill incessantly beneath
The unravelling thunder of its hooves –
Accoutrements which a phallus does not normally possess
But perhaps in this case they were retractable
Like the undercarriage of some large, cigar-shaped aircraft –
The Starlifter, for example, or the C-5A Galaxy.

See where it comes across 'the ontological divide
Separating men and women'!
The unbridled phallus in its frightening hauteur,
Gushing suds with each procreative snort –
Not the small, dog-skulled horse of the Greeks and the Etruscans,
But the horse of the Persians as noted by Herodotus,
Big, built thickly, hefty-headed,
Its two great globular hindquarters throbbing
Like the throats of rutting frogs.

The prancing pudendum curls its lip but says Yes to Life:
It is a yea-neigher.
Not only does it say 'ha-ha!' among the trumpets,
But in the landscaped gardens of fashionable country houses
It trumpets among the ha-has,
And the pulsing vein of its back is not afraid.

Though fleet-footed as an Arab it is stronger than a Clydesdale,
Shouldered like a Shire, bulk-bodied like a Suffolk –
A standing, foam-flanked reproach
To all those of us more appropriately represented
By the Shetland pony,
Or that shrunken, shrivelled toy horse with the mule-tail
Equus przewalskii, Przewalski's horse
From the Kobdo district of western Mongolia.

At nightfall the women of storm-swept lonely farms,
Or at casement windows of the grand houses aforesaid,
Or women anywhere who languish 'unfulfilled *qua* women',

Feel their ontological divide transformed to jelly
At the vibrant snuffle in the distance –
Long to subdue it, to overcome it, to pacify it,
Willing it homeward to its chosen stable,
Which will suffer its presence all the more exquisitely
For being neither deep nor wide enough wholly to contain

The unbridled ambition of the philosophical phallus.

Egon Friedell's Heroic Death

Egon Friedell committed suicide
By jumping from his window when he saw
Approaching Brownshirts eager to preside
At rites the recent *Anschluss* had made law.

Vienna's coffee-house habitués
By that time were in Paris, Amsterdam,
London, New York. Friedell just couldn't raise
The energy to take it on the lam.

Leaving aside the question of their looks,
The Jews the Nazis liked to see in Hell
Were good at writing and owned lots of books –
Which all spelled certain curtains for Friedell.

Friedell was cultivated in a way
That now in Europe we don't often see.
For every volume he'd have had to pay
In pain what those thugs thought the fitting fee.

Forestalling them was simply common sense,
An act only a Pharisee would blame,
Yet hard to do when fear is so intense.
Would *you* have had the nerve to do the same?

The normal move would be to just lie still
And tell yourself you somehow might survive,
But this great man of letters had the will
To meet his death while he was still alive.

So out into the air above the street
He sailed with all his learning left behind,
And by one further gesture turned defeat
Into a triumph for the human mind.

The civilized are most so as they die.
He called a warning even as he fell
In case his body hit a passer-by
As innocent as was Egon Friedell.

Homage to Rafinesque

The ichthyologist Constantine Rafinesque-Schmaltz
(Who was pleased to be known as quite simply Rafinesque)
And John James Audubon the famous student of birds
(Whose folios are generally thought too gorgeous for words
Although when opened they envelop your entire desk)
Teamed up in America as if they were dancing a waltz.

It was neither fish nor fowl crabbed their double act.
The flap in their cabin was caused by a humble bat
Which Rafinesque with the nearest thing to hand attacked,
Thus pounding Audubon's beloved violin out flat.

The revenge Audubon took was oblique but sure.
He returned from the Ohio River with drawings, life-size,
Of fish Rafinesque hadn't seen hide nor hair of before,
But belief in Audubon's pencil put scales on his eyes.
He published a book which his enemies loved for its faults.
To pay with his fame for a fiddle was clearly grotesque.
With the object of leading his friend up a similar creek
He might justly have fashioned a phoenix claw or orc beak,
But he showed the forbearance implied by his name, Rafinesque.
Now Audubon's plates are hoarded like gold in the vaults

And only the fish honour Constantine Rafinesque-Schmaltz.

Will Those Responsible Come Forward?

May the Lord have mercy on all those peoples
Who suffer from a perversion of religion –
Or, to put it in a less equivocating way,
Who suffer from an excess of religion –
Or, to come right out with it,
Who suffer from religion.

Let Him tell those catholic Protestants or protestant Catholics
Who in Northern Ireland go to bed on Saturday night
Looking forward to a morning of Holy Worship
That just this once they should make other plans –
Have a heavy cold, a stomach upset or a pulled hamstring
Severe enough to render them immobile,
With something similar for their children –
So that they will not be there to form a congregation
In a church just big enough for a small massacre.
Arrange this reprieve, Lord,
And if you can't manage that much then for Christ's sake
Hand the whole deal over to Allah.

May the Lord with the assistance of Allah
Give heed to the cries of those children in Beirut
Who have the dubious luck to be ten years old and under
While dwelling in the vicinity of a PLO faction
Currently being wiped out by another PLO faction,
And kindly swing it so that the incoming rockets
Do not dismember their small persons irreparably.
Children older than ten years we will give up on,
Not wanting the moon,
And their mothers, needless to say, are for the high jump.

Fix it, Lord. Get Al on to it,
And if it turns out to be more than you can handle
Raise Jehovah on the horn.

May the Lord and Allah with Jehovah's proverbial
In-depth back-up and sales apparatus
Make a concerted effort to cut the crap,
For the following reasons among others:

Lest at least two kinds of Christians during their annual shoot-out
Bisect an old lady who hears the word 'Duck!'
But can't hit the deck because of sciatica
(May her stoop be steep) –

Lest the Druze and the Jews or the Juze and the Drews,
When shelling each other from somewhere each side
Of a ridge or a bridge,
Cascade hot shrapnel on the intervening hospital
Whose patients suffer from mental disorders,
And thus exacerbate in those inherently unstable minds
An already acute sense of insecurity
(May their straitjackets be flak jackets) –

Lest Iraq and Iran or Iran and Iraq go to rack and ruin
Not just in the standard Islamic manner
Of finding each other insufficiently fanatical,
But with an ironic new wrinkle
By which the hitherto unapproachably sordid
Ayatollah or Arsola
Is upstaged by his own appointee,
That even more sadistic fuckwit and fruitcake
The Hayula or Payola,
Who has women tortured in front of their husbands

As a forceful reminder, no doubt supererogatory,
That you can't fight central mosque
(May their screams be deafening) –

Who also, if that doesn't do the trick,
Has the children tortured along with their mothers
(May they all go crazy quickly),
The object being to make the fathers admit
That they plotted the regime's overthrow –
A pretty fantastic charge when you consider
That the regime's overthrow hasn't yet been accomplished
By Allah functioning either on his tod
Or in combination with the Lord, Jehovah,
Buddha, the Great Spirit and each and every other
Recognized form of God –

Always supposing that They are working on it.
Always supposing that They care
About that or anything else.

But this is the sin of despair.

Echo Echo Echo

Changes in temperature entail turmoil.
Petits pois palpitate before they boil.
Ponds on the point of freezing look like oil.
And God knows what goes on below the soil.

God and the naturalists, who penetrate
With camera crews to depths as dark as fate
And shoot scenes hideous to contemplate
Where burrowing Attenboroughs fight and mate.

In outer space the endless turbulence
Seems too far gone to be at our expense.
One likes to think that if a bang's immense
It didn't happen in the present tense.

Still it's unnerving when two galaxies –
One Catherine wheel and one like a Swiss cheese –
Get stuck in with sharp elbows and scraped knees,
Cancelling out their twin eternities.

As for inside the atom here at home,
It makes the cosmos look like *jeu de paume*
Played out around the Houston Astrodome.
We might as well be back in ancient Rome.

Random, unjust and violent universe!
We feel, and those less ignorant feel worse,
Knowing that what's observed must soon disperse
And Phaethon's car turn out to be a hearse.

Hence, or despite that, our concern with form,
Though even here outclassed by nature's norm.
Snowflakes knock spots off Philibert de L'Orme
But something tells us that they are not warm.

Not that *we* are, compared with, say, the worms
Who live on lava, or are those the germs
That breed in butane and eat isotherms?
I'm not much good with scientific terms.

Even for Einstein it remained a dream
To unify the field, which makes it seem
Likely the rest of us won't get a gleam
Of how, or if, the whole works fit a scheme.

One merely hopes that we have made a start.
Our apprehensions might not melt the heart
Or even be heartfelt for the most part,
But from that insufficiency comes art.

We gather ourselves up from the abyss
As lovers after copulation kiss –
Lip-service which, while semaphoring bliss,
Puts in a claim that there was point to this.

Small wonder, therefore, that from time to time,
As dollar millionaires still nickel-and-dime,
The free-form poet knuckles down to rhyme –
Scared into neatness by the wild sublime.

The Anchor of the *Sirius*

Triangular Macquarie Place, up from the Quay,
Is half rainforest, half a sculpture park
Where can be found – hemmed in by palms and ferns,
Trees touching overhead – the Obelisk
From which, one learns, All Public Roads are Measured
Leading to the Interior of the Colony.
Skyscraper cliffs keep this green garden dark.

The Obelisk is sandstone. Thomas Mort
Is also present, bronze on a tall plinth –
His plain Victorian three-piece suit bulks large,
Befitting Sydney's first successful exporter
Of refrigerated foods – while, lower down
This plush declivity, one finds a bubbler
Superfluously shaded by a small
But intricate gun-metal *baldacchino*,
Sure-footed as a Donatello font.

Thus in a sculpture court less up to date
Yet cooler than MOMA's, leafier than the Frick,
One strolls encountering pieces carried out
In traditional materials and is lulled –
Till this free-standing object looms and startles
Like a Calder by Duchamp. It stops you cold,
The anchor of the *Sirius*. It hooks you
More firmly than the fluke which can't be seen
(Because, presumably, buried in the earth)
Could ever have snared the bottom of Sydney Cove.

One is amazed by how it is not old –
Which means the Colony's protracted birth
(The women were outscreamed by the flayed men)
Falls so far short of being long ago
It's hard to grasp. The anchor was brought back
From where the ship ended its history –
I think it tried to sail through Norfolk Island –

To where it began ours. Yes, the First Fleet
Dropped its first anchor just one hundred yards
(Or metres, as they say now) down the street –
And this is it, not much more touched by time
Than now by me, a yokel in the museum.

The crops failed. Phillip was no dynamo,
But Macquarie was, and men like Mort could double
The town's wealth in ten years. The scrub grew long
And lush like Joan Sutherland's throat. Success
Went overseas, took umpteen curtain calls,
Was toasted and had toast named after it,
And now the audience is here. Out on the harbour
Captain Cook II jam-packed with Japanese,
Their Nikons crackling like automatic flak,
Goes swanning past the well-remembered line
Where the submarine nets were when I was young,
Forty years ago – i.e. a full
Fifth of the time Port Jackson's had that name.

And after I'd grown up and gone away
Like the wool-clip to the other end of the world
(Where the wool was turned to suit-cloth and sent back
So Thomas Mort, full of ideas as Dickens,
Might look the part of the philanthropist)
The anchor of the *Sirius* had me pinned –
Spiked, rooted to the spot under these trees
Which filter what light's left by the glass towers
They put up yesterday so that the banks –
Algemene Bank Nederland NV,
Dresdner Bank AG, Banca Nazionale del Lavoro,
Sumitomo International Finance Australia –
Might catch through tinted windows like hot news
Digits conveying all they need to know,
Drawn down from space by ranks of VDUs
And here made manifest as a green glow –
New York and London, Hong Kong, Tokyo,
Sucked in at once to this same lightning rod –
Completing their great journey from afar
As a tired sinner comes at last to God,
As a ship comes in and drops anchor.

The Ferry Token

Not gold but some base alloy, it stays good
For one trip though the currency inflates –
Hard like the ferry's deck of seasoned wood,
The only coin in town that never dates.

Don Juan, as described by Baudelaire,
Before he crossed the Styx to the grim side
Paid Charon *son obole*, his ferry fare.
Was it this very token, worth one ride?

Of course it wasn't. This poor thing will buy
The traveller no myth beyond the dark
Leonine Pinchgut with one beady eye
Fixed on the brilliant, beckoning Luna Park.

At most it takes you back to Billy Blue
Whose ferry linked the Quay to the North Shore
Somewhere about the year of Waterloo –
And probably more after than before.

There's been so little time for grand events.
One ferry sank, but saying those who drowned
Contributed to our historic sense
Would be obscene and logically unsound.

Nevertheless nostalgia impregnates
This weightless disc as sunlight bleaches wood.
Our past is shallow but it scintillates –
Not gold but some base alloy, it stays good.

Funnelweb

The flame reflected in the welder's mask
Burns the board-rider's upstage fingertips
That cut a swathe across the curved sea wall
Inside the Banzai Pipeline's tubular swell.
Sopranos feel the same fire on their lips
Kissing Jochanaan as befits the task.

The crank-winged Chance-Vought F4-U Corsair
When turning tightly spilled white vortices
Behind its wing tips in the cobalt blue.
A mere machine, a Running W
As once brought stuntmen's horses to their knees,
And yet you can't deny it carved the air.

Phenomena like these, it will be said,
Are only incidental at the most
And mostly trivial, to say the least:
Less the confetti at the wedding feast
Than the box it came in, spice without the roast,
Beaches at Tarawa without the dead.

A saturation diver sets his seal
Where even fish can't see reflected flame.
A surfer in the folded tube may form
His signature unnoticed from the foam.
Night fighters' ailerons worked just the same
And Salome might think of her next meal.

True, but not true enough, in my belief.
These things though tenuous aren't set apart.
The casual grace note can't help but imply,
If not the outline of the melody,
Then anyway the impulse at its heart –
And do so all the more for being brief.

Stillness in movement is a waking dream
Movement in stillness has refined from strength.
The riverbank must make the drift apparent
Of swans at evening plugged into the current,
But lest they be disorganized at length
Just out of sight they steer to point upstream.

Wristy Makarova's Odette/Odile
(Two lovely people spinning on one toe)
Exemplifies the Body Beautiful
Consumed by its own power to appal.
Watch how the whiplash whirlwind sucks up snow –
A double helix drawn from sex appeal.

Woodcut adoring kings with narrowed eye
Quite clearly find the cradle-capped young Prince
Painful to look at, backed up by his nimbus.
Even His Mother, pierced by the columbus
And haloed in Her own right, seems to wince:
The sun is in the wrong part of the sky.

He could not save Himself, they said with scorn,
But always it has been supposed they erred
And that, armed by His power to distinguish
The star-bursts in His hands from human anguish,
He ultimately went out like a bird
The way that He came in when He was born.

Watching a dear friend go down fast with cancer
Like a raindrop down a window pane, I hold
Her hand of balsa clad with clear doped silk
Pulsating like the skin of simmering milk
Which must boil over soon and leave her cold.
Next time *I'm* coming back a necromancer.

The floorboards in Kyoto's Nijo-jo
Will sing like flocks of birds from their sleeved nails
When someone walks, however light in weight.
Thus Tokugawa shoguns dreamed at night
Equating sudden death with nightingales,
And paper walls seemed real, this being so.

Saito himself committed suicide
The long way round by using the short sword
Before the banzai charge went in at dawn.
Three thousand died before the sun went down.
All night it sounded like a psycho ward.
We sacked out with the corpses open eyed.

What happened the next morning broke your heart.
We saw the whole thing from above the beach.
Mothers threw living babies from the cliff.
The sick lined up to have their heads hacked off.
Those soldiers that the non-coms couldn't reach
Kissed a grenade and blew themselves apart.

Marines you'd swear would never shed a tear
On Saipan wept. And that was all she wrote.
We just got used to it, like swatting flies.
Not even Iwo came as a surprise.
The whole Jap nation would have cut its throat
I swear to God sure as I'm standing here.

For Lichtenberg, wit was a microscope,
Yet in between the lines he seemed to know
His fine analysis did not disperse,
But gave coherence to, the universe.
That strong light touch sums up the rococo:
An epoch blown from clear glass, not from soap.

So do the buildings of Cuvilliés,
The Wittelsbachs' great court-dwarf architect,
Whose play of curlicue and arabesque
Like flame reflected in the welder's mask
Suggests a brilliance beyond intellect,
Fulfilled creation singing its own praise.

His small theatre of the Residenz
In World War II was bombed to smithereens
Yet could be put back as it was, because
Its dazzling inner shell was lath and gauze,
A kit of plaster panels and silk screens
They stashed away until the world saw sense.

At Vegas, the last Grand Prix of the year
Before he died in Belgium, Gilles Villeneuve
Put on his helmet and I saw the sun
Fill up his tinted visor like white wine.
Few poets get the face that they deserve
Or, like Hart Crane, can travel in a tear.

Of course Villeneuve was handsome anyway –
The Rimbaud of the wheel just oozed romance –
But where his class showed was in how that beast
Ferrari drew sweet curves at his behest
Instead of leading him St Vitus' dance.
He charged the earth but gave back art for pay.

If she could *see* herself, the girl on skates –
But she must work by feel in the event,
Assured by how her heavy fingers burn
As in mid-air she makes the triple turn
Explosive effort was correctly spent
And from the whirlpool a way out awaits.

They say that Pipeline surfers deep in white
Whipped water when wiped out may sip the froth
Through pursed lips and thus drown less than they breathe
While buffeted their helpless bodies writhe,
Then once the ruined wave has spent its wrath
Swim resurrected up to the bright light.

Though children in deep shelters could not watch,
Pathfinder flares were sumptuous where they burned
And rustic simpletons found food for thought
In how those coloured chandeliers would float
As if the Son of Man had just returned –
Before the earthquake made them a hotchpotch.

Descending from heaped rubble, 'I composed
Der Rosenkavalier,' Strauss told GIs
Whose billet underneath the *Führerbau*
Reminded them of their hometown hoosegow.
At eighty he was right, if scarcely wise:
From where he stood the episode was closed.

And soon there was another Salome
To propagate his long *legato* phrases,
And, by their shapeliness made feverish,
Lift high the prophet's lopped head in a dish,
And taste the everlasting fire that rages
On those cold lips of *papier mâché*.

She's gone, perhaps to start again elsewhere.
The freezing fens lock up their latent heat.
The rime ice on the river to the touch
Splits in a gash benign neglect will stitch.
Full of potential like briquettes of peat
Atomic bombs enjoy conditioned air.

The Emperor's portrait had survived the blast.
We carried it to safety in the stream
And took turns holding it aloft. The fire
Arched overhead and we succumbed to fear.
The surface of the water turned to steam.
I must say we were very much downcast.

Emerging from a silo of spun spunk
To scan the killing ground with clustered eyes,
The funnelweb when she appears in person
Reveals a personality pure poison
Should you be tempted to idealize
Her gauze-lined bunker under the tree trunk,

And yet how sweet a tunnel in the mist!
Well might it fascinate as well as frighten.
Looking along such lustrous holes in space
Where indrawn starlight corkscrews down the sluice,
You'll feel your heart first hammer and then lighten
And think God was a gynaecologist.

The Sun so far has only twice touched Earth
With its unmitigated baleful stare.
Flesh turned to pizza under that hot look.
From all the forms of death you took pot luck,
But that by which the occasion was made rare
Showed later on in what was brought to birth.

At KZ Dachau the birthmarked young nun
Beseeching absolution for that place
Won't turn her full face to your chapel pew.
Only her murmurs will admonish you
For thinking to give up pursuit of grace
Simply because such dreadful things were done.

High over Saipan when another plane
Came back above us heading for Japan
As we flew south for home, I never saw
What would have been a chromium gewgaw,
But only what it casually began –
A long straight line of crystal flake cocaine.

Your progeny won't sit still to be told
Nor can you point out through the window how
Air battles of the past left vapour trails
Swirling and drifting like discarded veils,
Scarcely there then and not at all there now,
Except you feel the loss as you grow old.

Black-bottomed whiteware out of nowhere fast
The Shuttle takes fire coming back to us,
A purple storm with silence at the core.
Simmering down, it is the dodgem car
Daedalus should have given Icarus,
Whose wings – a bad mistake – were built to last.

To stay the course you must have stuff to burn.
For life, the ablative is absolute,
And though the fire proceeds against our wishes
Forms are implicit even in the ashes
Where we must walk in an asbestos suit:
A smouldering tip to which all things return.

We may not cavalierly lift the casque
Which separates us from the consequences
Of seeing how the godhead in full bloom
Absolves itself unthinkingly from blame.
It knows us as we know it, through our senses.
We feel for it the warmth in which we bask –
The flame reflected in the welder's mask.

A Valediction for Philip Larkin

You never travelled much but now you have,
Into the land whose brochures you liked least:
That drear Bulgaria beyond the grave
Where wonders have definitively ceased –
Ranked as a dead loss even in the East.

Friends will remember until their turn comes
What they were doing when the news came through.
I landed in Nairobi with eardrums
Cracked by the flight from Kichwa Tembo. You
Had gone, I soon learned, on safari too.

Learned soon but too late, since no telephone
Yet rings in the wild country where we'd been.
No media penetration. On one's own
One wakes up and unzips the morning scene
Outside one's tent and always finds it green.

Green Hills of Africa, wrote Hemingway.
Omitting a preliminary 'the',
He made the phrase more difficult to say –
The hills, however, easier to see,
Their verdure specified initially.

Fifty years on, the place still packs a thrill.
Several reserves of greenery survive,
And now mankind may look but must not kill
Some animals might even stay alive,
Surrounded by attentive four-wheel-drive

Toyotas full of tourists who shoot rolls
Of colour film off in the cheetah's face
While she sleeps in the grass or gravely strolls
With bloody cheeks back from the breathless chase,
Alone except for half the human race.

But we patrolled a less well-beaten trail.
Making a movie, we possessed the clout
To shove off up green hill and down green dale
And put our personal safety in some doubt
By opening the door and getting out.

Thus I descended on the day you died
And had myself filmed failing to get killed.
A large male lion left me petrified
But well alone and foolishly fulfilled,
Feeling weak-kneed but calling it strong-willed.

Silk brushed with honey in the hot noon light,
His inside leg was colonized by flies.
I made a mental note though wet with fright.
As his mouth might have done off me, my eyes
Tore pieces off him to metabolize.

In point of fact I swallowed Kenya whole,
A mill choked by a plenitude of grist.
Like anabolic steroids for the soul,
Every reagent was a catalyst –
So much to take in sent me round the twist.

I saw Kilimanjaro like the wall
Of Heaven going straight up for three miles.
The Mara river was a music hall
With tickled hippos rolling in the aisles.
I threw some fast food to the crocodiles.

I chased giraffes who floated out of reach
Like anglepoise lamps loose in zero g.
I chased a *mdudu* with a can of bleach
Around my tent until I couldn't see.
Only a small rhinoceros chased me.

The spectral sun-bird drew the mountain near,
And if the rain-bird singing *soon soon soon*
Turned white clouds purple, still the air was clear –
The radiant behind of a baboon
Was not more opulent than the full moon.

So one more tourist should have been agog
At treasure picked up cheaply while away –
Ecstatic as some latter-day sea dog,
His trolley piled high like a wain of hay
With duty-free goods looted from Calais.

For had I not enlarged my visual scope,
Perhaps my whole imaginative range,
By seeing how that deadpan antelope,
The topi, stands on small hills looking strange
While waiting for the traffic lights to change?

And had I not observed the elephant
Deposit heaps of steaming excrement
While looking wiser than Immanuel Kant,
More stately than the present Duke of Kent?
You start to see why I was glad I went.

Such sights were trophies, ivory and horn
Destined for carving into *objets d'art*.
Ideas already jumping like popcorn,
I climbed down but had not gone very far
Between that old Dakota and the car

When what they told me stretched the uncrossed space
Into a universe. No tears were shed.
Forgive me, but I hardly felt a trace
Of grief. Just sudden fear your being dead
So soon had left us disinherited.

You were the one who gave us the green light
To get out there and seek experience,
Since who could equal you at sitting tight
Until the house around you grew immense?
Your bleak bifocal gaze was so intense,

Hull stood for England, England for the world –
The whole caboodle crammed into one room.
Above your desk all of creation swirled
For you to look through with increasing gloom,
Or so your poems led us to assume.

Yet even with your last great work 'Aubade'
(To see death clearly, did you pull it close?)
The commentator must be on his guard
Lest he should overlook the virtuose
Technique which makes majestic the morose.

The truth is that you revelled in your craft.
Profound glee charged your sentences with wit.
You beat them into stanza form and laughed:
They didn't sound like poetry one bit,
Except for being absolutely it.

Described in English written at its best
The worst of life remains a bitch to face
But is more shared, which leaves us less depressed –
Pleased the condition of the human race,
However desperate, is touched with grace.

The seeming paradox is a plain fact –
You brought us all together on your own.
Your saddest lyric is a social act.
A bedside manner in your graveyard tone
Suggests that at the last we aren't alone.

You wouldn't have agreed, of course. You said
Without equivocation that life ends
With him who lived it definitely dead
And buried, after which event he tends
To spend a good deal less time with his friends.

But you aren't here to argue. Where you are
By now is anybody's guess but yours.
I'm five miles over Crete in a Tristar
Surrounded by the orchestrated snores
Induced by some old film of Roger Moore's.

Things will be tougher now you've proved your point,
By leaving early, that the man upstairs
Neither controls what happens in the joint
We call the world, nor noticeably cares.
While being careful not to put on airs,

It is perhaps the right time to concede
That life is all downhill from here on in.
For doing justice to it, one will need,
If not in the strict sense a sense of sin,
More *gravitas* than fits into a grin.

But simply staying put makes no one you.
Those who can't see the world in just one street
Must see the world. What else is there to do
Except face inescapable defeat
Flat out in a first-class reclining seat?

You heard the reaper in the Brynmor Jones
Library cough behind your swivel chair.
I had to hear those crocodiles crunch bones,
Like cars compressed for scrap, before the hair
Left on my head stood straight up in the air.

You saw it all in little. You dug deep.
A lesser man needs coarser stimuli,
Needs coruscating surfaces . . . needs sleep.
I'm very rarely conscious when I fly.
Not an event in life. To sleep. To die.

I wrote that much, then conked out over Rome,
Dreamed I'd been sat on by a buffalo,
Woke choking as we tilted down for home,
And now see, for once cloudless, the pale glow
Of evening on the England you loved so

And spoke for in a way she won't forget.
The quiet voice whose resonance seemed vast
Even while you lived, and which has now been set
Free by the mouth that shaped it shutting fast,
Stays with us as you turn back to the past –

Your immortality complete at last.

Jet Lag in Tokyo

Flat feet kept Einstein out of the army.
The Emperor's horse considers its position.
In Akasaka men sit down and weep
Because the night must end.

At Chez Oz I discussed my old friend's sex change
With a lovely woman who, I later learned,
Had also had one. The second movement
Of the Mahler Seventh on my Boodo Khan
Above the North Pole spoke to me like you.

Neutrinos from 1987A
Arrived in the Kamiokande bubble chamber
Three hours before the light. Shinjuku neon
Is dusted with submicroscopic diamonds.

Our belled cat keeps blackbirds up to scratch
With the fierce face of a tiger from the wall
Of the Ko-hojo in the Nanzen-ji, Kyoto.
You would not have been looking for me,
God told Pascal,
If you had not found me.

What will we do with those Satsuma pots
When the sun dies? Our Meissen *vieux Saxe* girl
Was fired three times. The car will be OK:
A Volkswagen can take anything.

An age now since I wrote about your beauty,
How rare it is. Tonight I am reminded.
Sue-Ellen Ewing says *Gomen nasai*.
Perhaps the Emperor's horse is awake also.
I think this time I've gone too far too fast.

The Light Well

*Nacimos en un país libre que nos legaron nuestros
padres, y primero se hundirá la Isla en el mar antes
que consintamos en ser esclavos de nadie.*

Fidel Castro, *La historia me absolverá*

From Playa Girón the two-lane blacktop
Sticks to the shoreline of the Bay of Pigs –
The swamp's fringe on your left showing the sea
Through twisted trees, the main swamp on your right –
Until the rocks and tangled roots give way
To the soft white sand of Playa Larga,
The other beach of the invasion. Here
Their armour got stopped early. At Girón
They pushed their bridgehead inland a few miles
And held out for two days. From the air
Their old B-26s fell in flames.
High-profile Shermans doddered, sat like ducks
And were duly dealt with. Fidel's tanks,
Fresh in from Russia and as fast as cars,
Dismembered everything the Contras had,
Even the ships that might have got them out.
Also the People, who were meant to rise –
Chuffed at the thought of being once again
Free to cut cane all day for one peso
On land owned by the United Fruit Company –
Unaccountably stayed where they were. The swamp
Didn't notice a thing. The crocodiles
Haven't given it a thought in years,
Though wayward bombs from 4.2″ mortars

Must, at the time, have made some awfully big
Holes in the mud. Apart from the vexed question
Of which genius ever picked it as the venue
For a military initiative whose chance
Paled beside that of a snowball in Hell,
The area holds no mysteries. Except one.
Somewhere about a mile along the road,
Look to the right and you can see a hint
Of what might be a flat spot in the swamp.
It is. A sketchy dirt track through the trees
Leads to a pool just forty feet across
Connected to the sea at such a depth
That though as clear as air and always calm
It shades down into darkness. Sufferers
From vertigo can't swim there. Parrotfish
Like clockwork paperweights on crystal shelves,
Their colour schemes preposterous, exchange
Positions endlessly. Shadows below
Look no more dense than purity compressed
Or light packed tight. Things were clear-cut
At that great moment of assault repulsed,
The victors proud yet chivalrous to a fault.
White flags, no matter how unsavoury
The hands that held them, were respected. Two
Of Batista's most notorious torturers,
Still wearing their original dark glasses
(Through which they'd both looked forward to a prompt
Resumption of a glittering career),
Were singled out and shot, but otherwise
Nobody missed a change of socks. They all
Got shipped back undamaged to Miami –
A better deal than they'd have handed out.
That day the Cuban revolution showed

A cleanliness which in the memory
Dazzles the more for how it has been spoiled:
What had to happen sullied by what might
Have been avoided, had those flagrant beards
Belonged to wiser heads – or so we think,
We who were young and thrilled and now are neither.
Credit where credit's due, though. Let's be fair.
Children cut cane here still, but go to school,
And don't get sick; or, if they do, don't die.
La cienega is a charnel house no longer,
And in this pool, which they call El Cenote,
Young workers float at lunchtime like tree frogs
Poised on an air column. Things have improved
In some ways, so when they get worse in others
It's easier to blame Reagan than accept
The plain fact that the concentrated power
Which makes sick babies well must break grown men –
The logic so obvious it's blinding.
From armchairs far away we watch the brilliant
Picture grow dim with pain. On the Isle of Pines
The men who wear dark glasses late at night
Are back in business. Anyone smart enough
To build a raft from inner tubes and rope
Would rather run the gauntlet of the sharks
On the off-chance of encountering Florida
Than take the risk of listening to one more
Speech by Fidel – who, in his unrelenting
Urge to find friends among the non-aligned
Countries, now heaps praise on the regime
Of the Ayatollah Khomeini. Russian oil
Pollutes Havana. How opaque, we feel,
Those erstwhile glories have become, how sad –
Preferring, on the whole, to leave it there

Than enter beyond one long, ravished glance
That cistern filled with nothing but the truth,
Which we partake of but may not possess
Unless we go too deep and become lost,
By pressure of transparency confounded –
Trusting our eyes instead of turning back,
Drawn down by clarity into the dark,
Crushed by the prospect of enlightenment,
Our lungs bursting like a revelation.

The Artificial Horizon

Deus gubernat navem

The artificial horizon is no false dawn
But a tool to locate you in the sky.
A line has been drawn.
If it tilts, it is you that are awry.
Trust it and not your eye.

Or trust your eye, but no further than it goes
To the artificial horizon.
Only if that froze
Would you look out for something on the level
And pray you didn't spot it too late.
To stay straight
You can't just follow your nose –

Except when the true horizon's there.
But how often is that?
The sea at sunset shades into the air.
A white cloud, a night black as your hat –
What ground you glimpse might be at an angle,
While looking flat.

So the artificial horizon is a court
Of appeal, your first line of defence
And last resort:
A token world whose import is immense.

Though it seem unreal,
If it moves it can't be broken.
Believe that it makes sense
Or else be brought up short.

The artificial horizon
Is your Dr Johnson:
It's got its own slant.

It says clear your mind of cant.

What Happened to Auden

His stunning first lines burst out of the page
Like a man thrown through a windscreen. His flat drawl
Was acrid with the spirit of the age –
The spy's last cigarette, the hungry sprawl
Of Hornby clockwork train sets in 'O' gauge,
Huge whitewashed slogans on a factory wall –
It was as if a spotlight when he spoke
Brilliantly pierced the histrionic smoke.

Unsentimental as the secret police,
Contemporary as a Dinky Toy,
On holiday in Iceland with MacNeice,
A flop-haired Cecil Beaton golden boy,
Auden pronounced like Pericles to Greece
The short time Europe had left to enjoy,
Yet made it sound as if impending doom
Could only ventilate the drawing room.

Splendidly poised above the ashtray's rim,
The silver record-breaking aeroplane
For streamlined utterance could not match him.
Oblique but no more often than the rain,
Impenetrable only to the dim,
Neurotic merely not to be insane,
He seemed to make so much sense all at once
Anyone puzzled called himself a dunce.

Cricket pavilion lust looked a touch twee
Even to devotees, but on the whole,
Apart from harsh reviews in *Scrutiny*,
All hailed his triumph in Cassandra's role,
Liking the *chic* he gave her, as if she
Wore ankle-strap high heels and a mink stole –
His ambiguity just further proof
Here was a man too proud to stand aloof.

By now, of course, we know he was in fact
As queer as a square grape, a roaring queen
Himself believing the forbidden act
Of love he made a meal of was obscene.
He could be crass and generally lacked tact.
He had no truck with personal hygiene.
The roughest trade would seldom stay to sleep.
In soiled sheets he was left alone to weep.

From the Kurfürstendamm to far Shanghai
He cruised in every sense with Isherwood.
Sadly he gave the talent the glad eye
And got out while the going was still good.
New York is where his genius went to die
Say those who disapproved, but though they could
Be right that he lost much of his allure,
Whether this meant decline is not so sure.

Compatriots who stuck it out have said
Guilt for his getaway left him unmanned,
Whereat his taproot shrivelled and went dead,
Having lost contact with its native land.
Some say it was the sharing of his bed
With the one man nobody else could stand
That did him in, since poets can't afford
The deadly risk of conjugal concord.

But Chester made bliss hard enough to take,
And Wystan, far from pining for his roots,
Gaily tucked into the unrationed steak.
An international figure put out shoots.
Stravinsky helped the progress of the rake:
Two cultural nabobs were in cahoots.
No, Auden ageing was as much at home
On the world stage as Virgil was in Rome,

If less than *salonfähig* still. Regret
By all accounts he sparingly displayed
When kind acquaintances appeared upset,
Their guest rooms wrecked as if by an air raid.
He would forgive himself and soon forget.
Pig-like he revelled in the mess he made,
Indecorous the more his work lost force,
Devoid of shame. Devoured, though, by remorse,

For had he not gazed into the abyss
And found, as Nietzsche warned, that it gazed back?
His wizardry was puerile next to this.
No spark of glamour touched the railway track
That took whole populations to the hiss
Of cyanide and stoked the chimney stack
Scattering ash above a vast expanse
Of industry bereft of all romance.

The pit cooled down but still he stood aghast
At how far he had failed to state the case
With all those tricks that now seemed so half-arsed.
The inconceivable had taken place.
Waking to find his wildest dreams outclassed
He felt his tongue must share in the disgrace,
And henceforth be confined, in recompense,
To no fine phrase devoid of plain prose sense.

The bard unstrung his lyre to change his tune,
Constrained his inspiration to repent.
Dry as the wind abrading a sand dune,
A tightly drafted letter of intent,
Each rubric grew incisive like a rune,
Merest suggestions became fully meant.
The ring of truth was in the level tone
He forged to fit hard facts and praise limestone.

His later manner leaves your neck-hair flat,
Not standing up as Housman said it should
When poetry has been achieved. For that,
In old age Auden simply grew too good.
A mortal fear of talking through his hat,
A moral mission to be understood
Precisely, made him extirpate the thrill
Which, being in his gift, was his to kill.

He wound up as a poor old fag at bay,
Beleaguered in the end as at the start
By dons appalled that he could talk all day
And not draw breath although pissed as a fart,
But deep down he had grown great, in a way
Seen seldom in the history of his art –
Whose earthly limits Auden helped define
By realizing he was not divine.

Last Night the Sea Dreamed It Was Greta Scacchi

Last night the sea dreamed it was Greta Scacchi.
It wakes unruffled, lustrous, feeling sweet –
Not one breath of scandal has ever touched it.

At a higher level, the rain has too much power.
Grim clouds conspire to bring about its downfall.
The squeeze is on, there is bound to be a shake-out.

The smug sea and the sky that will soon go bust
Look like antagonists, but don't be fooled:
They understand each other very well.

We are caught between the hammer and the anvil.
Our bodies, being umpteen per cent water,
Are in this thing up to the neck at least.

If you want to feel detached from a panorama,
Try the Sahara. Forget about Ayers Rock –
The sea was once all over it like a rash.

The water in the opal makes it lovely,
Also unlucky. If not born in October
You might be wearing a cloudburst for a pendant.

The ban on flash photography is lifted.
The reception area expectantly lights up.
No contest. It's just life. Don't try to fight it –

You'll only get wet through, and we are that
Already. Every dimple in the swell
Is a drop in the ocean, but then who isn't?

No, nothing about women is more sensual
Than their sea smell. Look at her lying there,
Taking what comes and spreading it on her skin –

The cat, she's using her cream as moisturizer.
Milt Jackson's mallets bounce on silver leaves.
Strafed by cool riffs she melts in silent music:

Once we walked out on her, but we'll be back.

Drama in the Soviet Union

When Kaganovich, brother-in-law of Stalin,
Left the performance barely halfway through,
Meyerhold must have known that he was doomed,
Yet ran behind the car until he fell.
In *Pravda* he'd been several times condemned
For Stubborn Formalism. The ill will
Of the All Highest himself was common knowledge,
Proved by a mud slide of denunciations
And rubbed in by the fact that the Great Teacher
Had never personally entered the theatre
Which this enemy of the people had polluted
With attitudes hostile to the State.

Thus Meyerhold was a dead man of long standing:
Behind the big black car it was a corpse
That ran, a skull that gasped for air,
Bare bone that flailed and then collapsed.
His dear friend Shostakovich later said
How glad he was that he had never seen
Poor Meyerhold like that. Which was perhaps
Precisely why this giant of his art
Did such a thing: to dramatize the fear
Which had already eaten him alive
And make it live.

Stalin, meanwhile,
Who didn't need to see how it was done
To know that the director's trick of staging
A scene so it could never be forgotten
Had to be stamped on, was the acknowledged master
Of the one theatrical effect that mattered –
He knew how to make people disappear.

So Meyerhold, having limped home, plummeted
Straight through the trapdoor to oblivion.
Nobody even registered surprise.
Specific memories were not permitted.
People looked vague, as if they didn't have them.
In due course his widow, too, was murdered –
Stabbed in the eyes, allegedly by thieves.

Budge up

Flowering cherry pales to brush-stroke pink at blossom fall
Like watermelon bitten almost to the rind.
It is in his mind because the skin is just that colour
Hot on her tight behind
As she lies in the bath, a Bonnard flipped like a flapjack.

His big black towel turns a naiad to a dryad,
No pun intended. Then,
An unwrapped praline,
She anoints herself with liberal Oil of Ulay.
It looks like fun.
Her curved fingers leave a few streaks not rubbed in.
He says: here, let me help.

The night is young but not as young as she is
And he is older than the hills.
Sweet sin
Swallows him at a gulp.

While cherry blossom suds dry on the lawn
Like raspberry soda
He attends the opening of the blue tulip
Mobbed at the stage door by forget-me-nots.

For a short season
He basks in her reflected glory.

Pathetic fallacy,
Dispelled by the clattering plastic rake.

Bring Me the Sweat of Gabriela Sabatini

Bring me the sweat of Gabriela Sabatini
For I know it tastes as pure as Malvern water,
Though laced with bright bubbles like the *acqua minerale*
That melted the kidney stones of Michelangelo
As sunlight the snow in spring.

Bring me the sweat of Gabriela Sabatini
In a green Lycurgus cup with a sprig of mint,
But add no sugar –
The bitterness is what I want.
If I craved sweetness I would be asking you to bring me
The tears of Annabel Croft.

I never asked for the wristbands of Maria Bueno,
Though their periodic transit of her glowing forehead
Was like watching a bear's tongue lap nectar.
I never asked for the blouse of Françoise Durr,
Who refused point-blank to improve her soufflé serve
For fear of overdeveloping her upper arm –
Which indeed remained delicate as a fawn's femur,
As a fern's frond under which cool shadows gather
So that the dew lingers.

Bring me the sweat of Gabriela Sabatini
And give me credit for having never before now
Cried out with longing.
Though for all the years since TV acquired colour
To watch Wimbledon for even a single day
Has left me shaking with grief like an ex-smoker
Locked overnight in a cigar factory,

Not once have I let loose as now I do
The parched howl of deprivation,
The croak of need.

Did I ever demand, as I might well have done,
The socks of Tracy Austin?
Did you ever hear me call for the cast-off Pumas
Of Hana Mandlikova?
Think what might have been distilled from these things,
And what a small request it would have seemed –
It would not, after all, have been like asking
For something so intimate as to arouse suspicion
Of mental derangement.
I would not have been calling for Carling Bassett's knickers
Or the tingling, Teddy Tinling B-cup brassiere
Of Andrea Temesvari.

Yet I denied myself.
I have denied myself too long.
If I had been Pat Cash at that great moment
Of triumph, I would have handed back the trophy
Saying take that thing away
And don't let me see it again until
It spills what makes this lawn burst into flower:
Bring me the sweat of Gabriela Sabatini.

In the beginning there was Gorgeous Gussie Moran
And even when there was just her it was tough enough,
But by now the top hundred boasts at least a dozen knockouts
Who make it difficult to keep one's tongue
From lolling like a broken roller blind.
Out of deference to Billie-Jean I did my best
To control my male chauvinist urges –

An objectivity made easier to achieve
When Betty Stove came clumping out to play
On a pair of what appeared to be bionic legs
Borrowed from Six Million Dollar Man.

I won't go so far as to say I harbour
Similar reservations about Steffi Graf –
I merely note that her thigh muscles when tense
Look interchangeable with those of Boris Becker –
Yet all are agreed that there can be no doubt
About Martina Navratilova:
Since she lent her body to Charles Atlas
The definition of the veins on her right forearm
Looks like the Mississippi river system
Photographed from a satellite,
And though she may unleash a charming smile
When crouching to dance at the ball with Ivan Lendl,
I have always found to admire her yet remain detached
Has been no problem.

But when the rain stops long enough for the true beauties
To come out swinging under the outshone sun,
The spectacle is hard for a man to take,
And in the case of this supernally graceful dish –
Likened to a panther by slavering sports reporters
Who pitiably fail to realize that any panther
With a topspin forehand line drive like hers
Would be managed personally by Mark McCormack –
I'm obliged to admit defeat.

So let me drink deep from the bitter cup.
Take it to her between any two points of a tie-break
That she may shake above it her thick black hair,

A nocturne from which the droplets as they fall
Flash like shooting stars –
And as their lustre becomes liqueur
Let the full calyx be repeatedly carried to me.
Until I tell you to stop,
Bring me the sweat of Gabriela Sabatini.

Fridge Magnet Sonnets

Except for the punctuation and capitalization, these sonnets were assembled on a refrigerator door entirely within the restrictions imposed by the Basic Magnetic Poetry Kit and the Cerebra Supplemental Kit. Whether the resulting, apparently unavoidable, pastiche of Wallace Stevens was dictated by a propensity in the mind of the author or by the nature of magnetic poetry would be nice to know. If the latter, there must now be refrigerators all over the world that look like the galley proofs of *Harmonium*.

I

I ribald sophist, you deft paragon,
Whet in our cloister languid dreams of sweet
Tongue-worship for the storm we cudgel on
With profligate palaver of bare feet.
But fiddle as we may, the shadows fall
Blue, tawdry, obdurate and lachrymose –
A torpid, adolescent caterwaul
Like tumid skin of a morose morass.
'So what?' you cry, and quashed I must eschew
Arid alacrity of epithet,
Be cool, austere, brusque, trenchant, true like you,
Not vapid and verbose as I am yet:
From here on in spurn brazen lusciousness,
Fetter my fecund zeal and chant fluff less.

II

Unctuous misanthrope, abscond to life!
Pant in a lather for a peachy breast.
Ascetic gynophobes usurp their lust,
Rip with the tacit rusty temporal knife
Of stultifying pallid acumen
The gorgeous mist of frantic puppy love
And enervate it to the putative.
No affable abeyance can supplant
Hot need, stalwart pariah and miscreant.
Let unrequited priapism, then,
Capriciously lambaste banal repose,
Ache, pound, boil, heave, drool juice and fulminate.
Delirious love is never delicate:
A florid blood-red spring rain shakes the rose.

Go Back to the Opal Sunset

Go back to the opal sunset, where the wine
Costs peanuts, and the avocado mousse
Is thick and strong as cream from a jade cow.
Before the passion fruit shrinks on the vine
Go back to where the heat turns your limbs loose.
You've worked your heart out and need no excuse.
Knock out your too-tall tent pegs and go now.

It's England, April, and it's pissing down,
So realize your assets and go back
To the opal sunset. Even autumn there
Will swathe you in a raw-silk dressing gown,
And through the midnight harbour lacquered black
The city lights strike like a heart attack
While eucalyptus soothes the injured air.

Now London's notion of a petty crime
Is simple murder or straightforward rape
And Oxford Street's a bombing range, to go
Back to the opal sunset while there's time
Seems only common sense. Make your escape
To where the prawns assume a size and shape
Less like a newborn baby's little toe.

Your tender nose anointed with zinc cream,
A sight for sore eyes will be brought to you.
Bottoms bisected by a piece of string
Will wobble through the heat-haze like a dream
That summer afternoon you go back to
The opal sunset, and it's all as true
As sandfly bite or jelly-blubber sting.

What keeps you here? Is it too late to tell?
It might be something you can't now define,
Your nature altered as if by the moon.
Yet out there at this moment, through the swell,
The hydrofoil draws its triumphant line.
Such powers of decision should be mine.
Go back to the opal sunset. Do it soon.

Lament for French Deal

feror ingenti circumdata nocte

God bless the nurses of the Sacred Heart
Who bring His great gift, morphine, to annul
The agony which tears French Deal apart.
Heaven be praised
That Science makes her once keen senses dull.

We thought of wattle sprays and willow wands
When we first saw French Deal in those young years –
Of frangipani petals and palm fronds.
Lord, she was sweet:
Gamblers and poets were both moved to tears.

To tears of lust as well, for though her face
Beat any angel's hollow, her loose limbs
And languorous figure had a pagan grace
To make a priest
Compose risqué new words for well-known hymns.

A gambler gave French Deal her name. Today,
Though sick himself, he sits beside her bed.
I know he will, while I am far away,
Kiss her goodbye
On my behalf as I would in his stead.

He named her for a racehorse that came in.
Fresh from the country, Janet was impressed
And as French Deal embraced a Life of Sin –
Since in those days
Free love was damned no sooner than confessed.

But not so at the Royal George Hotel,
Headquarters of the Downtown Push, for there
Bohemians defied the threat of Hell.
Lapsed Catholics
Sang blasphemously to the evening air.

Hot nights, cold beer and filtered cigarettes
Plucked proudly from the new-style flip-top box!
Philosophers pronounced, gamblers made bets –
It was a home
Away from home, that thieves' den by the docks.

Push women were the equals of their men,
Or so the theory went the men advanced
With all their other theories while, as then
Was still the rule,
The women were required to sit entranced.

Oasis faces in a boundless waste
Of words, and one face fairer than the rest:
Across the room, still smarting at the taste
Of my first beer,
I winced but gazed unblinking and felt blessed.

She was the gambler's girl and not to be
Approached by one so clearly short of clues,
But when I sailed away her memory
Smoked in my mind,
A brand evoking all I stood to lose.

The white light, the sweet heat, the open air,
The opal sunset and the sudden dawn,
You saw them all when she swept back her hair –
Her upraised arms
Outlined the paradise where we were born.

London was cold and girls in pubs would show
No skin below the neck except their hands.
Only blood shining out made their skins glow:
No sun shone in.
A man's eyes risked death in such frozen lands.

But come the second winter my despair
Cracked and dissolved. Out of the fog there stepped
French Deal and gathered me into her care.
Until the spring
It was together that we woke and slept.

She made it clear that she had come away
Only to show the gambler she was free.
For her this was a working holiday
From too much love,
A break from him. A bigger break for me,

My longed-for first great love affair unloosed
Not just desire but the desire to please.
Just as Narcissus was himself seduced
As he gazed down
To see the loved one's face in ecstasies,

I made her gasp and took it for applause:
It was my wretched ego I caressed.
No doubt I had confused effect and cause,
But equally
There could be no doubt I had Passed a Test.

Bursting with butch conceit I said goodbye.
She sailed home to be married. I stayed on,
And fifteen years unravelled before I
Saw her again.
Sydney had changed a lot while I was gone.

The Opera House was finished, there were tall
Buildings ablaze at night behind the Quay.
The Royal George was lost beyond recall
In concrete roads
Whose coils had squeezed it dry of mystery.

But one thing had remained the same: French Deal.
Tea on the lawn in my case proved unwise.
Unused to it, I judged the sun unreal.
Spread at our feet
Careening Cove was too bright for my eyes.

Dazzled I listened while she told me how
Marriage had come and gone. She had been ill
With meningitis but was better now.
She dropped a hint:
She and the gambler were true lovers still.

Long before sunset she took me inside
To lavish lotion on my burning skull.
I heard the ripple of the ebbing tide
Rocking a boat:
The chink of wind chimes and the slapping hull.

From that night on for fifteen years again
Whenever I flew home I came to tea,
And so in her life's prime the same two men
She started with
Shared her affection and her courtesy.

The gambler got the lion's share, of course:
To throw his life away yet keep her near
Was his reward for backing the right horse.
Each evening there
He warmed to her while it was morning here.

Conversely in my night she took the train
To Burwood where her girls thought her the best
Teacher in history and offset the pain
Of childlessness –
While he made sure he got a lot of rest.

Yes, all the time I toiled with diligence,
Apart from placing bets his only fame
He got from demonstrating in defence
Of a few trees –
His colleagues in the vegetation game.

Two men who scarcely added up to one,
One work-shy and the other a machine:
Both, when they sat beside her in the sun,
Were at their best.
Each was the better man he might have been.

Born of the fragile truce between us two,
Who never met except in her regard,
Her love life lasted yet was always new –
An ebb and flow
Like the tide at the foot of her front yard.

By rights we should all three have gone to hell
Together, but blind chance chose her to face
The silent forecast of her own death knell –
A cruel shadow
Which will soon, says the Sister's voice through space,

At last have done. The roses that I left
Fade in their vase. Bending to kiss her eyes
He can precisely see himself bereft
Where I must guess –
Yet I can paint the picture when she dies.

On High Street wharf at midnight she alone
Waits for the small white ferry with no crew
To grumble close. Its soft ropes on their own
Throw quiet loops.
Weightless she steps aboard as we will do

When our turn comes, gambler: but not tonight.
Tonight we are those two gulls overhead
Gliding against the wind to match our flight
With the ghost ship
That will not cross the harbour, but instead

Slips on the tide towards the open sea
Whose darkness, which already reaches deep
Into the brilliant city, soon will be
All that there is,
As she sails out across the curve of sleep –

Too far to follow, even for you and me.

The Eternity Man

Never filmed, he was photographed only once,
Looking up startled into the death-trap flash
Like a threatened life form.
Still underlining his copybook one-word message
With the flourish that doubled back under the initial 'E',
He was caught red-eyed with the stark white chalk in his hand
Writing Eternity.

Before he died in 1967
At the age of eighty-eight
He had managed to write it five hundred thousand times,
And always in copperplate script.
Few streets or public places in the city of Sydney
Remained unmarked by the man with a single obsession –
Writing Eternity.

Wherever you lived, sooner or later he'd reach you.
Hauling their billycarts up for the day's first run
Small boys swarmed when they came to the word
Arrestingly etched in the footpath.
It was self-protected by its perfect calligraphy –
The scrupulous sweep of a hand that had spent its lifetime
Writing Eternity.

He was born in a Balmain slum and raised underneath it,
Sleeping on hessian bags with his brothers and sisters
To keep beyond fist's reach of his dipso parents.
His name was Arthur Stace.
He had no one to use it apart from his family.
His fate was to die as a man and return as a portent,
Writing Eternity.

His sisters grew up to be prostitutes. He was a pimp,
But in 1930, in his early forties, on meths,
He heard the Reverend John Ridley at Burton Street
Baptist Church, Darlinghurst,
And scrapped his planned night in the down-and-out sanctuary.
The piss artist had his vocation revealed unto him –
Writing Eternity.

'I wish I could shout one word through the streets of Sydney!'
The Reverend Ridley shouted. 'Eternity! You
Have got to meet it! You! Where will you spend
Eternity?' Alone in his pew,
Avoided by all for his smell strong enough to see,
A man reborn saw the path stretch ahead he would stoop to,
Writing Eternity.

In New South Wales for more than a hundred years
We all had to learn that script in school,
But what school did he ever go to, and where
Did his chalk come from? How did he eat?
These nagging conundrums were mulled over endlessly
As he roamed unseen through the city without rhyme or reason
Writing Eternity.

In a blaze of glory the Thousand Year Reich was announced.
Old Bolsheviks shyly confessed with downcast eyes
And the first reffos arrived at Woolloomooloo.
Our troops sailed off to prop up the Middle East
Until Singapore fell and the Yanks overtipped for a taxi –
Yet still through the blacked-out streets he kept his own schedule
Writing Eternity.

But a mere word was ceasing to hold any terrors.
Belief in the afterlife faded. Where was God
When the Christmas snow came fluttering into the death camps?
Those kindling children, their piles of little shoes,
Condemned Divine Justice past hope of apology:
To rage at the storm and expect it to stop made more sense than
Writing Eternity.

He wrote it on the same night Hitler burned.
He wrote it as the Japanese cities melted
And the tanks rolled into Budapest.
While Sputnik skimmed through the stars he bent to his task
As if we believed there was still any Hell except history,
And Heaven could be rebuilt by one scuttling ratbag
Writing Eternity.

The rain didn't always wash his word away.
He sometimes used more than chalk. Near my place once
I found it fingertip-deep in the new white concrete.
It was lined with crimson enamel, a rune punched in
By a branding-iron from space. Down on one knee
I chipped out the paint with my penknife as if I could stop him
Writing Eternity.

He wouldn't have known. He didn't have time to go back,
Not even to visit his real bravura efforts
Which culminated in his famous Australia Square
Incised masterpiece filled with stainless steel.
Some snot-nosed kid with a grudge there would always be,
But he put all that behind him and kept on going,
Writing Eternity.

By the time he died I was half the world away
And when I came back I never gave him a thought.
It was almost fifty years after I unpicked it
That I pondered his word again,
On the dawn of the day when the laughing stock was yours truly
Who would have to go on alone and be caught in the spotlight
Writing Eternity.

From the thirty-third floor of the Regent I looked down naked.
The Opera House was sold out. I was afraid,
But the Harbour was flat calm all the way to the sea,
Its shaped, linked loops flush with silver,
And I suddenly saw what that showpiece of geology
Had really been up to ever since the magma cooled –
Writing Eternity.

That word again, and this time I could read it.
It said your life is on loan from those before you
Who had no chance, and before it is even over
Others will come to judge you, if only by
Forgetting your name; so better than glittering vainly
Would be to bend down in the dark half a million times
Writing Eternity.

Where will we spend it? Nowhere except here.
Life everlasting ends where it begins,
On Earth, but it is present at every moment.
We must seek grace now and not for ourselves alone
Was what that crazed saint meant in his ecstasy –
Since time is always, with chalk made from children's ashes,
Writing Eternity.

Reflections in an Extended Kitchen

Late summer charms the birds out of the trees
On to our lawn, where the cat gets them.
Aware of this but not unmanned, Matisse
Makes the whole room as sexy as the girl.

'Distributed voluptuousness,' he said,
Matching the decor to her lazy gaze.
Just book me on the first flight to Morocco.
You see what I see? Feathers on the grass.

Nothing so sordid in Henri's back yard
Where coloured shapes may touch, but not to crush.
Look at that death-trap out there, lined with roses!
We grew a free-fire zone with fertilizer.

Caught on the ground like the Egyptian Air Force
A wrecked bird on its back appears outraged:
It could have been a contender. What a world
Of slam-bang stuff to float one fantasy

Amongst her figured curtains, blobs for flowers,
Lolling unlocked in filmy harem pants!
Where did we see her first? That place they called
Leningrad. She looked like History's cure,

And even he could use that. When he turned
An artful blank back on his wife and child
They were arrested, leaving him to paint
In peace a world with no Gestapo in it –

A dream that came true. Agonies recede,
And if his vision hid harsh facts from him
It sharpens them for us. Best to believe
He served an indispensable ideal:

Douceur de vivre on a heroic scale –
Heaven on Earth, the Land of Oobladee,
Cloud Nine and Shangri-La hooked to the wall
As bolt holes for the brain, square wishing wells.

Suppose that like his brush my pen could speak
Volumes, our cat might stay in shape to pounce,
But only on the arm of that soft chair
You sit in now and where you would lie lulled,

An ageless, in-house *odalisque couchée*
Never to be less languorous than this,
Always dissolving in the air around you
Reality's cruel purr with your sweet whisper –

And nothing would be terrible again,
Nor ever was. The fear that we once felt
For daughters fallen ill or just an hour
Late home: it never happened. That dumb bird
Stayed in its tree and I was true to you.

In Praise of Marjorie Jackson

In 1999, the year before the Sydney Olympics,
Her face all laugh lines, regal in her scarlet coat,
The gold in her teeth aglow like her set of gold medals,
At the brand-new stadium she said exactly the right thing:
'What a heritage for our kids! It's lovely.'
As usual her words rang bells all over Australia.
She could always do that, tap into the national pride.

Fifty years back, she was the fastest kid in Lithgow.
She could run the boys into the earth,
And when she ran the legs off Fanny Blankers-Koen
(Who, visiting Sydney, expected to win in a walk)
The good citizens of Lithgow were not surprised –
Unlike the rest of Australia, whose collected sporting scribes,
When their mouths had returned to the normal, merely open,
     position,
Gave her an express train's name to match the way she ran –
She was the Lithgow Flash.
Young Marjorie, who could always do the right thing,
Went back to Lithgow with a modest, pre-cosmetic smile,
Quietly amused at the ratbag outside world.

Lithgow, hemmed in by its hills and one storey high
At its highest, didn't even have a running track.
They cleared her a stretch of ground to prepare for the Olympics.
Tired after work, she would train there in the dark:
Lit up by car headlights that turned the loitering fog
Into the nimbus of a legend about to happen
As she sailed like an angel through the clouds of her first glory,
The most brilliant thing Lithgow had ever seen –

The right thing, the thing she could always do
With a whole heart, putting one foot in front of the other
Like the fists of Jimmy Carruthers tapping a punchball.

At Helsinki she ran in metres instead of yards
So the stretch for the sprints was just that little bit longer
Each time, two ghosts of a chance for the others to catch her
After her start that uncoiled like Hector Hogan's –
But they never got near her.
In both events, she won scooting away like a wallaby
With its tail on fire, and collared those twin gold medals
With a smile for the camera that signalled her gratitude
To God and the world, to Finland, Australia and Lithgow –
The right smile, again the right thing exactly.

She came home in triumph, with ninety-six miles of people
From Sydney to Lithgow shouting congratulations –
The kind of acclaim that used to make Roman generals
Decide it might just be their turn to go for the title.
It would go to anyone's head, but it didn't to hers
Because it wouldn't have been the right thing:
She married her cyclist Peter and the people of Lithgow
Collected a total of seventy-seven pounds for the wedding –
The nearest she ever got to the big money
And the nearest she wanted.

When the last of Peter's health melted, what could she do
Except the right thing? She lent her undying lustre
To fundraising for leukaemia research.
She groomed herself as a speaker, walked with the poise
That only those who have danced on air can possess
(Or walked on water, like the RiverCat named for her

You can catch tomorrow from the Quay to Parramatta,
Watching the way its keels, like the spikes of a sprinter,
In their lightweight trajectory barely impinge on the world)
And still, with her seventieth year coming close to her heels,

She looked fit to make that spanking new surface at Homebush
Unroll from the balls of her feet like a belt going backwards
Into the past, into the headlight-lit mist
Where she was the quickest of all my fantastic girls –
Than Shirley Strickland, than even Betty Cuthbert she was quicker –
The very first of the fleet-foot females Movietone flung
Flying towards me but forever out of reach
Up there on the screen, their green and gold strip black and white
To the lens, but to my pre-teen eyes spilling fire
From the warmth of their bodies, the strength of their softness,
     the sweet
Line of their slimness propelled by the will to excel
And cold lamb cutlets for breakfast.

Yes, still in short pants I was out of my mind for them all,
But somehow I knew – I don't know, it was something about her –
That she – the unglamorous one but in motion a goddess –
That she was the one who, had I been able to catch her
And run at her side for a while as I gasped out my feelings,
Would have done the right thing,
And smiled without laughing before she raced on and away –

Or even said, even though it wasn't true,
That if I'd had the luck to have been born and brought up in Lithgow
Where the nights were cool, the stars were close and the people real,
I could have been a sprinter too,
And run for my country at the same amazing time

As the Lithgow Flash shot through like the Bondi Special
Into the language, and Australia rose to its feet –
Cheering the champion, which, even when all are equal,
And sometimes especially then, is the right thing to do.

Simple Stanzas about Modern Masters

If T. S. Eliot and Ezra Pound
Came back to life, again it would be found
One had the gab, the other had the gift
And each looked to the other for a lift.

The Waste Land, had not Pound applied his blue
Pencil, might well have seemed less spanking new.
Pound was a crackpot but that made his critical
Prowess particularly analytical.

Embarrassing, however, there's no doubt:
Increasingly too crass to have about.
While Eliot held discreetly right-wing views
Pound yelled obscenities about the Jews.

For Eliot, the time to cause a stir
Was past, and dignity was *de rigueur,*
But Pound preferred to hang out with the boys
In boots and black shirts who made lots of noise.

For Eliot the war brought veneration:
He seemed to speak for his adopted nation.
When Pound spoke it reminded Mussolini
What it had cost them to lose Toscanini.

Pound wound up in a cage and might have swung
Or died strapped down if he had not been sprung;
A big prize for the *Cantos* saved his neck
Though even he half-guessed they were a wreck.

The rackety campaign in Pound's support
Worked only because Eliot took thought
On how *il miglior fabbro* might best be
Saved for a dignified senility.

His tactic was to let it be inferred
That though he nowadays thought Pound absurd,
The established master and his erstwhile mentor
Were still somehow one creature, like a centaur.

One was the head, the other the hindquarters
(A point made by the more astute reporters)
But few dared to protest at a free pass
For such a well-connected horse's arse.

Pound in his dotage made no spark of sense
But Eliot, still staunch in his defence,
Remembered how it took a cocksure friend
To help unscramble radium from pitchblende.

Pound falling silent, Eliot sat in state.
Though some said what he did was etiolate,
Most regally he'd kept the palace rule –
Never lose sight of what you owe your fool.

Son of a Soldier

My tears came late. I was fifty-five years old
Before I began to cry authentically:
First for the hurt I had done to those I loved,
Then for myself, for what had been done to me
In the beginning, to make my heart so cold.

When the floodgates opened, the flood was not like rain.
With the undammed water came the sad refuse:
The slime, the drowned rats and the bloated corpse
Of the man whose absence had plugged up the sluice
That now gushed junk into my neat domain.

Not older by all that much than my dear daughters
He lay disfiguring a flower bed,
As if by bubbling gas a shallow grave
Of massacre had thrust up one of its dead,
Not to be washed clean by the clearest waters.

I took leave of my wife and knelt beside him
Who could have been my son, though I was his,
And everything he had not come back to tell me
About how everlasting true love is
Was a mouth of mud, so thick did woe betide him.

'Had you come home, I would not be what I am,'
I cried. 'I could have loved my mother less
And not searched for more like her among others,
Parched for a passion undimmed by distress
While you lay deep behind that looming dam.'

The wet earth swallowed him. This time his grave
Was marked: at least I knew now where he was.
I turned to meet her eyes. 'Let me explain,'
I said to her. 'My tears were trapped because
He left me to be tender, strong and brave

Who was none of those things. Inflamed by fright,
The love that he did not return to make
To the first woman I knew and could not help,
Became in me a thirst I could never slake
For one more face transfigured by delight,

Yet needing nothing else. It was a doomed quest
Right from the start, and now it is at an end.
I am too old, too raddled, too ashamed.
Can I stay in your house? I need a friend.'
'So did I,' she said truly. 'But be my guest:

God knows I too have waited wasted years
To have my husband home. Our parents wept
For history. Great events prised them apart,
Not greed, guilt, lies and promises unkept.
Pray they come not too late, these healing tears.'

The house we live in and that man-sized mound
Are a long walk between, yet both are real.
Like family life, his flowers have their weeds
To save them from a sanitized ideal.
I hope this balance holds until the ground

Takes me down, too. But I fear they will go on thronging,
Those pipe-dream sprites who promise a fresh start –
Free, easy furies haunting a cot-case
That never lived, or loved, with a whole heart –
Until for one last time I die of longing.

What will I tell her then, in that tattoo
Of the last breath, the last gasp, the death rattle?
The truth: that in my life stolen from him
Whose only legacy was a lost battle,
The one thing that belonged to me was you.

Where the Sea Meets the Desert

Antony and Cleopatra swam at Mersa Matruh
In the clear blue shallows.
Imagine the clean sand, the absence of litter –
No plastic bottles or scraps of styrofoam packing,
No jetsam at all except the occasional corpse
Of a used slave tossed off a galley –
And the shrieks of the dancing Queen as the hero splashed her
While her cheer-squad of ladies-in-waiting giggled on cue,
The eunuchs holding the towels.
With salt in her eyes did she wrinkle the perfect nose
Of which Pascal would later venture the opinion
That had it been shorter (he didn't say by how much)
History would have been different?
They were probably both naked. What a servant saw
Did not count. They might even have boffed each other
Right there at the water's edge like a pair of dolphins
Washed up in the middle of a mad affair,
With her unable to believe the big lunk would ever
Walk away from this, and him in his soul
Fighting to forget that this was R&R
And there was still the war.

There is always the war. The Aussies in Tobruk
Could hear the German bombers at El Adem
Warming up on the airfield
For the five-minute flight that is really the only distance
Between bliss and blitz.
Ears still ringing from kookaburras and whipbirds
Were heckled by Heinkels.

When Antony eyeballed her Coppertone tits and bum
He was looking at Actium.

Shake it, lady.
Shake it for the Afrika Korps.
Where the sea meets the desert there is always,
There is always the war.

The Lions at Taronga

The leaves of Tower Bridge are rigged to open
For any taxi I might chance to catch.
They say that when the ravens leave the Tower

It means they'll use my rain-stained study skylight
As a toilet. I can see Canary Wharf,
A Russian rocket packed around with boosters

Lit up to launch at dawn from Baikonur.
The Blade of Light is cleared for butterflies
To crash-land. When that lens-shaped office block

Is finished it will bend a ray from space
To burn the *Belfast* like a sitting duck.
I've known the NatWest Tower since it was knee-high

To the Barbican, another high-tech know-how
HQ that used to look like the last word.
From my place I can see last words in vistas

As far downriver as the spreading spikes
Of the Dome, some sad bitch of a sea urchin
Losing its battle with a stray Dutch cap

While hothouse pleasure boats leak foreign voices
Like tourist minibuses nose to tail
In the corridors of Buckingham Palace.

Been there, done that. The Queen, she hung one on me.
I've got it in a box. The box to frame
My body will be built here, like as not,

And probably quite soon. I've lived in London
For longer than some people live all told.
Except for the way out, I know it backwards.

So at night when the lions at Taronga
Roar in my memory across the water
I feel the way they must have felt, poor bastards –

Gone in the teeth. The food dead. On display
All day and every day. Sleep in a fortress.
Every familiar walkway leads to strangers.

Dream Me Some Happiness

John Donne, uneasiest of apostates,
Renouncing Rome that he might get ahead
In life, or anyway not wind up dead,
Minus his guts or pressed beneath great weights,

Ascribed his bad faith to his latest flame
As if the fact she could be bent to do
His bidding proved that she would not stay true:
Each kiss a Judas kiss, a double game.

Compared with him, the mental muscle-man,
Successors who declared his numbers rough
Revealed by theirs they found the pace too tough:
The knotty strength that made him hard to scan

Left him renowned for his conceits alone,
Figments unfading as the forms of death
Prescribed for Catholics by Elizabeth –
Tangles of gristle, relics of hair and bone.

Brought back to favour in an anxious time
Attuned to his tormented intellect,
By now he charms us, save in one respect:
Framing his women still looks like a crime.

We foist our fault on her we claim to love
A different way. Pleased to the point of tears,
She tells us that the real world disappears.
Not quite the Donne thing, when push comes to shove:

He wrote betrayal into her delight.
We have a better reason to deceive
Ourselves as we help her help us believe
Life isn't like that: at least, not tonight.

Deckard Was a Replicant

The forms of nature cufflinked through your life
Bring a sense of what Americans call closure.
The full-blown iris swims in English air
Like the wreckage of an airbag jellyfish
Rinsed by a wave's thin edge at Tamarama:
The same frail blue, the same exhausted sprawl,
The same splendour. Nothing but the poison
Is taken out. In the gallery, that girl
Has the beauty that once gave itself to you
To be turned into marriage, children, houses.
She will give these things to someone else this time.

If this time seems the same time, it's because
It is. The reason she is not for you
Is she already was. Try to remember
What power they have, knowing what sex is for:
Replacing us. The Gainsborough chatelaine
She studies wears a shawl dipped in the hint
Of jacaranda blossoms, yet it might
Remind her of sucked sweets, or the pale veins
Of her own breasts. Setting the Thames on fire,
The tall white-painted training ship from Denmark
Flaunts the brass fittings of the little ferry
That took you as a child to Kirribilli
On its way to Wapping, then the Acheron
And Hades. Those gulls that graze the mud
Took sixty years to get here from Bundeena.

At an average speed of forty yards an hour
They barely moved. It seems you didn't either.
You stood still with your head wrapped in the armour
Of perception's hard-wired interlocking habits.
Ned Kelly was the ghost of Hamlet's father.
Dazzled by lipstick pulped from waratahs,
The smoker coughs, having been born again.

Lucretius the Diver

Things worn out by the lapse of ages tend
Toward the reef, that motley wrecking crew
Of living polyps who, to get ahead,
Climb ruthlessly all over their own dead,
But facts like those Lucretius never knew:
He merely meant we can't long buck the trend
That winds up hard against a watershed.

Horace had godly names for every breeze.
Ovid himself was stiff with sacred stuff.
Virgil talked turkey just once, about bees.
Of ancient wits Lucretius alone,
Without recourse to supernatural guff,
Uncannily forecast the modern tone –
Viewing the world as miracle enough.

Imagine him in scuba gear, instead
Of whatever kit a Roman poet wore –
To find his fruitful symbol for the grave
Not just inevitable but alive
Would surely suit him down to the sea floor.
Suspended before such a flower bed
He'd bubble with delight beneath the wave.

The reef, a daughter, and the sea, its mother,
In a long, white-lipped rage with one another
Would shout above him as he hung in space
And saw his intuition had been right:
Under a windswept canopy of lace,
Even down there in that froth-filtered light,
The World of Things is clearly the one place –

Death lives, life dies, and no gods intervene.
It's all so obvious, would be his thought:
But then, it always was, at least to him,
And why the rest of them were quite so dim
On that point is perhaps a theme we ought
To tackle, realizing it could mean
Our chances going in are pretty slim

Of drawing comfort from a Golden Age
So lethally haphazard no one sane
Could contemplate the play of chance was all
There was to life. That took the featherbrain
Lucretius seemed to them, and not the sage
He seems to us, who flinch from his disdain
As he stares seaward at the restless wall

Of ruined waves, the spray that falls like rain.

One Man to Another

Salute me! I have tamed my daughter's face
With hot oil, and my honour has been saved.
It's not to be defied that I have slaved.
She talks a lot less now she knows her place.

Most of her mouth can still move, and one eye
Could stare in hatred if she wanted to.
I'm proud to say her protests have been few
Apart from that absurd initial cry.

That was the evil spirit leaving her.
She really should have dealt with it herself.
She said she'd rather end up on the shelf
Than marry our best choice. What thoughts occur

To girls nowadays! Next they will want a say
In what to wear and when to buy a book.
Here, take your mother's mirror. Take a look.
What have you got in store for me today?

You thought to shake my faith? Well, you have found
My faith shakes you, and will again, I swear,
If you continue with that hangdog air:
If you continue with that whining sound.

Can't you be grateful we still keep you here?
We could have sent you out there to the dust
Where people fight for every cowpat crust.
We don't ask for a grin from ear to ear,

But now no man would want you, we still do,
So cut the sulky pout. To many another
Far worse than this has happened. Ask your mother.
I don't know what the world is coming to.

See how she slinks inside. If not with grace
She seems to have accepted, more or less,
Some limit to a woman's wilfulness.
The lesson hurt us both, but met the case.

Salute me! I have tamed my daughter's face.

Stolen Children

From where I sit for cool drinks in the heat
The Covent Garden Jumpzone seems to fling
Kids over rooftops in a bungee dive
The wrong way, and the thrill it is to swing
Straight up and down you see when they arrive,
In Heaven as on Earth, with kicking feet,

And so depart. One flier takes the pip
By somersaulting in her harness when,
High overhead, there is a moment's pause
For rubber to recuperate. Not then,
But later, as she signals for applause
With a slow stride instead of a last flip,

The penny drops. I've seen this girl before.
Above the birthplace of the Son of God
It had pleased Botticelli to impose
The perfect circle of a trained cheer-squad
Dancing barefoot with light fantastic toes
As angels do, the cloudless blue their floor.

The second from the left was my dream girl.
Outside, Trafalgar Square filled up with snow.
Winter in England was a culture shock
More ways than one. The gallery's warm glow
Seemed concentrated in a flowing frock,
A flash of ankle gleaming like a pearl.

Back down with us, she saunters past my chair.
About thirteen, with more than blips for breasts,
She wasn't born before I saw her first
On a glass board surfing the troughs and crests
Of the air waves. Nor was her mother. Worst
Of all is how the longing lingers there

Yet leaves us nothing else to bless at last
Except our luck that we were not insane.
The *Standard* says the missing girls are still
Not found. A man is held. The writers strain
The law's pale letter, closing for the kill
As once the mob did, not far in the past.

Suppose he did it, don't I know that face?
I shave it every morning. The same eyes
Plead innocent. In his case, one loose screw
Switched the desire a priest can't neutralize
To children, and permitted him to do
What we don't dream of even when God's grace

Stuns us with glory walking in the sky.
Grace, but not justice. If an impulse makes
Mere fools of most but monsters of the rest,
A balance sheet of what it gives and takes
Implies a mediator who knows best
If you can just surrender. Nor can I.

Think of the fathers, praying. They must know
No one exists to listen who did not
Choose them for this, but where else can they ask
The same exemption all the others got
By chance? They beg for mercy from a mask.
Had it a mind, they'd not be weeping so.

Time to go home. The things I tried to tell
My own two daughters churn in my hot head.
The stranger won't come on like Captain Hook.
He'll laugh like me, crack jokes, yet want you dead.
Good story, Dad. I turn for one last look
At Paradise, and how we rose and fell.

Young Lady in Black

The Russian poets dreamed, but dreamed too soon,
Of a red-lipped, chalk-white face framed in black fur:
Symbol of what their future would be like –
Free, lyrical and elegant, like her.
In the love songs of their climacteric
I met you before I met you, and you were
The way you are now in these photographs

Your father took outside the Hermitage.
You stand on snow, and more snow in the air
Arrives in powdered form like rice through space.
It hurts to know the colour of your hair
Is blacker than your hat. Such is the price
Figments exact by turning real: we care
Too much. I too was tricked by history,

But at least I saw you, close enough to touch,
Even as time made touch impossible.
The poets never met their richly dressed
Princess of liberty. The actual girl
Was lost to them as all the rest was lost:
Only their ghosts attended the snowfall
The camera stopped when you stood in the square,

Fiction made fact at long last and too late.
My grief would look like nothing in their eyes.
I hear them in the photographs. The breath
Of sorrow stirs the cold dust while hope dies
The worst way, in the vision of rebirth,
As by whole generations they arise
From pitted shallows in the permafrost

And storm the Winter Palace from the sky.
Each spirit shivering in a bead of light,
They fall again for what they once foretold –

For you, dawn burning through its cloak of night.
They miss what I miss, and a millionfold.
It all came true, it's there in black and white:
But your mouth is the colour of their blood.

In Town for the March

Today in Castlereagh Street I
Felt short of breath, and here is why.
From the direction of the Quay
Towards where Mark Foy's used to be,
A glass and metal river ran
Made in Germany and Japan.
Past the facade of David Jones
Men walked their mobile telephones,
Making the footpath hideous
With what they needed to discuss.
But why so long, and why so loud?
I can recall a bigger crowd
In which nobody fought for space
Except to call a name. The face
To fit it smiled as it went by
Among the ranks. Women would cry
Who knew that should they call all day
One face would never look their way.
All this was sixty years ago,
Since when I have grown old and slow,
But still I see the marching men,
So many of them still young then,
Even the men from the first war
Straight as a piece of two-by-four.
Men of the Anzac Day parade,
I grew up in the world you made.
To mock it would be my mistake.
I try to love it for your sake.
Through cars and buses, on they come,
Their pace set by a spectral drum.

Their regimental banners, thin
As watercolours fading in
The sun, hint at a panoply
Dissolving into history.
As the rearguard outflanks Hyde Park,
Wheels right, and melts into the dark,
It leaves me, barely fit to stand,
Reaching up for my mother's hand.

Six Degrees of Separation from Shelley

In the last year of her life I dined with Diana Cooper
Who told me she thought the best thing to do with the poor
Was to kill them. I think her tongue was in her cheek
But with that much plastic surgery it was hard to tell.

As a child she had sat on the knee of George Meredith,
More than forty years after he published *Modern Love*.
Though she must have been as pretty as any poppet
Who challenged the trousers of Dowson or Lewis Carroll,

We can bet Meredith wasn't as modern as that.
By then the old boy wouldn't have felt a twinge
Even had he foreseen she would one day arrive
In Paris with an escort of two dozen Spitfires.

The book lamented his marriage to one of the daughters
Of Peacock. Peacock when young rescued Shelley
From a coma brought on through an excess of vegetarianism
By waving a steak under his sensitive nose.

Shelley never quite said that the best thing to do with the rich
Was to kill them, but he probably thought so.
Whether the steak was cooked or raw I can't remember.
I should, of course. I was practically there:

The blaze of his funeral pyre on the beach at night
Was still in her eyes. At her age I hope to recall
The phial of poison she carried but never used
Against the day there was nothing left to live for.

Occupation: Housewife

Advertisements asked 'Which twin has the Toni?'
Our mothers were supposed to be non-plussed.
Dense paragraphs of technical baloney
Explained the close resemblance of the phoney
To the Expensive Perm. It worked on trust.

The barber tried to tell me the same sheila
With the same Expensive Perm was pictured twice.
He said the Toni treatment was paint-sealer
Re-bottled by a second-hand car dealer
And did to hair what strychnine did to mice.

Our mothers all survived, but not the perms.
Two hours at most the Toni bobbed and dazzled
Before the waves were back on level terms,
Limp as the spear-points of the household germs
An avalanche of Vim left looking frazzled.

Another false economy, home brew
Seethed after nightfall in the laundry copper.
Bought on the sly, the hops were left to stew
Into a mulch that grunted as it grew.
You had to sample it with an eye-dropper,

Not stir it with a stick as one mum did.
She piled housebricks on top, thinking the gas
Would have nowhere to go. Lucky she hid
Inside the house. The copper blew its lid
Like Krakatoa to emit a mass

Of foam. The laundry window bulged and broke.
The prodigy invaded the back yard.
Spreading across the lawn like evil smoke
It murdered her hydrangeas at a stroke
And long before the dawn it had set hard.

On a world scale, one hardly needs to note,
Those Aussie battlers barely had a taste
Of deprivation. Reeling from the boat
Came reffo women who had eaten goat
Only on feast days. Still, it is the waste

I think of, the long years without our men,
And only the Yanks to offer luxuries
At a price no decent woman thought of then
As one she could afford, waiting for when
The Man Himself came back from Overseas.

And then I think of those whose men did not:
My mother one of them. She who had kept
Herself for him for so long, and for what?
To creep, when I had splinters, to my cot
With tweezers and a needle while I slept?

Now comes the time I fly to sit with her
Where she lies waiting, to what end we know.
We trade our stories of the way things were,
The home brew and the perm like rabbit fur.
How sad, she says, the heart is last to go.

The heart, the heart. I still can hear it break.
She asked for nothing except his return.
To pay so great a debt, what does it take?
My books, degrees, the money that I make?
Proud of a son who never seems to learn,

She can't forget I lost my good penknife.
Those memories of waste do not grow dim
When you, for Occupation, write: Housewife.
Out of this world, God grant them both the life
She gave me and I had instead of him.

Jesus in Nigeria

Let him so keen for casting the first stone
Direct a fast ball right between her eyes,
So it might be from one quick burst of bone,
Not from a mass of bruises, that she dies.

I'm pleased to see, of all you without sin,
The cocky dimwit is so young and strong
Who won the draw to let the games begin.
He looks the type, unless I'm very wrong,

Who'll hog the glory with his opening shot.
With any luck at least he'll knock her out.
His rivals in this miserable lot
Are hard-pressed to jump up and down and shout.

That old one there has just put out his back
Lifting a boulder he could barely throw
For half a yard without a heart attack,
But you can bet, just to be in the show,

He'd shuffle up and drop it on her head.
I hate to take my father's name in vain
But God almighty, how they want her dead:
How sure they are that she should die in pain.

The woman taken in adultery:
It's one of the best stories in my book.
Some scholars call it the essential me.
If my writ ran here, you could take a look.

Alas, it doesn't. I wield little power
Even with my bunch, let alone with yours.
Long, long ago I had my public hour.
My mission failed. The maniacs and bores

Took over. I still weep, but weep in fear
Over a world become so pitiless
I miss that blessed soldier with the spear
Who put an early end to my distress.

Merely a thug and not a mental case,
He showed the only mercy I recall.
A dumb but reasonably decent face:
The best that we can hope for, all in all.

Step up, young man. Take aim and don't think twice.
No matter what you both believe is true,
Tonight she will be with me in Paradise.
I'm sorry I can't say the same for you.

The Place of Reeds

Kogarah (suppress the first 'a' and it scans)
Named by the locals for the creek's tall reeds
That look like an exotic dancer's fans
When dead, was where I lived. Born to great deeds

I stripped the fronds and was a warrior
Whose arrows were the long thin brittle stem
With a stiff piece of copper wire or
A headless nail to make a point for them.

The point went in where once the pith had been
Before it crumbled. The capillary
Was open at the other end. Some keen
Constructors mastered the technology

For fitting in a feathery tailpiece,
But they made model aeroplanes that flew.
Mine didn't, and my shafts, upon release
Wobbled and drifted as all missiles do

With nothing at the back to guide their flight.
Still, I was dangerous. My willow bow
Armed an Odysseus equipped to smite
Penelope and let her suitors go.

The creek led through a swamp where each weekend
Among the tangled trees we waged mock war.
At short range I could sometimes miss a friend
And hit the foe. Imagine Agincourt

Plus spiders, snakes and hydroponic plants.
I can't forget one boy, caught up a tree
By twenty others, peeing his short pants
As the arrows came up sizzling. It was me.

Just so the tribesmen, when our ship came in
Bringing the puffs of smoke that threw a spear
Too quick to see, realized they couldn't win.
It was our weaponry and not their fear

Defeated them. As we who couldn't lose
Fought with our toys, their young men dived for coins
From the wharf across the bay at La Perouse,
Far from us. Now, in age, my memory joins

Easy supremacy to black despair
In those enchanted gardens that they left
Because they knew they didn't have a prayer:
Lately I too begin to feel bereft.

Led by the head, my arrow proves to be
My life. I took my life into my hands.
I loosed it to its wandering apogee,
And now it falls. I wonder where it lands.

Hard-Core Orthography

In porno-speak, reversion to the Latin
Consoles us. 'Cum.' *Cum laude* we construe
As an audible orgasm. By that pattern,
Cum grano salis overturns the salt
With a thrashing climax when her urge to screw
Right there at dinner must be satisfied.
Cum vulpibus vulpinandum. While with foxes –
Caught *in flagrante*, high-heeled shoes flung wide
In satin sheets – do as the foxes do.
With aching wrist and pouting like a dolt,
Linguistically we still tick the right boxes:
You made *mecum*, she moans as she comes to.
Thus moved, her airbag lips look cumbersome
In the best sense. Maybe she's not so dumb.
Dum spiro, spero. How was it for you?

Flashback on Fast Forward

The way his broken spirit almost healed
When he first saw how lovely she could look,
Her face illuminated by a book,
Was such a holy moment that he kneeled
Beside her; and the way his shoulders shook
Moved her caressing hand. Their love was sealed.

They met again. A different, older place
Had drawn her to its books, but still the glow
Of white between the words lit up her face
As if she gazed on freshly fallen snow.
He knew his troubled heart could not forego,
Not even for her sake, this touch of grace.

He asked her hand in marriage. She said yes.
Later he often said she must have known
To be with him was to be left alone
With the sworn enemy of happiness,
Her house a demilitarized zone
At best, and peace a pause in the distress.

When finally it broke her, he helped bring
Her back to life. Give him that much at least:
His cruelty was but a casual thing,
Not a career. Alas, that thought increased
His guilt he'd talked her into sheltering
Him safe home from the storm that never ceased,

Nor ever would. And so the years went by,
And, longer wed than almost all their friends,
Always in silence they would wonder why,
And sometimes say so. When a marriage ends,
They noticed, it's from good will running dry,
Not just from lack of means to make amends.

He could not save himself: that much she knew.
Perhaps she'd felt it forty years before
When he quaked where he knelt, and what was more
She was aware that saying 'I love you'
To one who hates himself can only store
Up trouble earthly powers can't undo.

But revelation can. There at the start,
It came again to mark their closing years.
Once more, and this time through and through, his heart
Was touched. The ice he half prized turned to tears
As the last hailstone melts and disappears
In rain. By just a glass door set apart,

She in her study, he in the garden, they
Looked separate still, but he saw, in her eyes,
The light of the white paper. How time flies
Revealed its secret path from their first day.
He did a dance to make her look his way.
She smiled at him, her devil in disguise,

Almost as if at last he had grown wise.

From Robert Lowell's Notebook

Notes for a Sonnet

Stalled before my metal shaving mirror
With a locked razor in my hand I think of Tantalus
Whose lake retreats below the fractured lower lip
Of my will. Splinter the groined eyeballs of our sin,
Ford Madox Ford: you on the Quaker golf course
In Nantucket double-dealt your practised lies
Flattering the others and me we'd be great poets.
How wrong you were in their case. And now Nixon,
Nixon rolls in the harpoon ropes and smashes with his flukes
The frail gunwales of our beleaguered art. What
Else remains now but your England, Ford? There's not
Much Lowell-praise left in Mailer but could be Alvarez
Might still write that book. In the skunk-hour
My mind's not right. But there will be
Fifty-six new sonnets by tomorrow night.

Revised Notes for a Sonnet

On the steps of the Pentagon I tucked my skull
Well down between my knees, thinking of Cordell Hull
Cabot Lodge Van du Plessis Stuyvesant, our gardener,
Who'd stop me playing speedway in the red-and-rust
Model A Ford that got clapped out on Cape Cod
And wound up as a seed shed. Oh my God, my God,

How this administration bleeds but will not die,
Hacking at the ribcage of our art. You were wrong, R. P.
Blackmur. Some of the others had our insight, too:
Though I suppose I had endurance, toughness, faith,
Sensitivity, intelligence and talent. My mind's not right.
With groined, sinning eyeballs I write sonnets until dawn
Is published over London like a row of books by Faber –
Then shave myself with Uncle's full-dress sabre.

Notes for a Revised Sonnet

Slicing my head off shaving I think of Charles I
Bowing to the groined eyeball of Cromwell's sinning will.
Think too of Orpheus, whose disembodied head
Dumped by the Bacchants floated singing in the river,
His love for Eurydice surviving her dumb move
By many sonnets. Decapitation wouldn't slow me down
By more than a hundred lines a day. R. P. and F. M. F.
Play eighteen holes together in my troubled mind,
Ford faking his card, Blackmur explicating his,
And what is love? John Berryman, if you'd had what it took
We could have both blown England open. Now, alone,
With a plush new set-up to move into and shake down,
I snow-job Stephen Spender while the liquor flows like lava
In the parlour of the Marchioness of Dufferin and Ava.

R. S. Thomas at Altitude

The reason I am leaning over
At this pronounced angle is simply
That I am accustomed to standing
On Welsh hillsides
Staring out over escarpments stripped
And pitiless as my vision,
Where God says: Come
Back to the trodden manure
Of the chapel's warm temptation.
But I see the canker that awaits
The child, and say no.
I see the death that ends
Life, and say no.
Missing nothing, I say
No, no.
And God says: you can't
Say no to me, cully,
I'm omnipotent.
But I indicate the
Flying birds and the
Swimming fish and the trudging
Horse with my pointing
Finger and with customary
Economy of language, say
Nothing.
There is a stone in my mouth,
There is a storm in my
Flesh, there is a wind in
My bone.

Artificer of the knuckled, globed years
Is this your answer?
I've been up on this hill
Too long.

Edward Estlin Cummings Dead

what time el Rouble & la Dollar spin
'their' armies into ever smaller change,
patrolling Kopeks for a Quarter search
& Deutschfranc, after decimating Yen
inflates with sterling Rupee in a ditch

(what time, i.e., as moneys in their 'death'
throes leave room for unbought souls to breathe)

that time, perhaps,
                    I'm him believing (i.
e., cummings
    hold it
    CUMMINGS) dead (
p   e   g   g   e   d   o   u   t
) & I will leave him lie

Symptoms of Self-Regard

As she lies there naked on the only hot
Day in a ruined August reading Hugo Williams,
She looks up at the window cleaner.
Who has hesitantly appeared.

Wishing that he were Hugo Williams
She luxuriates provocatively,
Her fantasy protected by the glass
Or so she thinks.

Would that this abrasive oaf
Were Hugo Williams, she muses –
Imagining the poet in a black Armani
Bomber jacket from *Miami Vice*,
His lips pursed to kiss.

Suddenly, convulsively, she draws
The sheet up over herself
And quivers, having at last realized
That it really *is* Hugo Williams.

He sinks out of sight,
His poem already written.
He signs it 'Hugo Williams'.
The blue overalls have come in handy.

He takes off his flat cap,
Letting his silken hair fall free.
Hugo Williams has gone back to being handsome.
The poet has come down to earth.

Richard Wilbur's Fabergé Egg Factory

If Occam's razor gleams in Massachusetts
In time the Pitti Palace is unravelled:
An old moon re-arising as the new sets
To show the poet how much he has travelled.

Laforgue said missing trains was beautiful
But Wittgenstein said words should not seduce:
Small talk from him would at the best be dutiful –
And news of trains, from either man, no use.

Akhmatova finds echoes in Akhnaten.
The vocables they share *a fortiori*
Twin-yolk them in the selfsame kindergarten
Though Alekhine might tell a different story.

All mentioned populate a limpid lyric
Where learning deftly intromits precision:
The shots are Parthian, the victories Pyrrhic,
Piccarda's ghost was not so pale a vision,
But still you must admit this boy's got class –

His riddles lead through vacuums to a space
Where skill leans on the parapet of farce
And sees Narcissus making up his face.

After Such Knowledge

Great Tom: Notes Towards the Definition of T. S. Eliot
by T. S. Matthews

I saw him when distaste had turned to nightmare
    Near the end of this interminable book:
    As if the terraced cloudscape were a staircase
And he himself yet palpable, his sandals,
    Achillean by asphodel uplifted,
    Propelled their burden's effortless ascent –
A tuft of candid feathers at each shoulder
    Proclaiming him apprentice, cherished fledgling
    To overhanging galleries of angels.
And so, the poet first and I behind him,
    But only he a freedman hieing homeward,
    My quarry turned towards me. I cried 'Master!
We all knew you could make it!' and embraced him –
    Since, being both Sordello and Odysseus,
    I forgot my teacher's substance was a shadow,
And gathered uselessly the empty air.
    'Just passing through?' he chuckled as I teetered,
    Perhaps to ease the anguish of my gesture.
'If I were you I wouldn't plan on staying,
    Unless you don't mind falling through the scenery.'
    His smile, admonitory yet seraphic,
Suggested Pentecost, the truce of Advent,
    The prior taste unspeakably assuaging
    Of the ineluctable apotheosis.
'You remember T. S. Matthews, Sir?' I asked.
    'T. S. Who?' 'He's written your biography.'

'Matthews . . . I suppose I knew him vaguely.
A *Time* man. Is it awful?' A platoon
   Of cherubim flashed past us on the banister,
   Posteriors illumined by the marble:
The welcoming committee for Stravinsky,
   As yet some years below but toiling skyward.
   'Not quite as bad as most have said, but still
A pretty odious effort.' Here I wavered.
   Around his neck, the excalfactive Order
   Of Merit infumated, argentine,
But the gaze above, both placent and unsleeping,
   Entlastende without tergiversation,
   Compelled the apprehension it prevented.
And I: 'It hasn't got that many facts
   Which can't be found in places more reputed –
   Notably your widow's thoughtful preface
To the MS of *The Waste Land*. That aside,
   The speculative content can add little
   To the cairn of innuendo stacked already
By Sencourt's *T. S. Eliot: A Memoir*.'
   I paused. And he: 'Poor Robert was a pest,
   I'm sad to say. Well, all right: what's the fuss then?'
I caught a sudden flicker of impatience,
   Familiar yet ineffable. 'Sir, nothing;
   For nothing can come of nothing. Matthews puzzles
Repellently about those thousand letters
   You wrote to Emily Hale, but has no answers.'
   And he, diverted: 'Nor will anybody,
For another fifty years. I can't believe, though,
   A full-blown book enshrines no more than these
   Incursions void of judgment. Therefore speak.'
And I: 'He rates his chances as a critic –
   Allowing you your gift, he dares to offer

Conjectures that your ear verged on the faulty.
You said, for instance, of St Magnus Martyr,
    Its walls contained inexplicable splendour.
    He calls that adjective cacophonous.'
'He calls it *what*?' 'Cacophonous.' 'I see.'
    And I: 'The strictures go beyond irreverence.
    His animus is manifest. Your consort
He terms "robust" at one point; elsewhere, "ample";
    Yet cravenly endorses in his foreword
    Her telling him in such a forthright manner
To render himself scarce.' A gust of laughter,
    Subversive of his sanctity, perturbed him.
    He conjured from the gold strings of his harp
An autoschediastic lilt of love
    Which might have once been whistled by Ravel.
    And he: 'She did that, did she? Excellent.'
I said, 'The pride you feel is not misplaced:
    Your wish that no biography be written
    Will not be lightly flouted. Forced to yield,
Your wife will choose her author with great scruple
    Yet most of us who wish your memory well
    By now share the opinion that permission
To undertake the task must soon be granted
    Lest unofficial books like this gain ground,
    Besmirching the achievement of a lifetime.'
And he: 'I'm sure the lass will do what's best.
    One's not allowed to give advice from here
    And care for earthly fame is hard to summon.
It may, perhaps, however, please Another
    To whisper in her ear.' He turned away,
    Declaring as he faded 'It's surprising,
But this place isn't quite as Dante said –
    It's like the escalator at High Holborn,

Except there's no way down.' So he departed,
Dissolving like a snowflake in the sun,
    A Sibyl's sentence in the leaves lost –
    Yet seemed like one who ends the race triumphant.

What About You? Asks Kingsley Amis

When Mrs Taflan Gruffydd-Lewis left Dai's flat
She gave her coiffe a pat
Having straightened carefully those nylon seams
Adopted to fulfil Dai's wicked dreams.
Evans didn't like tights.
He liked plump white thighs pulsing under thin skirts in
    packed pubs on warm nights.

That's that, then, thought Evans, hearing her Jag start,
And test-flew a fart.
Stuffing the wives of these industrial shags may be all
Very well, and *this* one was an embassy barroom brawl
With Madame Nhu.
Grade A. But give them that fatal twelfth inch and they'll
    soon take their cue

To grab a yard of your large intestine or include your glans
Penis in their plans
For that Rich, Full Emotional Life you'd thus far ducked
So successfully.
Yes, Evans was feeling . . . Mucked-
up sheets recalled their scrap.
Thinking barbed thoughts in stanza form after shafting's
    a right sweat. Time for a nap.

The North Window

To stay, as Mr Larkin stays, back late
Checking accessions in the Brynmor Jones
Library (the clapped date-stamp, punch-drunk, rattling,
The sea-green tinted windows turning slate,
The so-called Reading Room deserted) seems
A picnic at first blush. No Rolling Stones
Manqués or Pink Floyd simulacra battling
Their way to low-slung pass-marks head in hands:
Instead, unpeopled silence. Which demands

Reverence, and calls nightly like bad dreams
To make sure that that happens. Here he keeps
Elected frith, his thanedom undespited,
Ensconced against the mating-mandrill screams
Of this week's Students' Union Gang-Bang Sit-in,
As wet winds scour the Wolds. The moon-cold deeps
Are cod-thronged for the trawlers now benighted,
North. The inland cousin to the sail-maker
Can still bestride the boundaries of the way-acre,

The barley-ground and furzle-field unwritten
Fee simple failed to guard from Marks & Spencer's
Stock depot some time back. (Ten years, was it?)
Gull, lapwing, redshank, oyster-catcher, bittern
(Yet further out: shearwater, fulmar, gannet)
Police his mud-and-cloud-ashlared defences.
Intangible revetments! On deposit,
Chalk thick below prevents the Humber seeping

Upward to where he could be sitting sleeping,
So motionless he lowers. Screwed, the planet
Swerves towards its distant, death-dark pocket.
He opens out his notebook at a would-be
Poem, ashamed by now that he began it.
Grave-skinned with grief, such Hardy-hyphened diction,
Tight-crammed as pack ice, grates. What keys unlock it?
It's all gone wrong. Fame isn't as it should be –
No, nothing like. 'The town's not been the same',
He's heard slags whine, 'since Mr Larkin came.'

Sir John arriving with those science-fiction
Broadcasting pricks and bitches didn't help.
And those Jap PhDs, their questionnaires!
(Replying 'Sod off, Slant-Eyes' led to friction.)
He conjures envied livings less like dying:
Sharp cat-house stomp and tart-toned, gate-mouthed yelp
Of Satchmo surge undulled, dispersing cares
Thought reconvenes. In that way She would kiss,
The Wanted One. But other lives than this – .

Fantastic. Pages spread their blankness. Sighing,
He knuckles down to force-feed epithets.
Would Love have eased the joints of his iambs?
He can't guess, and by now it's no use trying.
A sweet ache spreads from cramp-gripped pen to limb:
The stanza next to last coheres and sets.
As rhyme and rhythm, tame tonight like lambs,
Entice him to the standard whirlwind finish,
The only cry no distances diminish

Comes hurtling soundless from Creation's rim
Earthward – the harsh *recitativo secco*
Of spaces between stars. He hears it sing,
That voice of utmost emptiness. To him.
Declaring he has always moved too late,
And hinting, its each long-lost blaze's echo
Lack-lustre as a Hell-bent angel's wing,
That what – as if he needed telling twice –
Comes next makes this lot look like Paradise.

SELECTED VERSE LETTERS

To Martin Amis: a letter from Indianapolis

Dear Mart, I write you from a magic spot.
The dullsville capital of Indiana
At this one point, for this one day, has got
Intensity in every nut and spanner.
Soon now the cars will sing their vast Hosanna
And pressure will produce amazing grace.
Drake-Offenhauser! A. J. Foyt's bandanna!
Velazquez painting Philip at the chase
Saw something like these colours, nothing like this race.

Ten thirty. Half an hour before the start.
The press-box at the Brickyard is up high.
We sit here safely, emperors set apart,
And kibbitz down as those about to die
Cry *Morituri* . . . Yes, but so am I,
And so are you, though not now. When we're older.
Where death will be the last thing we defy,
These madmen feel it perching on their shoulder:
The tremble of the heat is tinged with something colder.

But that's enough of talk about the weather.
To rail against the climate's not good form.
My subject ought to be the latest feather
Protruding from your cap. I mean the Maugham.
I offer you, through gritted teeth, my warm
Congratulations on another coup.

Success for you's so soon become the norm,
Your fresh young ego might be knocked askew.
A widespread fear, I find. Your father thinks so too.

The prize's terms dictate an expedition
To distant lands. That makes you Captain Kirk
Of Starship *Enterprise*. Your Five-Year Mission:
To Boldly Go etcetera. You can't shirk
The challenge. This award's not just a perk:
Queer Maugham's £500 are meant to send
Your mind in search of fodder for your work
Through any far-flung way you care to wend.
Which means, at present rates, a fortnight in Southend,

So choosing Andalusia took nerve.
It's certainly some kind of foreign part.
A bit close-flung, perhaps, but it will serve
To show you the left knee, if not the heart,
Of European Culture. It's a start.
Like Chesterfield advising his young son
(Who didn't, I imagine, give a fart)
I'm keen to see your life correctly run.
You can't just arse around forever having fun.

The day's work here began at 6 a.m.
The first car they pumped full of gasoline
And wheeled out looked unworldly, like a LEM.
A Mass was said. 'The Lord is King.' The scene
Grew crammed with every kind of clean machine.
An Offenhauser woke with shrieks and yells.
The heart-throb Dayglo pulse and Duco preen
Of decals filled the view with charms and spells
As densely drawn and brilliant as the Book of Kells.

BORG WARNER. BARDAHL. 'Let the Earth rejoice.'
'May Christ have mercy.' LODESTAR. OLSONITE.
America exults with sponsored voice
From Kitty Hawk to ultra-Lunar flight.
RAYBESTOS. GULF. Uptight and out of sight!
The Cape. BELL HELMETS. Gemini. Apollo!
Jay Gatsby put his faith in the green light.
Behold his dream, and who shall call it hollow?
What genius they have, what destinies they follow!

The big pre-race parade comes down the straight
While hardened press-men lecherously dote
On schoolgirl majorettes all looking great
In boots and spangled swimsuits. Flags denote
Their provenance. The band from Terre Haute
Is called the Marching Patriots. Purdue
Has got a drum so big it needs a float.
And now the Dancing Bears come prancing through,
Their derrières starred white and striped with red and blue.

From Tucson, Kokomo and Tuscaloosa,
From over the state line and far away,
Purveying the complete John Philip Sousa
The kids have come for this one day in May
To show the watching world the USA
Survives and thrives and still knows how to cock its
Snoot. Old Uncle Sam is A-OK –
He's strutting with bright buttons and high pockets.
Hail, Tiger Band from Circleville! Broad Ripple Rockets!

Objectively, perhaps, they do look tatty.
This continent's original invaders
Were not, however, notably less ratty.

Torpedoes in tin hats and leather waders,
Hard bastards handing beads around like traders –
Grand larceny in every squeak and rattle.
The whole deal was a nightmare of Ralph Nader's,
A corporate racket dressed up as a battle:
The locals kissed the Spaniard's foot or died like cattle.

The choice between the New World and the Old
I've never found that clear, to tell the truth.
Tradition? Yes indeed, to that I hold:
These bouncing brats from Des Moines and Duluth
Seem short of every virtue except youth.
But really, was there that much more appeal
In stout Cortez's lack of ruth and couth
Simply because it bore the papal seal?
It's art that makes the difference, and Art means the Ideal:

Velazquez (*vide supra*) for example.
You're visiting the Prado, I presume?
Well, when you do, you'll find a healthy sample
Abstracted from his *oeuvre* from womb to tomb.
The key works line one giant, stunning room:
Group portraits done in and around the Court
Whose brilliance cleans your brains out like a broom.
Bravura, yes. But products, too, of thought:
An inner world in which the Kings ruled as they ought,

Not as they did. His purpose wasn't flattery
Or cravenly to kiss the royal rod.
He just depicted the assault and battery
Of Habsburg policies as acts of God,
Whose earthly incarnation was the clod
That currently inhabited the throne.

He deified the whole lot on his tod,
Each royal no-no, nincompoop and crone.
Great Titian was long gone. Velazquez was alone.

Alone, and hemmed about by mediocrities
(Except for once when Rubens came to town),
He must have felt as singular as Socrates
But didn't let the pressure get him down.
He slyly banked his credit with the Crown
Until he was allowed a year abroad
(In Rome, of course. In Venice he might drown.)
To raise his sights by study. An award
The King well knew would be a hundredfold restored.

Conquistadores in their *armadura*
The drivers now are standing by their cars.
Unholy soldiers (but in purpose purer),
They look as if they're shipping out for Mars.
It's hard to tell the rookies from the stars:
When suited-up and masked, they seem the same.
White skin grafts are the veteran's battle scars.
For A. J. Foyt the searing price of fame
Was branded round his mouth the day he ate the flame.

A year back young Swede Savage swallowed fire.
He took six months to die. It goes to show
How hot it is inside a funeral pyre
And just how hard a row the drivers hoe.
I can't believe they're in this for the dough.
The secret's not beyond, but in, the fear:
A focal point of grief they get to know
Some other place a million miles from here –
The dream Hart Crane once had, to travel in a tear.

Eleven on the dot. The zoo gets hit
By lightning. Lions whelp and panthers panic.
The fastest qualifiers quit the pit
No more than hipbone-high to a mechanic
And take the track. The uproar is Satanic.
By now the less exalted have departed,
But still the sound is monumental, manic.
Librarians would hear it broken-hearted.
And this lap's just for lining up. They haven't started.

Around the speedway cruising on the ton
(Which means for Indy cars, they're nearly stalling)
They blaze away like spaceships round the Sun –
A shout of thunder like Valhalla falling.
(I'm running out of epithets: it's galling.
I've never heard a noise like this before.)
They're coming round again. And it's appalling –
The moment when you can't stand any more,
The green light goes! Geronimo! Excelsior!

It's gangway for the new apocalypse!
They're racing at two hundred miles an hour!
The likelier contenders get to grips
Like heavy cavalry berserk with power
And three-time-winner Foyt already rips
Away to lead the field by half a mile
As up the ante goes. Down go the chips.
No one but Rutherford can match that style,
And he starts too far back. I'll tell you in a while

The way it all comes out, but now I've got
To set this screed aside and keep a check
From lap to lap on who, while driving what,

Gets hits by whom or ends up in a wreck.
A half a thousand miles is quite a trek –
Though even as I'm jotting down this line
A. J.'s got someone breathing down his neck . . .
Yes, Rutherford's McLaren, from row nine,
Has moved up more than twenty places. Heady wine!

Since Johnny Rutherford is from Fort Worth
And Foyt from Houston, they are Texans twain:
The both of them behind the wheel since birth,
The both of them straight-arrow as John Wayne.
This thing they're doing's technically insane
And yet there's no denying it's a thrill:
For something fundamental in the brain
Rejoices in the daring and the skill.
The heart is lifted, even though the blood may chill.

It's SOME TIME LATER. On the victory dais
Glad Rutherford gets kissed and plied with drink.
It looks a bit like supper at Emmaus.
Unceasing worship's damaging, I think:
One's standards of self-knowledge tend to sink.
I'd like to try it, though, I must confess.
Perhaps a little bit. Not to the brink.
Nor would that heap of lolly cause distress:
Three hundred thousand dollars – not a penny less.

Until halfway, the prize belonged to Foyt.
His pretty GILMORE RACING ketchup-red
Coyote skated flatter than a quoit,
The maestro lying down as if in bed.
He only led by inches, but he led –
Until his turbo-charger coughed white smoke.

The car kept running quickly while it bled,
But finally – black flag. For Foyt, no joke:
Unless he had his money on the other bloke.

The Coming Boy on his eleventh try
At winning the '500' finished first.
A perfect journey. No one had to die.
On looking back, I think about the worst
Catastrophe was that an engine burst.
The empty Brickyard bakes in silent heat,
The quarter-million race-fans have dispersed,
And I have got a deadline I must meet:
I have to tell the story of the champion's defeat.

Velazquez was ennobled in the end.
(Old Philip, fading fast, could not refuse
The final accolade to such a friend.)
His background was examined for loose screws
(Against the blood of craftsmen, Moors or Jews
Bureaucracy imposed a strict embargo)
And in a year or so came the good news,
Together with the robes and wealthy cargo
They used to hang around a Knight of Santiago.

Encumbered thus, he sank into the grave.
The man is dead. The artist is alive.
For lonely are the brilliant, like the brave –
Exactly like, except their deeds survive.
My point (it's taken ages to arrive)
Is simply this: enjoy the adulation,
But meanwhile take a tip from Uncle Clive
And amplify your general education.
There's more than literature involved in cultivation.

Tomorrow in the London afternoon
I'll miss your stubby, Jaggerish appearance
And wish you back in Fleet Street very soon.
Among the foremost ranks of your adherents
I'm vocal to the point of incoherence
When totting up your qualities of mind.
You've even got the rarest: perseverance.
A wise adviser ought to be resigned,
Unless he keeps the pace hot, to being left behind.

'We're given Art in order not to perish
Faced with the Truth.' Or words to that effect.
An apophthegm of Nietzsche's which I cherish:
He sees how these two areas connect
Without conceding that they intersect.
Enough for now. Go easy, I implore you.
It all abides your questing intellect.
The Heritage of Culture, I assure you,
Like everything, you lucky sod, is all before you.

To Tom Stoppard: a letter from London

To catch your eye in Paris, Tom,
I choose a show-off stanza from
    Some Thirties play
Forgotten now like Rin Tin Tin.
Was it *The Dog Beneath the Skin*?
    Well, anyway

Its tone survives. The metres move
Through time like paintings in the Louvre
    (Say loov, not loover):
Coherent in their verbal jazz,
They're confident of tenure as
    J. Edgar Hoover.

Pink fairies of the sixth-form Left,
Those Ruined Boys at least were deft
    At the actual writing.
Though history scorns all they thought,
The nifty artefacts they wrought
    Still sound exciting.

Distinguishing the higher fliers
Remorselessly from plodding triers
    Who haven't got it,
Such phonic zip bespeaks a knack
Of which no labour hides the lack:
    A child could spot it.

And boy, you've got the stuff in bales –
A Lubitsch-touch that never fails.
   The other guys
Compared to you write lines that float
With all the grace of what gets wrote
   By Ernest Wise.

The Stoppard dramaturgic moxie
Unnerves the priests of orthodoxy:
   We still hear thicks
Who broadcast the opinion freely
Your plays are only sketches really –
   Just bags of tricks.

If dramas do not hammer themes
Like pub bores telling you their dreams
   The dense don't twig.
They want the things they know already
Reiterated loud and steady –
   Drilled through the wig.

From all frivolity aloof,
Those positivist killjoys goof
   Two ways at once:
They sell skill short, and then ignore
The way your works are so much more
   Than clever stunts.

So frictionless a *jeu d'esprit*,
Like Wittgenstein's philosophy,
    Appears to leave
Things as they are, but at the last
The future flowing to the past
    Without reprieve

Endorses everything you've done.
As Einstein puts it, The Old One
    Does not play dice,
And though your gift might smack of luck
Laws guide it, like the hockey puck
    Across the ice.

Deterministic you are not,
However, even by a jot.
    Your sense of form
Derives its casual power to thrill
From operating at the still
    Heart of the storm.

For how could someone lack concern
Who cared that gentle Guildenstern
    And Rosencrantz
(Or else the same names rearranged
Should those two men be interchanged)
    Were sent by chance

To meet a death at Hamlet's whim
Less grand than lay in store for him,
    But still a death:
A more appalling death, in fact
Than any king's in the Fifth Act –
    Even Macbeth?

In south-east Asia as I type
The carbuncle is growing ripe
    Around Saigon.
The citadels are soon reduced.
The chickens have come home to roost.
    The heat is on,

And we shall see a sickness cured
Which virulently has endured
    These thirty years:
The torturers ran out of jails,
The coffin-makers out of nails,
    Mothers of tears,

While all the Furies and the Fates
Unleashed by the United States
    In Freedom's name
Gave evidence that moral error
Returns in tumult and in terror
    The way it came.

But now the conquerors bring peace.
When everyone is in the police
    There's no unrest.
Except for those who disappear
The People grin from ear to ear –
    Not like the West.

Rejecting both kinds of belief
(Believing only in the grief
    Their clash must bring)
We find to use the words we feel
Adhere most closely to the real
    Means everything.

I like the kind of jokes you tell
And what's more you like mine as well –
    Clear proof of nous.
I like your stylish way of life.
I've thought of kidnapping your wife.
    I like your house.

Success appeals to my sweet tooth:
But finally it's to the truth
    That you defer –
And that's the thing I like the best.
My love to Miri. Get some rest.
    A tout à l'heure.

To Craig Raine: a letter from Biarritz

Dear Craig, I've brought your books down to the sea
In order to catch up with what you've done
Since first I gasped at your facility
For writing Martian postcards home. The sun
Illuminates *The Onion, Memory*
Two pages at a time. The beach girls run
With naked bosoms on my low horizon
And yet yours are the lines I've got my eyes on.

Not all the time perhaps, but none the less
It's fair to say I'm utterly drawn in.
When praising your alchemical prowess
One hardly knows the best place to begin.
Your similes are struck with such success
At least one bard has called your gift a sin.
You spot resemblances with a precision
Not normally conferred by human vision.

What I admire and envy most, however,
Is your unflinching hunger for the real.
Proportionate you are but pallid never.
With strength of knee unknown to the genteel
You push on with your passionate endeavour
To sweep aside the veil of the ideal
And view the actual world on a straight footing
In every aspect, even the off-putting.

'Your stomach's got no eyes,' a man once said
Who'd guessed I didn't like how oysters look.
For you I'd stand that saying on its head:
Your eyes have got no stomach. They can brook,
Nay revel in, sights that would strike me dead
And make me queasy even in a book.
I'd like to call it sorcery or knavery
But all too clearly it's a kind of bravery.

You'd need it, too, if you were here today,
I think I might just mention at this point.
For every sweet young curved hip on display
There squeaks a fearsomely arthritic joint.
Those oiled old hands will never smooth away
The cellulite and wrinkles they anoint,
And many of the bare breasts on parade
Sensationally fail to make the grade.

Squeezed flat and creased like empty toothpaste tubes
Or else inflated to degrees grotesque –
To sum up this array of has-been boobs
The only adjective is Düreresque.
That woman sports a pair of Rubik's cubes.
That woman there could use hers as a desk.
At these exhausted sources of lactation
Words can't convey my lack of fascination.

But back again to literary matters.
One or two critics, I have lately noted,
Are showing signs of going mad as hatters
At hearing you so often praised and quoted.

The strictest of them taciturnly natters
Of how you could well find yourself demoted:
You are too popular and should tread warily.
Also, he says, your lines end arbitrarily.

I always thought *his* ended when the bell
Rang on his Olivetti. Never mind.
Your stanza forms still check out pretty well,
Even if arbitrarily inclined.
They break no rules as far as I can tell.
There are no wasted words that I can find.
In later works your rhythm grows less striking
But that might mean strong rhythm's to my liking.

Speaking of form and rhythm, incidentally,
Two water nymphs so beautiful I bet
The sight of them would paralyse you mentally
Are playing tennis. It seems I'm the net.
They must be highly privileged parentally:
Such clear skins and fine bones you only get
When there's a solid family tradition
Of no-expense-spared, well-thought-out nutrition.

Needless to say that with these two the breasts
From every viewpoint seem in A1 shape,
Though no doubt if it came to tactile tests
There'd be a yielding, as with a ripe grape.
Praise God that they've got those where we've got chests
I muse, while being careful not to gape –
A bald and overweight old coot from Sydney
Who cops a Frog tart's let ball in the kidney.

Now they've pranced off and plunged into a wave
Which warmly fondles them as who would not.
Their gaiety of mood has left mine grave,
Preoccupied with man and his brief lot.
I think of time's hourglass and bladed stave,
Of how we waste the few days that we've got,
Of how my youth is gone and shan't return.
I must turn over or my back will burn.

I'm writing now in the supine position,
A posture more conducive to high thoughts
Of Culture and the means of its transmission.
From here on in I think you'll find all sorts
Of pundits prophesying the perdition
Awaiting you, complete with boils and warts,
If you should go on proving so appealing
To the unclean, unthinking and unfeeling.

I don't imply, I hasten to assure you,
Your fate's to be a pop star like Kate Bush.
Though seas of spellbound faces stretch before you
The bodies underneath won't pee or push.
I know the more you're buttered up the more you
Will stay as untouched as the Hindu Kush.
Endowed with inspiration of such purity
You'd gladly follow it back to obscurity.

It's obvious that you're a heavyweight:
Your harshest critics can't say otherwise.
Your status would remain inviolate
Though Jeff Nuttall should praise you to the skies.

In that regard you've got it on a plate,
Whence comes the shamrock tinge of certain eyes.
While hitting the jackpot in all essentials
You've managed to hang on to your credentials.

You write intensely *and* you're entertaining.
For those of us less apt to do the first,
Apart from silence there's one course remaining –
Which is to do the second. At the worst
(And when this happens it's no use complaining)
The public clamours to be reimbursed,
But on the whole there's some cause to be proud
If what one writes makes people laugh aloud.

Or so I think when critics in terms drastic
Inform the world my feet are half trochaic.
It seems my scansion's absolutely spastic.
Even my best iambics are spondaic.
The poor fool's sense of rhythm is elastic!
His diction is archaic Aramaic!
As for his rhymes, let's send him back to Kogarah! Hell,
The stuff he drivels isn't even dogarahhell!

It's useless to invoke the semi-vowel
And point out 'bevel' *is* a rhyme for 'Devil'.
The cloth-eared scribes who write prose with a trowel
Will smugly wonder if I'm on the level.
One really might as well throw in the towel.
Fulke Greville's brother was called Neville Greville . . .
No, let the critics stew in their pale juice:
A joke's a joke and it needs no excuse.

Far out on their twin-fin potato chips
The young star surfers sprint to climb astride
A wave as smooth as spit feels on your lips
And when it breaks you see them there inside –
Born acrobats trained to their fingertips.
Meanwhile here at the thin edge of the tide
A man pretending he's a submarine
To please his children's also in the scene.

A Boudin painted by Tiepolo,
A beige and azure fresco two miles long;
The sky brushed pink, the *sable d'or* aglow,
The plump swell dimpled like a silver gong;
The beach lit by *le ciel*, laved by *les flots*,
An airy glittering shantung sarong,
Unfolds into the south where with a stain
Of Monet nenuphars France turns to Spain.

And though down there the Basques will bomb your car,
Up here they are a people touched with grace.
They know the sweet years only go so far
And life is more than just a pretty face.
However poor and sick and old they are
The sun shines for them, too. They have a place.
A fact which would provoke me to deep thinking
Were not the sun now on the point of sinking.

Clear plum juice simmers in the solar disc.
The soft light off the pale blue water stipples
With gold the green cliff-clothing tamarisk.
The breathing sea sends in its silken ripples.

High on the sea wall the last odalisque
Looks down with mute approval at her nipples.
La mer, la mer, toujours recommencée.
But that's enough of versing for one day.

I'll get up now and put on thongs and hat.
I'll gather up your books and these few pages.
I'll shake and roll my tatty rattan mat
And up the cliff *trottoir* by easy stages
I'll dawdle with a feeling of that's that –
Great talents may write poems for the ages,
But poetasters with their tongues in fetters
When all else fails at least can still write letters.

To Gore Vidal at Fifty

To Gore Vidal at – how should I commence?
The trick is to strike sparks and still make sense.
To Gore Vidal at fifty – sounds a lot.
Should I be flippant about that, or not?
To Gore Vidal at fifty years of age –
That slights the sprite, though it salutes the sage.
To Gore Vidal at fifty years of youth –
A trifle twee, but closer to the truth,
Since you (I speak in awe, not animosity)
Remain the incarnation of precocity,
A marvellous boy whose man-sized aureola
Still scintillates like fresh-poured Pepsi-Cola
(If I can mention safe from repercussions
The formula that Nixon sold the Russians),
Whose promise is renewed in the fulfilling,
A teenage thrill that goes on being thrilling,
A pledge kept firm with no recourse to perjury
Save incidental, mainly dental, surgery.
And yet you will admit you are no chicken.
Admit? Insist. The Peter Panic-stricken
Might cling to childhood out of self-delusion,
But that or any similar confusion
You've always held in absolute contempt –
The only absolute that you exempt
From your unwearyingly edifying
Assault on mankind's thirst to be undying:
A hope you've never ceased to make a mock of
Or boldly nominate what it's a crock of.
Small wonder you admire that far-off era
The clear lens of your style brings that much nearer,

In which, as Flaubert wrote (and here I quote,
Or, rather, quote what you said Flaubert wrote)
The gods were dead and Christ was not yet born,
A quick, cold night dividing dusk from dawn,
When man was quite alone, with nothing holier
To call his own than clear-eyed melancholia –
That penetrating gaze into infinity
Revealing it devoid of all divinity
And transcendental only in its endless
Detachment from our dread of feeling friendless –
A universe which neither plans our grief
Nor pampers us in payment for belief,
But rings its changes utterly unheeding
Though sadist die in bed or saint lie bleeding.
Committed in its course beyond retrieval,
Indifferent to all talk of good and evil,
Unreachable by prayer, untouched by curses,
It tirelessly assembles and disperses,
Created and destroyed and recreated –
Reduced, reprocessed and repristinated;
Its victories defeats, retreats advances,
Its triumphs tragedies, disasters dances,
Its involuted curves of time and distance
All adding up to one fierce, flat insistence –
That its immensities will still be there
When we are not. It simply doesn't *care*.
This is the void that you with the cool grace
Of your prose style help teach us how to face.
This is the pit from which none can escape
Your wit lights up that we might see its shape.

But to convince the world the soul of Marcus
Aurelius must perish with his carcass
Was hard even for him. Most men prefer
To hide their heads in warm sand and not stir.
That public probity, not sexuality,
Is really the foundation of morality –
That justice plays no active part in fate,
Not even when fate leads to Watergate –
That all the prayers and powers of the Kennedys
Buy not one moment's rest from the Eumenides –
That Caesar is not God, nor the good Lord
Someone who walks and talks like Gerald Ford –
With facts like these we find it hard to grapple,
And much prefer to think Eve plucked the apple
Specifically so that redemptive love,
Beamed down on her descendants from above,
Could ease the pangs of her initial blunder
And make us grateful as we knuckle under.
My own view is that mankind would be worse
Than ever should that cloud of dreams disperse,
But your view is the one we're here to praise
For how it penetrates the wishful haze
Which forms when all-too-human self-delusion
Allied with solipsism breeds confusion –
A mist that men call vision as they grope
And choking on it give the name of hope.
So dense a fog will be a long time thinning
So let's call your work thus far a beginning,
And for our own sake wish your life that too –
And, friends before, years more be friends to you.

The Great Wrasse: for Les Murray at sixty

Mask wet and snorkel dry, I'm lying loose
On the glass roof of time, and forty years
Straight down I see it teeming, the bombora
Of Manning House. Tables like staghorn coral
Chewed at by schools of poets. Frensham girls
(Remember Xanthe Small and Joanne Williamson,
Those blouses and tight skirts? *You little beaut*
We breathed into our fried rice. God, what dreams:
By now they must be grandmothers) glide by
Like semicircle angelfish. Psychologists
With teeth like wahoos turn their heads as one,
Torn from discussion of the Individual,
Their Watch Committee late-lunch seminar
Prorogued *pro tem.*
                 Poised Andersonian squid
Explain to freshettes peeping from their shells
If dualism allows no real division
There can be no real connection. Fusiliers,
Trevallies, sweetlips, damselfish, hussars
Patrol in Balbos, split up, feed, re-form,
Waved at by worshipping anemones.
The food chain and the mating dance, the mass
Manoeuvring, the shape-up and the shake-out,
The pretty faces pumping pain through spines:
It's all there, displayed in liquid crystal,
No further than my fingertips adrift
(A year in time is just an inch in space) –
And there *you* are, and I can see you now
For what you were, most brilliant of the bunch,
The Great Wrasse.

       But to know that, I had first
To see the thing itself, in all its glory,
Five years ago. Sleeping on Lizard Island,
My family was recovering its strength
From too long in the cold. On the second day
We woke at noon and rolled into the water
To join the turtles feeding on the seagrass
Between the beach and sandbar. Serious fish
Were just around the point, at the big bommie.
We drifted off the platform at the back
Of the launch and let the current take us over
A chunk of reef that came up to arm's length:
Just what the doctor ordered. We could see
The whole aquarium in action, hear
The parrotfish at work on the hard coral
Like journalists around the Doric porch
Of some beer-froth tycoon whose time had come
To be cast out of Toorak.
        Then it was there –
Beside us, as if to share our view:
Materializing, as is its marvellous way,
With no preliminary fanfare,
Like an air-dropped marching band that opens up
Full blast around your bed. *Lord, I can see*,
I said in silence, smiling around my rubber
Dummy like a baby. Powered by pearls
On fire inside its emerald envelope,
The Wrasse comes on like a space invader
In docking mode, filling the vision full:
The shock of its appearance stops the swimmer
Dead in the water, flippers frozen solid,
Stunned by a sudden nearness so aloof.

As if the Inca, walking his lion's walk
In soft shoes, were to pass by from behind
Preoccupied by his divinity,
So with this big fish and its quiet storm,
Its mute Magnificat.
                    Bigger fish yet
Plumb deep holes of the Outer Barrier –
Potato cod in mottled camouflage
Like Japanese Army Kawasaki fighters
Parked in the palms, *franc-tireur* Tiger sharks
With Kerry Packer smiles, the last few marlin
To keep their swords – but nothing quite as massive
As the daddy of all wrasses, the Daimyo number,
Shows up at the bombora, and nothing as bright
Is known the whole reef over.
                              Over the reef,
You realize, is where this fish belongs –
Above it and not of it. Nothing is written there,
Enjoyed or cherished. Even the beautiful,
There in abundance, does not know itself.
'Sex is a Nazi' you once wrote, and so
It is here. Killing to grow up so they can screw,
Things eat, are eaten, and the crown-of-thorns
Starfish that eats everything looks like
A rail map of the Final Solution,
But all it adds to universal horror
Is its lack of colour.
                       Even in full bloom
The reef is a *jardin des supplices*:
The frills, the fronds, the fans, the powder puffs
Soften the razor's edge, the reign of terror.
Lulled by the moon snail and the Spanish dancer
With choreography by Carlos Saura,

By feathery platoons of *poules de luxe*
Cute as the kick-line of the Tropicana,
The tourist feels this is the show for him –
Atlantis in an atrium, a rumpus room
For slo-mo willy-willies of loose chips
From bombed casinos, a warehouse arcade
For love seats, swansdown pouffes and stuffed banquettes
That he could snuggle up to like a prayer
Of Hasidim against the Wailing Wall
And soothe his fevered brow in yielding plush –
But only an expert should ever touch it
Even with rubber gloves.
                        Buyer beware,
The forms of death are not just for each other
But for us too, and not all are as ugly
As the stonefish, toadfish, puffer and striped Toby
In his leather jacket. Even a child can see
That these are kitted out for bio war:
They pull the face of neurotoxic venom.
But the cone shells that beg to be picked up
By writers are like antique fountain pens
Proust might have held except he would have written
A short book, and that dreamboat with the sulk
Like Michelle Pfeiffer lolling in the glass
Elevator in *Scarface* is a breed
Of butterfly whose class would set you raving
At closer quarters, anguish cloaked in floating
Come-hither chiffon veils that spell curtains
At the first kiss.
                   Rising above it all,
A benign airship poised over New York –
The *Hindenburg* without the *Hakenkreuz*
Or parking problems – just by its repose

The dawdling Wrasse siphons up Hell's Kitchen
And turns it to serenity, the spectrum
Of helium in Rutherford's radon tube,
The clear, blue light of pure polonium,
The green, fused sand of Trinity, the silent
Summary, the peaceful aftermath.
Something, someone, must be the focal emblem,
The stately bearer of the synthesis
To make our griefs make sense, if not worthwhile.
That the young you, in a red-striped sloppy joe
Like Sydney Greenstreet cast as Ginger Meggs
Progressing through the Quad the very year
Of the first Opera House Lottery draw,
Would be the Great Wrasse, few could guess
But now all know, glad that the time it took
Was in their lives, and what you made of it –
Those new and strange and lovely living things,
Your poems – theirs to goggle at when born:
Born from your mouth.
                    Born fit to breathe our sea,
Which is the air I surface to drink in
(My mask a nifty hat by Schiaparelli)
Having seen wonders – how our lives once were,
Nature's indifference, time's transparency,
Fame's cloud of pigment, fortune's blood-tipped needles,
And finally, most fabulous of all,
A monumental fish that speaks in colours,
Offering solace from within itself.

To Leonie Kramer, Chancellor of Sydney University: A Report on My Discipline, on the Eve of My Receiving an Honorary Degree, 1999

The brief is to report on what's been done –
Or, if it hasn't, to report on that –
In my field over twenty years. The gun
Is to my head and I will eat my hat
Sooner than flinch, but my job's too much fun,
Too fissile, for a *précis* to get at.
Leonie, let's be frank. My discipline
Is serious like Jack Benny's violin.

Mine is no academic bailiwick:
In fact it is defined by being not one.
Gowned bigwigs might well find it a bit thick
To see my name among theirs. 'That's a hot one,'
They'll mutinously mutter. '*This* Osric
Fronting a field of study: has he got one?'
They're right, I haven't; but I do this stuff
On the assumption they aren't right enough.

My territory's the chattering hedgerow
Between the neat fields forming the landscape
Of proper scholarship. By now we know
The ecosystem winds up out of shape
When too much science grabs the soil to grow
The *pouffe*-sized pumpkin and the pre-shrunk grape.
We've organized the land to serve society
So thoroughly we've wiped out its variety.

Too bad, some say. We can't eat singing birds –
You see the way my metaphor is tending –
Or cope with hedgehogs roaming round in herds:
The cost of feeding them would be mind-bending.
The same goes double for the world of words:
The era of the ragged edge is ending.
The kind of writing we can't classify
Might fairly soon have barely room to die.

I mourn its passing, and guess you do too,
Or A. D. Hope would not have dedicated
His Roman letter to you. Knowing you
Would get a kick from being celebrated
In such a *jeu d'esprit*, a tiramisu
Designed to leave you nothing but elated,
Our mightiest poet tossed off something lightweight,
Not doubting that that weight would be the right weight.

Of all Hope's poetry I found that letter
The most amazing thing he'd written, ever.
Had Byron ever done the same thing better?
Had even Auden been so clearly clever?
From then on I was Hope's eternal debtor,
Convinced, despite the times, the time is never
To let one's literary ambition stifle
The urge to squander talent on a trifle.

Always supposing talent's what one's got –
But let's take that for now as a *donnée*
And ask if those of us who, on the spot,
Can put a phrase together in a way
That gets attention ought to, or ought not,
Feel so responsible for what we say
We don't say anything, however witty,
That might not please the Nobel Prize committee.

I think not. Literature is out of hand.
With so much genius jostling for position
Shakespeare would have to fight for room to stand,
Dante to kneel and pray. A mass emission
Of deathless texts leaves nothing *an den Rand
Geschrieben*. All's composed on the condition
We read it with the awe-struck, furrowed brow
We'd read the classics with if we knew how.

None of which means, of course, I want books burned.
Heine foresaw the bonfire in Berlin.
Men who burn books burn men: that much we learned
Sifting the ashes of the loony bin.
Now that some form of sanity's returned
We should be glad the age we're living in
Accords great writers every accolade
From the T-shirt to the ticker-tape parade.

The only problem is, no other kind
Of writer *except* great's thought worth attention.
This attitude, in matters of the mind,
To my mind robs us of a whole dimension.
Intelligence just isn't that refined:
It's less a distillate than a suspension,
An absinthe we'd knock back in half a minute
Without the cloud of particles within it.

Just so, a living culture is a swarm
Of moments that provide its tang and tingle:
Unless it's fuelled by every minor form
From dirty joke to advertising jingle
It ends up like Dame Edna's husband, Norm,
Stiff as a post. I think John Douglas Pringle
Was first to spot our language, at its core,
Owed its *élan* to how a wharfie swore.

Shifting that notion further up the scale
We soon discover it applies worldwide.
The casual jotting priced for a quick sale
Can be a bridesmaid that outshines the bride.
There is a vantage point beyond the pale:
To pull the inside job from the outside
Confers on essayist or rogue reviewer
The plus of knowing where to put the skewer.

Nor need he specialize in kicking ass
(*Pro tem* to bluster *à l'américaine*).
In fact a gadfly's likely to sound crass
If all he ever does is dish out pain,
Just as to pump the anaesthetic gas
Of adulation backfires on the brain –
Dooming the sycophant to a sclerosis
Off-putting as the cynic's halitosis.

The voice I favour questions *and* enjoys.
No pushover, it's ready to submit.
It homes on a clear signal through the noise
Kicked up by the tumultuous cockpit
We call the Arts, and from the girls and boys
It separates the men and women. Wit,
When true, well knows a show of cleverness
Means least when it is most meant to impress,

And yet a comprehensive lack of flair
By no means guarantees the truly serious.
It takes a cool, hard head to be aware
How art is in its essence a mysterious
Compound engendered by a gift as rare
As hen's teeth of the base and the imperious.
It takes an artist, though that appellation
Seldom adorns his dodgy reputation.

Just such an artist was my most revered
Role model from the old world Hitler wrecked,
Alfred Polgar, who, as the menace neared,
Focused despair to such a fine effect
His *feuilletons* teem with all that disappeared.
Schatzkammer snow-domes of the intellect,
Polgar's packed paragraphs reintegrate
A time bomb getting set to detonate.

He and the other refugees who scattered
To the Earth's four corners not excluding ours
Personified the unity left shattered
Where once they had devoted first-rate powers
To the ephemeral as if it mattered.
Their fate proved that it had. The topless towers
Of Ilium arise from the hubbub
Of the bazaar, the throb of the nightclub.

It is the wasted talents that I sing,
The ones that might have climbed to high renown,
Have done great things, had they done the done thing
And steered clear of the *demi-monde* downtown.
A nation needs them the same way a king
Lost on the heath should listen to his clown,
Lest literature withdraw to a top shelf
And vivid language serve only itself.

Australia Felix, sea-girt land most fair –
Fair go, fair suck, fair prospects of success
For all – there's an equality more rare
Even than these, though it be cherished less:
A mental life that everyone may share.
Its secret lies in the receptiveness
Of how we speak, our tongue that makes a poet
In two weeks of a taxi-driving Croat.

Whole cultures in our time razed to the ground
Enriched us with their homeless destitute,
A thriving proof the Promised Land is found
Where all is hallowed save the absolute.
That thought revives my hopes as, with one bound,
Like Emile Mercier's Wocko the Beaut,
I fly to my reward at your fair hand.
Lady, I'm blushing. Will there be a band?

from Angels Over Elsinore

Windows Is Shutting Down

Windows is shutting down, and grammar are
On their last leg. So what am we to do?
A letter of complaint go just so far,
Proving the only one in step are you.

Better, perhaps, to simply let it goes.
A sentence have to be screwed pretty bad
Before they gets to where you doesnt knows
The meaning what it must of meant to had.

The meteor have hit. Extinction spread,
But evolution do not stop for that.
A mutant languages rise from the dead
And all them rules is suddenly old hat.

Too bad for we, us what has had so long
The best seat from the only game in town.
But there it am, and whom can say its wrong?
Those are the break. Windows is shutting down.

Angels Over Elsinore

How many angels knew who Hamlet was
When they were summoned by Horatio?
They probably showed up only because
The roster said it was their turn to go.

Another day, another Dane. Too bad,
But while they sang their well-rehearsed lament
They noticed his good looks. Too soon, too sad,
This welcome home for what seemed heaven sent.

Imagine having been with him down there!
But here I dream, for angels do not yearn.
They take up their positions in the air
Free from the passions of the earth they spurn.

Even their singing is done less from joy
Than duty. But was this the usual thing?
Surely they gazed on that recumbent boy,
Clearly cut out one day to be a king,

And sang him to his early rest above
With soaring pride that they should form the choir
Whose voices echoed all the cries of love,
Which, even when divine, implies desire?

But soft: an ideal world does not exist.
Hamlet went nowhere after he was dead.
No angel sighed where lovers never kissed,
And there was nothing in what his friend said.

Hamlet himself knew just what to expect:
Steady reduction of his body mass
Until the day, his very coffin wrecked,
Some clown picked up his skull and said, 'Alas.'

No, there would be no music from on high.
No feather from a wing would fall, not one.
Forget it all, even the empty sky –
What's gone is gone, sweet prince. What's done is done.

Exit Don Giovanni

Somewhere below his pride, the Don's bad dreams
Fashioned the statue that would take him down.
Deep underground, the tears were there in streams.
The man who had the only game in town,

In Spain, in Europe, when it came to love,
Sensed that there had to be a reckoning.
The boundaries he claimed to soar above
Meant nothing to him except everything.

Why the defiant stance, if not from shame?
And why deny that truth, if not from fear?
The bodice-ripper made his famous name
By staying buttoned up. His whole career

Came back to haunt him in a stony glance.
Transfixed, he followed where the statue led.
Below, tips of hot tongues began to dance.
Further below, it was a sea of red.

There was a jetty. Next to it, a raft
Held every name on Leporello's list,
Even from just last week. The statue laughed
And left. The women, modelled out of mist,

Were images, as they had always been
To him, but strong enough to ply the sweeps.
They would not meet his eye, having foreseen
What waited for him on the burning deeps.

A long way out, they paused, and one by one
They disappeared, each hinting with a smile,
But not to him, their work had been well done.
He was alone. To cry was not his style,

But then he reached down through the surface fire
Into the water. Almost with relief
He learned at last the flames of his desire
Had floated on the ocean of his grief.

Had he known sooner, what would that have meant?
Less to regret, and little to admit?
The raft burned: final stage of his descent.
Hell was on Earth. Now he was out of it.

My Father Before Me

Sai Wan War Cemetery, Hong Kong

At noon, no shadow. I am on my knees
Once more before your number and your name.
The usual heat, the usual fretful bees
Fitfully busy as last time I came.

Here you have lain since 1945,
When you, at half the age that I am now,
Were taken from the world of the alive,
Were taken out of time. You should see how

This hillside, since I visited it first,
Has stayed the same. Nothing has happened here.
They trim the sloping lawn and slake its thirst.
Regular wreaths may fade and reappear,

But these are details. High on either side
Waves of apartment blocks roll in so far
And no further, forbidden to collide
By laws that keep the green field where you are,

Along with all these others, sacrosanct.
For once the future is denied fresh ground.
For that much if no more, let God be thanked.
You can't see me or even hear the sound

Of my voice, though it comes out like the cry
You heard from me before you sailed away.
Your wife, my mother, took her turn to die
Not long ago. I don't know what to say –

Except those many years she longed for you
Are over now at last, and now she wears
The same robes of forgetfulness you do.
When the dreams cease, so do the nightmares.

I know you would be angry if I said
I, too, crave peace. Besides, it's not quite so.
Despair will ebb when I leave you for dead
Once more. Once more, as I get up to go,

I look up to the sky, down to the sea,
And hope to see them, while I still draw breath,
The way you saw your photograph of me
The very day you flew to meet your death.

Back at the gate, I turn to face the hill,
Your headstone lost again among the rest.
I have no time to waste, much less to kill.
My life is yours; my curse, to be so blessed.

A Gyre from Brother Jack

The canvas, called *A Morning Long Ago*,
Hangs now in Dublin's National Gallery
Of Ireland, and for capturing the flow
Of life, its radiant circularity,
Yeats painter leaves Yeats poet beaten flat.
I hear you saying, 'How can he say that?'

But look. Here is the foyer of a grand
Theatre. It is always interval.
On the upper level, brilliant people stand.
What they have seen inside invests them all
With liquid light, and some of them descend
The sweet, slow, curving, anti-clockwise bend

Of staircase and go out into that park
Where yet another spectacle has formed:
A lake made bright by the oncoming dark.
And at the left of that, white wings have stormed
Upward towards where this rondeau begins.
Birds? Angels? Avatars? Forgiven sins?

He doesn't say: the aspect I like best.
William had theories. Jack has just the thrill.
We see a little but we miss the rest,
And what we keep to ponder, time will kill.
The lives we might have led had we but known
Check out at dawn and take off on their own

Even as we arrive. Sad, it might seem,
When talked about: but shown, it shines like day.
The only realistic general scheme
Of the divine is in this rich display –
Proof that the evanescent present tense
Is made eternal by our transience.

Woman Resting

Sometimes the merely gifted give us proof
Born artists have a democratic eye
That genius gets above, to stand aloof,
Scorning to seize on all that happens by

And give it the full treatment. Look at her,
Mancini's woman, as she rests her head
In white impasto linen. Cats would purr
To think of lying curled up on that bed

Warmed by her Monica Bellucci skin.
Her mouth, like Vitti's in *La Notte*, breathes
A sulky need for more of the same sin
That knocked her sideways. Silently, she seethes.

She's perfect, and he's well up to the task
Of illustrating her full bloom of youth.
Why isn't she immortal, then? you ask.
Look at her bedside table for the truth.

Carafe, decanter, bottle, beaker, all
Are brushed in with the same besotted touch:
Not just as clutter which, were it to fall,
Would break and be swept up. He cares too much

About the world around her. While she dreams,
The room dreams too, as if it too were spent
From pleasure. In the end, nothing redeems
This failure to make her the main event.

Manet's Olympia is no great shakes
For beauty beside this one, but transcends
Her setting with exactly what it takes:
The fire that starts where general interest ends.

Out for the count, Miss Italy sleeps on,
So lovely that we check the artist's name,
Vow to remember it, and then are gone,
Forgetting one who never found his fame

Because his unrestricted sympathy
Homogenised existence. Art must choose
What truly merits perpetuity
From everything that we are bound to lose.

Even a master's landscape, though devoid
Of people, has a human soul in view:
His own. A focused vision is employed
To say: behold what I alone can do.

Picking the mortal to immortalise,
The great paint objects only to abet
Their concentration on what lives and dies.
Faced with a woman that they can't forget

They make sure we can't either. Should she rest,
Her daylight hours still dominate the room.
We see her waking up and getting dressed.
Her silence hits us like the crack of doom.

But this girl, drowned in decor, disappears
From memory, which doesn't care to keep
A pretty picture long, so save your tears.
I shouldn't try to wake her. Let her sleep,

And let Mancini, suave but second rate,
Sleep with her, as in fact he might have done –
Some recompense for his eventual fate
Of scarcely mattering to anyone.

Sunday Morning Walk

Frost on the green.
The ducks cold-footing it across the grass
Beside the college moat

Meet a clutch of matrons
In freeze-dried Barbours
Walking their collies
Freshly brushed by Gainsborough.

Buoyed by the world's supply
Of rosemary sprigs
Packed under glass,

The moorcock emerging from the reeds
Does a hesitation step
As though dancing to Piazzolla.
Cool shoes, if I may say so.

In front of the boat-houses
The rowers rigging fulcrums to the shells
Bite off their gloves
To push in pins,

And the metal shines
Just short of a glitter
Because the light, though Croesus-rich,
Is kiss-soft.

Under the bridge, the iron ribs
Form a pigeon loft,
A pit-lane of sports saloons
Testing their engines.

The final year
Of the finishing school for swans
Passes in review,
Watched by the cob, his nibs,

Who at Bayreuth once
Had a glide-on role
In *Lohengrin*,
But this is better.

Winter regatta,
Unspoiled by even
Yesterday's litter
Spilling from the bins,

Is it any wonder
That I never left you?
Remember this day,
It's already melting.

Natural Selection

The gradual but inexorable magic
That turned the dinosaurs into the birds
Had no overt, only a hidden, logic.
To start the squadrons climbing from the herds
No wand was ever waved, but afterwards
Those who believed there must have been a wizard
Said the whole show looked too well-planned for hazard.

And so it does, in retrospect. Such clever
Transitions, intricate beyond belief!
The little lobsters, in their mating fever,
Assaulted from the sea, stormed up the cliff,
And swept inland as scorpions. But if
Some weapons freak equipped their tails for murder
He must have thought sheer anguish all in order.

Source of all good and hence of evil, pleasure
And hence of pain, he is, or else they are,
Without a moral sense that we can measure,
And thus without a mind. Better by far
To stand in awe of blind chance than to fear
A conscious mechanism of mutation
Bringing its fine intentions to fruition

Without a qualm about collateral horror.
The peacock and the tapeworm both make sense.
Nobody calls the ugly one an error.
But when a child is born to pain intense
Enough to drive its family all at once
To weep blood, an intelligent designer
Looks like a torture garden's beaming owner.

No, give it up. The world demands our wonder
Solely because no feeling brain conceived
The thumb that holds the bamboo for the panda.
Creation, if the thing's to be believed –
And only through belief can life be loved –
Must do without that helping hand from Heaven.
Forget it, lest it never be forgiven.

Under the Jacarandas

Under the jacarandas
The pigeons and the gulls
Pick at the fallen purple
That inundates the grass
For two weeks in October.

Although the splash of colour
Should seem absurdly lush,
Soon you get used to it.
You think life is like that,
But a clock is ticking.

The pigeons and the gulls
Don't even know how good
They look, set off like this.
They get it while it's there.
Keep watching and you'll learn.

The Victor Hugo Clematis

In our garden, the Victor Hugo clematis
Grows among masses of small pink roses
Prettier than it is, but not as stately.
There's a royal lustre to its purple petals:
Long splinters of amethyst
Arranged like the ribs of a Catherine wheel
In a disc that is almost all space,
And the edge of every petal
Is curved like the volutes in any of the four
Propellers of the *Normandie*,
Those museum-forecourt-filling pieces of sculpture
(37 tons each of cast manganese bronze)
That transmitted the electric
Power to the water,
Giving the ship her all-conquering speed,
Not to mention her teeth-rattling vibration
Even in First Class –
The cost of elegance, as the Victor Hugo clematis
Costs me my equilibrium,
Until I wonder: don't I mean the narrow-bladed
More-wood-than-metal airscrew
Of a WWI Armée de l'Air bomber?
Say a Breguet 14, faster than a Fokker D. VII?
Perhaps that would be better:
I grow uncertain, I have to look things up,
And stuff that I thought I knew for sure
Turns out to be wrong.

Inelegantly reclining in my liner chair
As the evening sunlight finally fades,
I watch the flowers, that were never really my thing,
Glowing their last and blacking out closer
And closer to me
(When the dancing finished in the Grand Salon
At one o'clock in the morning
They brought back and unrolled the half-ton weight
Of the world's biggest ocean-going carpet
To cover the parquetry floor
Copied from the throne-room in Versailles)
While the great poet's record-breaker of a funeral
Still stretches halfway across Paris –
Well, it does in my mind –
And the rockets and flares go up to look for Gothas –
I can see the colours burst and fall, going dry
Like the baby dribble of cherubim
On a black velvet bib –
And the pinwheel flower, even in silhouette,
Drills a sibilant echo of Cocteau's voice through my brain's ruins:
The Victor Hugo clematis is a madman that thinks
It is Victor Hugo.

Mystery of the Silver Chair

As if God's glory, with just one sun-ray,
Could not burn craters in a chromosome,
We call it kindly when it works our way,
And, some of us with tact, some with display,
Arrange the house to make it feel at home.

With votive tokens we propitiate
Almighty God. Just to be neat and clean –
Running the water hot to rinse the plate,
Chipping the rust-flakes from the garden gate –
These things are silent prayers, meant to be seen.

Strange, though, when parents with a stricken child
Still cleanse the temple, purify themselves.
They were betrayed, but how do they run wild?
With J-cloth and a blob of Fairy Mild
They wipe the white gloss of the kitchen shelves.

They, least of all, are likely to let go
Completely, like the slovens down the street:
The ones who could conceal a buffalo
In their front lawn and you would never know,
Yet somehow they keep their Creator sweet.

Unjust, unjust: but only if He's there.
The girl with palsy looks you in the eye,
Seeming to say there is no God to care.
Her gleaming wheel-chair says He's everywhere,
Or why would the unwell try not to die?

And why would those who love them give the best
Years of their lives to doing the right thing?
Why go on passing a perpetual test
With no real hope and with so little rest?
Why make from suffering an offering?

Why dust the carpet, wash the car, dress well?
If God were mocked by those who might do that
With ample cause, having been given Hell
To live with, we could very quickly tell –
Somebody would forget to feed the cat.

Sometimes they do. Sometimes the spirit kneels.
But when those with the least take pride the most,
We need to bend our thoughts to how it feels.
Shamed by those scintillating silver wheels,
We see the lightning of the Holy Ghost.

The Genesis Wafers

Genesis carried wafers in her hold
To catch the particles sent from the sun.
Diamond, sapphire, gold
Were those fine webs, as if by spiders spun
Beside whom specks of dust would weigh a ton.

A million miles from Earth, in the deep cold,
The particles collected in the skeins.
Diamond, sapphire, gold,
They flowered like tiny salt pans in the rains –
Fresh tablecloths distressed with coffee stains.

Back in the lab, the altered wafers told
A story of how poetry is born:
Diamond, sapphire, gold
Serenities invaded by stuff torn
From the incandescent storm that powers the dawn.

Museum of the Unmoving Image

The objects on display might seem to lack
Significance, unless you know the words.
The final straw that broke the camel's back,
The solitary stone that killed two birds.

Does this stuff really merit a glass case?
A tatty mattress and a shrivelled pea,
A shadow that somebody tried to chase,
A rusty pin that somehow earned a fee?

That gilded lily might have looked quite good
Without the dust that you won't see me for.
But where's the thrill in one piece of touched wood?
I think we've seen that uncut ice before.

A strained-at gnat, how interesting is that?
The bat from hell looks pitifully tame,
As do the pickled tongue got by the cat,
The ashes of the moth drawn to the flame.

Spilled milk, rough diamond, gift horse, gathered moss,
Dead duck, gone goose, bad apple, busted flush –
They're all lined up as if we gave a toss.
Try not to kill each other in the crush.

They've got an annexe for the big events:
Burned boats and bridges, castles in the air,
Clouds for your head to be in, rows of tents
For being camp as. Do we have to care?

What does this junk add up to? Look and learn,
The headphones say. They say our language grew
Out of this bric-a-brac. Here we return
To when the world around us shone brand new,

Lending its lustre to what people said;
Their speech was vivid with specific things.
It cries out to be brought back from the dead.
See what it was, and hear what it still sings.

Statement from the Secretary of Defense

This one we didn't know we didn't know:
At least, I didn't. You, you might have known
You didn't know. Let's say that might be so.
You knew, with wisdom granted you alone,

You didn't know. You say, but don't say how,
You knew we didn't know about abuse,
By us, in gaols of theirs that we run now.
Well, now we all know. I make no excuse:

In fact it's far worse than you think. You thought
You knew how bad it was? If you could see
The photos in this classified report
You'd know you knew, as usual, less than me.

You want to see a stress position? Look
At how I crouch to meet the President
And tell him this has not gone by the book.
How do I know he won't know what I meant?

I just know what he'll say, with hanging head:
'They don't know what pain is, these foreign folks.
Pain is to know you don't know what gets said
Behind your back, except you know the jokes.'

I feel for that man in his time of trial.
He simply didn't know, but now he knows
He didn't, and it hurts. Yet he can smile.
Remember how that Arab saying goes –

The blow that doesn't break you makes you strong?
They'll thank us when they get up off the mat.
They didn't know we knew what they knew. Wrong.
Even our women can do stuff like that.

Fair-weather friends who called our cause so good
Not even we could screw it, but now say
We've managed the impossible – I've stood
All I can stand of petty spite today,

So leave no room for doubt: now that we know
We might have known we didn't know, let's keep
Our heads. Give history time, and time will show
How flags wash clean, and eagles cease to weep.

The Australian Suicide Bomber's Heavenly Reward

Here I am, complaining as usual to Nicole Kidman
('Sometimes I think that to you I'm just a sex object')
While I watch Elle MacPherson model her new range
Of minimalist lingerie.
Elle does it the way I told her,
Dancing slowly to theme music from *The Sirens*
As she puts the stuff on instead of taking it off.
Meanwhile, Naomi Watts is fluffing up the spare bed
For her re-run of that scene in *Mulholland Drive*
Where she gets it on with the brunette with the weird name.
In keeping with the requirements of ethnic origin
Naomi's partner here will be Portia de Rossi,
Who seems admirably hot for the whole idea.
On every level surface there are perfumed candles
And wind chimes tinkle on the moonlit terrace:
Kylie and Dannii are doing a great job.
(They fight a lot, but when I warn them they might miss
Their turn, they come to heel.)
Do you know, I was scared I might never make it?
All suited up in my dynamite new waistcoat,
I was listening to our spiritual leader –
Radiant his beard, elegant his uplifted finger –
As he enthrallingly outlined, not for the first time,
The blessings that awaited us upon the successful completion
Of our mission to obliterate the infidel.
He should never have said he was sorry
He wasn't going with us.
Somehow I found myself pushing the button early.
I remember his look of surprise
In the flash of light before everything went sideways,

And I thought I might have incurred Allah's displeasure.
But Allah, the Greatest, truly as great as they say –
Great in his glory, glorious in his greatness, you name it –
Was actually waiting for me at the front door of this place
With a few words of his own. 'You did the right thing.
Those were exactly the people to lower the boom on.
Did they really think that I, of all deities,
Was ever going to be saddled with all that shit?
I mean, *please*. Hello? Have we met?'
And so I was escorted by the Hockeyroos –
Who had kindly decided to dress for beach volleyball –
Into the antechamber where Cate Blanchett was waiting
In a white bias-cut evening gown and bare feet.
High maintenance, or what?
No wonder I was feeling a bit wrecked.
'You look,' she said, 'as if you could use a bath.'
She ran it for me, whisking the foam with her fingertips
While adding petals of hydrangeas and nasturtiums.
Down at her end, she opened a packet of Jaffas
And dropped them in, like blood into a cloud.

Diamond Pens of the Bus Vandals

Where do bus vandals get their diamond pens
That fill each upstairs window with a cloud
Of shuffled etchings? Patience does them proud.
Think of Spinoza when he ground a lens.

A fog in London used to be outside
The bus, which had to crawl until it cleared.
Now it's as if the world had disappeared
In shining smoke however far you ride.

You could call this a breakthrough, of a sort.
These storms of brilliance, light as the new dark,
Disturb and question like a pickled shark:
Conceptual art free from the bonds of thought,

Raw talent rampant. New York subway cars
Once left poor Jackson Pollock looking tame.
Some of the doodlers sprayed their way to fame:
A dazzled Norman Mailer called them stars.

And wasn't Michelangelo, deep down,
Compelled to sling paint by an empty space,
Some ceiling he could thoroughly deface?
The same for Raphael. When those boys hit town

Few of its walls were safe. One cave in France
Has borne for almost forty thousand years
Pictures of bison and small men with spears –
Blank surfaces have never stood a chance

Against the human impulse to express
The self. All those initials on the glass
Remind you, as you clutch your Freedom Pass,
It's a long journey from the wilderness.

The Zero Pilot

On the *Hiryu*, Hajime Toyoshima
Starred in the group photos like Andy Hardy,
He was so small and cute.
His face, as friendly as his first name
(In Japanese you say 'Hajime' at first meeting),
Could have been chirping, 'Hey, why don't we
Put the show on right here in the barn?'
After Pearl Harbor he was one of the great ship's heroes
And the attack on Darwin promised him yet more glory,
But his engine conked out over Melville Island
From one lousy rifle bullet in the oil system.
Caught by natives, he should have done it then,
If not beforehand when the prop stopped turning.
Instead of hitting the silk
He could have nosed over and dived into the ground
But he didn't. When the natives closed in
He could have shot himself with his .32
But he didn't do that either.
Under interrogation he was offered chocolate
Which he ate instead of turning down.
What was he thinking of?
He didn't get it done
Until a full two and half years later –
After the Cowra breakout, which he helped
To lead, madly blowing a stolen bugle,
Psyched up to guide his party of frantic runners
All the way to Japan. Upon recapture
He finally did it with a carving knife,
Sawing at his own throat as if to cancel
That sweet, rich taste of surrender,

The swallowed chocolate. His ruined Zero
Is on display in Darwin. The empty bulkhead
Is torn like silver paper where the engine roared
That once propelled him through the startled sky
At a rate of roll unknown to Kittyhawks.
Paint, cables, webbing, instruments and guns:
Much else is also missing,
But the real absence is his,
And always was.
'Hajime' is short for
'Our acquaintanceship begins:
Until now, we did not know each other.
From this day forth, we will.'
Well, could be,
Though it mightn't be quite that easy.
Buried at Cowra,
He probably never knew
That the *Hiryu* went down at Midway,
Where the last of his friends died fighting –
Still missing the cheery voice
Of their mascot, named always to say hello,
Who never said goodbye.

Iron Horse

The Sioux, believing ponies should be pintos,
Painted the ones that weren't.
When they saw the Iron Horse
They must have wondered why the palefaces
Left its black coat unmarked.
Bruno Schulz said an artist must mature
But only into childhood.
He called our first perceptions
The iron capital of the adult brain.
I would like to think my latest marquetry
Was underpinned by Debussy's *Images*
Or the chain of micro-essays
In Adorno's *Minima Moralia*,
But a more likely progenitor
Entered my head right here in Sydney:
The first aesthetic thrill that I remember.
In a Strand Arcade display case
A tiny but fine-detailed model train
Ran endlessly around a plaster landscape.
On tip-toe, looking through the panorama
Rather than down on it, I formed or fed
Lasting ideals of mimesis, precision
And the consonance of closely fitted parts
Combined into a work that had coherence
Beyond its inseparable workings.
Later, at the flicks, when the Iron Horse
Was attacked by yelping braves,
I heard their hoof-beats on a marble floor,
And later still, having read about steam power
In my *Modern Marvels Encyclopedia*,

When I realised the little train
Had been pulled by an illusionary loco –
Directly turned by an electric motor,
The wheels propelled the rods and not vice versa –
My seeing through the trick only increased
The recollection of intensity,
Immensity compressed into a bubble,
The macrosphere in miniature.
But mere shrinkage didn't work the magic:
There had to be that complicated movement
Of intricate articulation
As in an aero-engine like the Merlin
Or the H-form Napier Sabre.
In the Hermitage, a Fabergé toy train
Was not so precious, didn't even go,
Was hopelessly disfigured by its jewels.
It left me with pursed lips and shaking head,
Surprised they even bothered
And full of pity for the royal children
Deceived by their bonanza every Christmas –
A wampum headband set with amethysts,
A solid silver tomahawk –
Into equating workmanship with wealth.
Full of boutiques that try to do the same,
The Strand Arcade is still there,
Commendably preserved if over-polished,
But the train is gone for good –
Except where, in my mind,
Forever turning back and yet forever
Continuing its *tour d'horizon*
Of a world threatened by a race of giants,
It snickers behind the glass
I stained with the acid of my fingertips.

Grace Cossington Smith's Harbour Bridge

Grace Cossington Smith, Grace Cossington Smith,
Your name is yet one to be conjuring with.
You painted the Bridge well before it was finished
And still the excitement remains undiminished,
Your patchwork of pigments enhancing its myth.

Grace Cossington Smith, Grace Cossington Smith,
Your skill was the essence, the fulcrum and pith
Of all that we love about classical art
Embracing the modern and making it part
Of the total adventure that starts in the heart.

Grace Cossington Smith, Grace Cossington Smith,
Your moniker honours your kin and your kith.
The studies you made of the Bridge uncompleted
Add up to a triumph that can't be repeated:
The lattice-work elements reach for each other
Like Damon and Pythias, brother to brother,
Imprinting the sky with the future before it
Was certain, and you were the one who foresaw it.
The polychrome grains of our grey megalith –
You put them together, Grace Cossington Smith.

When We Were Kids

When we were kids we fought in the mock battle
With Ned Kelly cap guns and we opened the cold bottle
Of Shelley's lemonade with a Scout belt buckle.
We cracked the passion fruit and sipped the honeysuckle.

When we were kids we lit the Thundercracker
Under the fruit tin and we sucked the all day sucker.
We opened the shoe box to watch the silk-worms spinning
Cocoons of cirrus with oriental cunning.

When we were kids we were sun-burned to a frazzle.
The beach was a griddle, you could hear us spit and sizzle.
We slept face down when our backs came out in blisters.
Teachers were famous for throwing blackboard dusters.

When we were kids we dive-bombed from the tower.
We floated in the inner tube, we bowled the rubber tyre.
From torn balloons we blew the cherry bubble.
Blowing up Frenchies could get you into trouble.

When we were kids we played at cock-a-lorum.
Gutter to gutter the boys ran harum-scarum.
The girls ran slower and their arms and legs looked funny.
You weren't supposed to drink your school milk in the dunny.

When we were kids the licorice came in cables.
We traded Hubba-Bubba bubblegum for marbles.
A new connie-agate was a flower trapped in crystal
Worth just one go with a genuine air pistol.

When we were kids we threw the cigarette cards
Against the wall and we lined the Grenadier Guards
Up on the carpet and you couldn't touch the trifle
Your Aunt Marge made to go in the church raffle.

When we were kids we hunted the cicada.
The pet cockatoo bit like a barracuda.
We were secret agents and fluent in pig Latin.
Gutsing on mulberries made our lips shine like black satin.

When we were kids we caught the Christmas beetle.
Its brittle wings were gold-green like the wattle.
Our mothers made bouquets from frangipani.
Hard to pronounce, a pink musk-stick cost a penny.

When we were kids we climbed peppercorns and willows.
We startled the stingrays when we waded in the shallows.
We mined the sand dunes in search of buried treasure,
And all this news pleased our parents beyond measure.

When we were kids the pus would wet the needle
When you dug out splinters and a piss was called a piddle.
The scabs on your knees would itch when they were ready
To be picked off your self-renewing body.

When we were kids a year would last forever.
Then we grew up and were told it was all over.
Now we are old and the memories returning
Are like the last stars that fade before the morning.

Only Divine

Always the Gods learned more from humankind
Than vice versa. So it was bound to be:
It takes a troubled heart to make a mind.
Stuck with their beautiful stupidity,

The Gods were peeved to find themselves outclassed
Even in pleasure, which was their best thing.
Sky-walking Zeus, the Bright One, was aghast
To find that men could laugh and weep and sing

For love, instead of merely chasing tail
The way he did when he came down to earth:
Driving his lightning bolt in like a nail,
Shouting the place down with unsubtle mirth.

Sometimes he stole earth-men's identities.
His acrobatics in a borrowed face
Drew some applause for their raw power to please
But none at all for foreplay, tact or grace.

By Jove! By Jupiter! He heard the names
Men gave him change. The world grew less impressed
Than he was with his simple fun and games,
The gold medallions on his hairy chest.

Back in the clouds, he brooded for as long
As Gods can. If he couldn't have the tears
Of mortals, he could copy a love song.
To learn one took him several hundred years,

But time, like sorrow, doesn't count up there.
He got quite good at it, and now he sings
Sinatra standards that sound pretty fair
Against a backing track complete with strings.

Virgin Minerva, born out of his brain
To stave off Vulcan with a single slap,
Borrowed more fetching versions of disdain
Better designed to milk the thunderclap

Of lust. Her heavenly suitors pay for shoes
She might wear only once, or not at all.
Pretending they know how it feels to lose,
Prospective lovers, outside in the hall,

Compare TAG Heuer watches while they scuff
Their Gucci loafers on the marble floor.
In love, real men have taught them, things get rough:
A show of grief might get you through her door.

Inside, she lies back on her Zsa-Zsa pink
Chaise-longue while Aphrodite dishes dirt.
Feigning to taste the whisky sours they drink,
They smile as if a memory could hurt.

Does Atlas need those Terminator shades?
Poseidon's wet-suit, what good does it do?
Is gold-crowned Phoebe on her roller blades
Really as cute as when the world was new?

And here comes Hera in her Britney kit,
And there goes Hermes on his superbike.
The stuff they have! You wouldn't credit it,
And all top of the range. What are they *like*?

Like us, without the creativity
Stirred by the guilt that hangs around our necks.
Their only care the void of their carefree
Millennia of unprotected sex,

Uncomprehendingly they quote our books.
Their gull-wing sports cars and their Gulfstream jets,
The bling-bling wasted on their perfect looks –
It's all ours. Gleaming as their long sun sets,

The Gods are gaudy tatters of a plan
Hatched by our ancestors to render fate
More bearable. They end as they began,
Belittled in our thoughts that made them great.

Lock Me Away

In the NHS psychiatric test
For classifying the mentally ill
You have to spell 'world' backwards.
Since I heard this, I can't stop doing it.
The first time I tried pronouncing the results
I got a sudden flaring picture
Of Danny La Rue in short pants
With his mouth full of marshmallows.
He was giving his initial and surname
To a new schoolteacher.
Now every time I read the *Guardian*
I find its columns populated
By a thousand mumbling drag queens.
Why, though, do I never think
Of a French film composer
(Georges Delerue, pupil of
Darius Milhaud, composed the waltz
In *Hiroshima, Mon Amour*)
Identifying himself to a policeman
After being beaten up?
But can I truly say I never think of it
After I've just thought of it?
Maybe I'm going stun:
Dam, dab and dangerous to wonk.
You realise this ward you've led me into
Spelled backwards is the cloudy draw
Of the ghost-riders in the sky?
Listen to this palindrome
And tell me that it's not my ticket out.
Able was I ere I saw Elba.
Do you know who I am, Dr Larue?

Bigger than a Man

Bigger than a man, the wedding tackle
Of the male blue whale is a reminder
There can be potent spouses who stay true.

As he nuzzles up behind her
He gives hard evidence that he is always keen,
And when they have lain face to face awhile

Like two blimps that have seen *The Blue Lagoon*,
He brings the Sunday papers up to bed.
With a whole globe of ocean for a boudoir

Their pillow talk has not been much recorded,
But there have been some transcripts:
'Baweeng bok eeng,' he sings, and she:

'Baweeng chock. Eeng bawok eeng chunk.'
Some experts think that 'eeng' must mean 'again':
She asks for more of what he always gives.

Well, that would fit, as his impressive member
Lodges in her blancmange-lined sleeping bag.
There are no blue whale marriage guidance counsellors

Except perhaps one, seen alone near Cape Town.
She sang 'eeng', always with a plangent cadence.
She sang 'eeng' only. 'Eeng eeng. Eeng eeng eeng.'

Publisher's Party

for Posy Simmonds

Young ladies beautiful as novelists
Were handing out the nibbles and the drinks.
Butch writers with bald heads and hairy wrists
Exchanged raised eyebrows, nudges, knowing winks,
Hints broader than their beams.
The tall dark knockout who prowled like a lynx
With the chicken satay cooled the optimists –
Her polite smile said *as if* and *in your dreams*.

One writer never sought her violet eyes.
He concentrated on the parquet floor.
Ungainly yet of no impressive size,
Lacking in social skills, licensed to bore,
He was the kind of bloke
A girl like her would normally ignore,
Unless, of course, he'd won the Booker Prize.
Alas, he had. I can't think of a joke –

Only of how she lingered there until
He woke up to the full force of her looks;
Of how we rippled with a jealous thrill,
All those of us who'd also written books
Out of an inner need;
And now a panel-game of hacks and crooks
Had staked him out for her to stalk and kill –
As if the man could write, and she could read.

They live in Docklands now: a top-floor flat
They can see France from. Yes, they live there, too:
A house in the Dordogne. Stuff like that
I honestly don't care about, do you?
But then I see her face
Beside his in the papers. Strange, but true –
Blind chance that picked his fame out of a hat
Had perfect vision when it gave him grace.

My new book's hopeless and I'm getting fat.

Literary Lunch

Reciting poetry by those you prize –
Auden, MacNeice, Yeats, Stevens, Charlotte Mew –
I trust my memory and watch your eyes
To see if you know I am wooing you
With all these stolen goods. Of course you do.

Across the table, you know every line
Does service for a kiss or a caress.
Words taken out of other mouths, in mine
Are a laying on of hands in formal dress,
And your awareness measures my success

While marking out its limits. You may smile
For pleasure, confident my love is pure:
What would have been an exercise in guile
When I was young and strong, is now for sure
Raised safely to the plane of literature,

Where you may take it as a compliment
Unmixed with any claims to more delight
Than your attention. Such was my intent
This morning, as I planned what to recite
Just so you might remember me tonight,

When you are with the man who has no need
Of any words but his, or even those:
The only poem that he cares to read
Is open there before him. How it flows
He feels, and how it starts and ends he knows.

At School with Reg Gasnier

Gasnier had soft hands that the ball stuck to
And a body swerve off either foot
That just happened, you couldn't see him think.
He wasn't really knock-kneed
But he looked that way when he ran,
With his studded ankles flailing sideways
Like the hubcaps of a war chariot.
At tackling practice we went at him in despair
And either missed or fell stunned,
Our foreheads dotted with bleeding sprig-marks.
So glorious were his deeds
That the testimonials at school assembly
On the day after the match
Went on like passages from Homer.
He put Sydney Tech on the football map.
There were whole GPS teams he went through
Like a bat through a dark cave.
Sydney High, with backs the size of forwards,
Only barely stopped him,
And they practically used land mines.
Wanting to be him, I so conspicuously wasn't
That I would brood for hours in the library,
One kid from Kogarah utterly wiped out
By the lustre of another.
Later on, as a pro, he won national fame.
His shining story followed me to England:
I couldn't get away from the bastard.
By the time I got a slice of fame myself –
And we're talking about the echo of a whisper –
His nephew Mark was playing:

Clear proof that the gift was in the blood.
Reg is retired now
And not writing as many poems as I am,
But give me my life again and I would still rather
Be worshipped in the school playground
By those who saw him score the winning try,
A human dodgem snaking through a bunch of blokes
All flying the wrong way like literary critics –
Or at least I think so,
Now that I can't sleep without socks on.

At Ian Hamilton's Funeral

Another black-tie invitation comes:
And once again, the black tie is the long
Thin one and not the bow. No muffled drums
Or stuff like that, but still it would be wrong
To flout the solemn forms. Fingers and thumbs
Adjust the knot as I recall the song
About the gang that sang 'Heart of My Heart'.
Death brings together what time pulled apart.

In Wimbledon, a cold bright New Year's Eve
Shines on the faces that you used to know
But only lights the depth to which they grieve
Or are beginning to. The body-blow
You dealt us when you left we will believe
When it sinks in. We haven't let you go
As yet. Outside the church, you're here with us.
Whatever's said, it's you that we discuss.

We speak of other things, but what we mean
Is you, and who you were, not where you are.
No one would call the centre of the scene
That little box inside the big black car.
Two things we wish were true: you made a clean
Getaway, and you have not gone far.
One thing we're sure of: now the breath is fled
You aren't in there, you're somewhere else instead –

Safe in a general memory. We file
Inside. The London literati take
Their places pew to pew and aisle to aisle
At murmured random. Nothing is at stake
Except the recollection of your smile.
All earned it. Who most often? For your sake
Men wrote all night, and as for women, well,
How many of them loved you none can tell.

Those who are here among us wear the years
With ease, as fine-boned beauty tends to do.
It wasn't just your looks that won the tears
They spill today when they remember you.
Most of us had our minds on our careers.
You were our conscience, and your women knew
Just by our deference the man in black
Who said least was the leader of the pack.

Dressed all your life for mourning, you made no
Display. Although your prose was eloquent,
Your poetry fought shy of outward show.
Pain and regret said no more than they meant.
Love sued for peace but had nowhere to go.
Joy was a book advance already spent,
And yet by day, free from the soul's midnight,
Your conversation was a sheer delight.

Thirsty for more of it, we came to drink
In Soho. While you read his manuscript
You gave its perpetrator time to think
Of taking up another trade. White-lipped
He watched you sneer. But sometimes you would blink
Or nod or even chuckle while you sipped
Your Scotch, and then came the acceptance fee:
The wit, the gossip, the hilarity.

You paid us from your only source of wealth.
Your finances were always in a mess.
We told each other we did good by stealth.
In private we took pride in a success:
Knowing the way of life that wrecked your health
Was death-defying faith, not fecklessness,
We preened to feel your hard-won lack of guile
Rub off on us for just a little while.

For lyric truth, such suffering is the cost –
So the equation goes you incarnated.
The rest of us must ponder what we lost
When we so prudently equivocated.
But you yourself had time for Robert Frost –
His folksy pomp and circumstance you hated,
Yet loved his moments of that pure expression
You made your own sole aim if not obsession.

Our quarrel about that's not over yet,
But here today we have to let it rest.
The disagreements we could not forget
In life, will fade now and it's for the best.
Your work was a sad trumpet at sunset.
My sideshow razzmatazz you rarely blessed
Except with the reluctant grin I treasured
The most of all the ways my stuff was measured.

Laughter in life, and dark, unsmiling art:
There lay, or seemed to lie, the paradox.
Which was the spirit, which the mortal part?
As if in answer, borne aloft, the box
Goes by one slow step at a time. The heart
At last heaves and the reservoir unlocks
Of sorrow. That was you, and you are gone:
First to the altar, then to oblivion.

The rest is ceremony, and well said.
Your brother speaks what you would blush to hear
Were you alive and standing with bowed head.
But you lie straight and hidden, very near
Yet just as far off as the other dead
Each of us knows will never reappear.
You were the governor, the chief, the squire,
And now what's left of you leaves for the fire.

Ashes will breed no phoenix, you were sure
Of that, but not right. You should hear your friends
Who rise to follow, and outside the door
Agree this is a sad day yet it ends
In something that was not so clear before:
The awareness of love, how it defends
Itself against forgetfulness, and gives
Through death the best assurance that it lives.

Press Release from Plato

Delayed until the sacred ship got back
From Delos, the last hour of Socrates
Unfolded smoothly. His time-honoured knack
For putting everybody at their ease

Was still there even while the numbness spread
Up from his feet. All present in the cell
Were much moved by the way he kept his head
As he spoke less, but never less than well.

Poor Crito and Apollodorus wept
Like Xanthippe, but not one tear was his
From start to finish. Dignity was kept.
If that much isn't certain, nothing is.

I only wish I could have been there too.
When, later on, I wrote down every word,
I double-checked – the least that I could do –
To make it sound as if I'd overheard.

But let's face facts. He lives because of me.
That simple-seeming man and what he meant
To politics and to philosophy –
These things have not survived by accident.

Deals to be done and details to discuss
Called me elsewhere. I'm sorry for that still.
He owed a cock to Aesculapius.
Socratic question: guess who paid the bill?

Ramifications of Pure Beauty

Passing the line-up of the narrow-boats
The swans proceed downriver. As they go
They sometimes dip and lift an inch or so.
A swan is not a stick that merely floats
With the current. Currents might prove too slow
Or contrary. Therefore the feet deploy:
Trailed in the glide, they dig deep for the thrust
That makes the body bob. Though we don't see
The leg swing forward and extend, it must
Do so. Such a deduction can't destroy
Our sense-impression of serenity,
But does taint what we feel with what we know.

Bounced from up-sun by Focke-Wulf 'Long Nose'
Ta-152s, Pierre Clostermann
Noted their bodies 'fined down by the speed':
And so they were, to his eyes. Glider wings,
Long legs and close-cowled engine made the pose
Of that plane poised when stock-still. In the air,
High up and flat out, it looked fleet indeed.
What pulled it through the sky was left implied:
You had to know the turning blades were there,
Like the guns, the ammo and the man inside
Who might have thought your Tempest pretty too –
But not enough to stop him killing you.

The crowds for Titian cope with the appeal
Of flayed Actaeon. Horror made sublime:
We see that. Having seen it, we relax
With supine ladies. Pin-ups of their time,
Surely they have no hinterland of crime?
Corruption would show up like needle-tracks.
No, they are clean, as he was. All he knew
Of sin was painting them with not much on.
Even to fill a Spanish contract, he
Fleshed out the abstract with the sumptuous real –
Brought on the girls and called it poetry.
Philip II felt the same. Why think
At this late date about the mortal stink
Of the war galley, graceful as a swan?

The Serpent Beguiled Me

Following Eve, you look for apple cores
Along the riverbank, tossed in the mud.
Following Adam down long corridors,
You swing your torch to look for spit and blood.

He got his chest condition when he learned
Contentment made her curious. He thought
He was enough for her, and what he earned
Would keep her pinned while he played covert sport.

Alas, not so. She claimed that privilege too,
And even, under wraps, nursed the same pride
In taking satiation as her due –
A cue to call herself dissatisfied.

That rate of change was coded by the tree
Into the fruit. The instant thrill of sin
Turned sweet release to bitter urgency:
His fig leaf was flicked off, and hers sucked in.

From that day forth, the syrup she gave down
Smacked of the knowledge that she felt no shame.
The modesty for which she won renown
Was feigned to keep her freedom free of blame.

There was a time when, if he had not worn
Her out, she would have lain awake and wept.
Why was the truth, we ask, so slow to dawn?
He should have guessed it from how well she slept.

And when she turned to him, as she did still,
Though the old compulsion was no longer there,
The readiness with which she drank her fill
Told him in vain her fancy lay elsewhere.

He never faced the fact until she went.
He tracked her down and asked her what was wrong.
For once she said exactly what she meant:
'It was perfect. It just went on too long.'

State Funeral

In memory of Shirley Strickland de la Hunty

Famous for overcoming obstacles
She finally finds one that checks her flight.
Hit by the leading foot, a hurdle falls:
Except when, set in concrete, it sits tight.

Not that she hit too many. Most she cleared,
Her trailing leg laid effortlessly flat.
As in repose, at full tilt she appeared
Blessed with a supple grace. On top of that

She studied physics, took a good degree,
Had several languages to read and speak.
Alone, she wasn't short of company:
In company she shone. She was unique

Even among our girl Olympians
For bringing the mind's power and body's poise
To perfect balance. Ancient Greeks had plans
Along those lines, but strictly for the boys.

Her seven medals in three separate Games
Should have been eight, but she retired content.
In time she sold the lot to feed the flames
Of her concern for the Environment.

Civic responsibility: but one
Kind of pollution lay outside her scope
To counteract. The races she had run
Were won now by sad cyborgs fuelled with dope.

It started in the East. The State required
Results that only science could supply.
The female victims, suitably rewired
For victory, could do everything but fly.

And if some wept for how they changed, too bad.
The doctors did what they were ordered to
And told the chosen ones they should be glad:
Drink this, and it will make a man of you.

The plague spread to the West, where money talked.
Poor women, like poor men, had much to gain
Through muscle. The bad bottle was uncorked.
They plucked their chins and thought it worth the pain.

Perhaps it was, yet one glimpse of Flo-Jo
Coiled in her starting blocks told you the cost.
Transmuted to a charging buffalo,
She mourned with painted nails for what she'd lost.

But more was lost than that. The time had come
When no one could be trusted any more
Because to play it straight seemed simply dumb,
And who remembered how things were before?

Desire beats scruple into second place.
Gratification makes a fool of thrift.
The only rules are Rafferty's. The race
Is to the sly that once was to the swift.

A brighter future, back there in the past,
Flared for a moment but it flickered out.
It speaks, our flag that flutters at half mast,
Of final silence. Let it silence doubt:

When Shirley raced, the wings on her spiked shoes
Were merely mythical, like Mercury's.
She did it unassisted, win or lose.
The world she did it in died by degrees

While she looked on. Now she is spared the sight
At last. The bobby-dazzler won't be back,
Who ran for love and jumped for sheer delight
In a better life and on a different track –

We have too much if she is what we lack.

This Is No Drill

Out on my singing teacher's patio
While waiting for my lesson, I sat smoking,
And on the flag-stone about three feet from my chair
A scoop of bird shit suddenly appeared.
It looked like a nouvelle cuisine hors d'oeuvre,
A brown-green snail-pulp dollop on a bed
Of mascarpone hardening to meringue
As I watched, stupefied. I searched the sky
And there was nothing. Clean sweep. Been and gone.
So high up that it flies with the U-2s
And sees the Earth's curve, this bird calculates
Trajectories with so much to factor in –
Cloud density, speed, height, wind over target –
The wonder is it didn't miss by miles.
Instead, the point of impact was so close
The shock wave took the air out of my lungs.
Inside the house I croaked scales, and remembered
That day in the Piazza Santa Croce –
It must be thirty years back, maybe more –
When I got taken out by such a load
I felt the weight, and had to sit around
While the gunk dried on my brand new jacket. Why
These sneak attacks? We give them enough aid.
At least Prometheus and Tippi Hedren
Could see them coming. This is something else.
What do they want, a seat at the UN?
And no use asking if I would have died
Had this one nailed me. When a man is bald
And soon to face an aria from *Tosca*,

It's not as if he needs a pile of crap
Dumped on his head from fifty thousand feet
By some Stealth fowl. And spare me the assurance
That it wipes off. I didn't sign up for this.

Fires Burning, Fires Burning

Over Hamburg
The Lancaster crews could feel the heat
Through the sides of the aircraft.
The fire was six thousand feet high.

At Birkenau
When burning a lot of bodies, the SS found
The thing to do was to put down a layer
Of women first.
They had more fat in them.

In Tokyo
Some people who survived in a canal
Saw a horse on fire running through the streets.
But few who saw it were left to remember anything:
Even the water burned.

In New York
Some couples, given the choice
Between the flames and a long fall,
Outflanked the heat and went down holding hands.
Come with me, you imagine the men saying,
I know a quicker way.

In Sydney
Next to my mother's coffin
I gave thanks that she would shortly meet
A different kind of fire,
Having died first, and in due time.

Yusra

The Public Morals Unit of Hamas
Saw Yusra al-Azzuri, bold as brass,
In Gaza City, walk with her betrothed,
Her sister also present. Half unclothed,

All three behaved as if beyond the reach
Of justice. Laughing, dancing on the beach,
They almost touched. They thought to drive away.
The Unit followed them without delay.

Her young man drove. Beside him as they fled,
Yusra died quickly in a hail of lead.
The other two were hauled out of the car
And beaten senseless. With an iron bar,

The riddled corpse of Yusra, as the worst
Offender, was assaulted till it burst.
She would have prayed for death. It can be said,
Therefore, it was a blessing she was dead

Already. Thus we look for just one touch
Of grace in this catastrophe. Too much
To bear, the thought that those young men were glad
To be there. Won't the memory drive them mad?

Could they not see the laughter in her face
Was heaven on earth, the only holy place?
Perhaps they guessed, and acted from the fear
That Paradise is nowhere if not here.

Yusra, your name too lovely to forget
Shines like a sunrise joined to a sunset.
The day between went with you. Where you are,
That light around you is your life, Yusra.

Private Prayer at Yasukuni Shrine

An *Oka* kamikaze rocket bomb
Sits in the vestibule, its rising sun
Ablaze with pride.
Names of the fallen are on CD-ROM.
The war might have been lost. The peace was won:
A resurrection after suicide.

For once I feel the urge to send my thoughts
Your way, as I suppose these people do.
I see the tide
Come in on Papua. Their troop transports,
The beach, our hospital. Over to you:
Why was one little miracle denied?

After they made our nurses wade waist deep
They picked their targets and they shot them all.
The waves ran red.
Somehow this is a memory I keep.
I hear the lost cries of the last to fall
As if I, too, had been among the dead.

Those same troops fought south to the Golden Stairs,
Where they were stopped. They starved, and finally
The last few fed
On corpses. And the victory would be theirs
If I were glad? That's what you're telling me?
It would have been in vain that your son bled?

But wasn't it? What were you thinking when
Our daughters died? You couldn't interfere,
I hear you say.
That must mean that you never can. Well, then,
At least I know now that no prayers from here
Have ever made much difference either way,

And therefore we weren't fighting you as well.
Old people here saw the *Missouri* loom
Out in the bay
And thought the end had come. They couldn't tell
That the alternative to certain doom
Would be *pachinko* and the cash to play

A game of chance, all day and every day.
In that bright shrine you really do preside.
What you have said
Comes true. The DOW is down on the Nikkei.
The royal baby takes a buggy ride.
The last war criminal will die in bed.

Naomi from Namibia

In the Brisbane Botanical Gardens,
Walking the avenue of weeping figs,
You can see exuded latex stain the bark
Like adolescent sperm. A metamorphosis:
The trunks must be full of randy boys.

At home, the Java willows
When planted alongside a watercourse
Were said to stem the breeding of mosquitoes.
Here, they have nothing else to do
Except to stand there looking elegant
In Elle MacPherson lingerie.

From the walkway through the mangrove mud-flats
Spread south from overwhelming Asia,
You can see the breathing tubes of Viet Cong crabs
And imagine Arnie hiding from the Predator
Like a mud-skipper playing possum,
Although he did that, of course, in South America.
Below the tangled branches, bubbles tick.

For a century and a half, the giant banyan
Has grown like a cathedral heading downwards,
As a dumb Chartres might slowly dive for cover
Through shallows clear as air. In India
At least a dozen families would be dying
By inches in its colonnades.

At the kiosk, Naomi from Namibia
Serves me a skimmed-milk strawberry milkshake.
She has come here to lead her ideal life,
Like almost all these trees.
They get to stay, but she has to go back.

William Dobell's Cypriot

The Cypriot brought his wine-dark eyes with him
Along with his skin and hair. He also brought
That shirt. Swathes of fine fabric clothe a slim
Frame with a grace bespeaking taste and thought.

Australia, 1940. There were few
Men native-born who had that kind of style.
Hence the attention Dobell gave the blue
Collar and cuffs, to make us pause awhile

And see a presence that did not belong.
This sitter, sitting here, caught by this hand?
Caught beautifully. No, there is nothing wrong
About this transportation to Queensland

Of ancient subtleties. It's merely odd.
A man whom he had loved and seen asleep
The painter painted naked, a Greek god.
But then he had the sudden wit to keep

The clothes, and thus the heritage, in the next
Picture. A window from a men's-wear store,
It doubles as the greatest early text
Of the immigration. What we were before

Looks back through this to what we would become.
We see a sense of nuance head our way
To make the raw rich, complicate the sum
Of qualities, prepare us for today.

Now that the day is ours, the time arrives
To remember destiny began as chance,
And history is as frail as human lives.
A young and foreign smile, love at first glance:

Painter and painted possibly first met
Just because one admired the other's tie.
A year old then, I live now in their debt.
This is the way they live. I too will die.

Ghost Train to Australia

Container Train in Landscape, 1983–84
by Jeffrey Smart

I won't this time. Silent at last and shunted
Into its siding in the Victorian Arts Centre,
The container train started its journey in Yugoslavia
Two years before it arrived in Gippsland
Among trees that echo Albert Namatjira.

The containers echo First World War dazzle paint
Whose solid planes of colour fooled submarines.
Everything in the picture echoes something,
Yet it all belongs to the painter's unifying vision.
How does he do that? Perhaps as a consolation

For not being Piero della Francesca
And lacking Christ's birth to celebrate in Arezzo,
He can alter the order of modern history's pages
Though we might need our memories to catch him in the act:
All trains in Europe, for example, even today,

When they are drawn by electric locos and made of metal,
Remind us of boxcars full of unbelieving people
And the scenes on the platform when the train pulled in.
No amount of lusciously applied colour
Can cover all that stark grey squalor up

Or take away the shadow on a train's fate.
Simply because it is a European train,
Even if it goes all the way to Australia
And terminates among the eucalypts
In a lake of perfect sunlight the whole sky deep

And everybody gets off and there are no searchlights
Or whips or wolf-hounds or cold-eyed efficient doctors
And the fathers go to work on the Snowy River
And the mothers learn the lemon meringue pie
And the children, after they have had their tonsils out,

Get Shelley's lemonade and vanilla ice-cream
And all grow up to be captain of the school,
And the local intellectuals fly in like fruit-bats
To lecture the new arrivals about genocide,
The train, the train, the wonderful train

That found visas for all aboard and now finally sits
Shining in the bush like five bob's worth of sweets –
Jaffas, Cherry Ripes, Hoadley's Violet Crumble Bars
Glittering in the original purple and gold wrappers –
Is still the ghost train. I'm sorry, I didn't mean to.

Les Saw It First

I swam across the creek at Inverell.
The guard of jacarandas bled their blue
Into the water. I recall it well,
But partly I do that because of you.

I was a city boy. A country trip
Was rare, and so the memories were sparse.
I helped to plait a cracker for a whip,
But when I swung the thing it was a farce.

At Tingha, where they used to mine the tin,
I searched for sapphires all day and found none.
I briefly rode a horse and barked my shin
When I got off, and couldn't stand the sun

That bleached the fence-rails to a dry, pale grey
A hundred years before and there they were,
Just looking wooden and what can you say?
Sit on a stump and blink into the blur.

I had been long away when I looked back
Through your books and at last saw what I'd seen:
The blue-tongue in the gum beside the track,
The headless black snake limp as Plasticine.

The snake was in a trench they called a race.
Somebody threw it there when it was dead.
Now I remember how fear froze my face
When, further on, I found its yawning head.

The country built the city: now I know.
Like it or not, it got to even me,
And not just through the Royal Easter Show,
But the hard yakka of its poetry.

Now I can hear the shouts of the young men
Out after rabbits with a .22.
I wasn't there long, but I'm there again,
Collecting trinkets as the magpies do.

It's part of me, and partly because of you.

Signed by the Artist

The way the bamboo leans out of the frame,
Some of its leaves cut short by the frame's edge,
Makes room for swathes of air which you would think,
If it were sold in bolts, would drape like silk.
Below, where one pond spills from the stone ledge
Into the next, three carp as white as milk
Glow through the water near the painter's name,
A stack of characters brushed in black ink.

The open spaces and the spare detail
Are both compressed into that signature:
He made his name part of the work of art.
Slice of crisp leaf, smooth flourish of fish fin
Are there to show you he is very sure
Of how the balance of things kept apart
Can shape a distance. On a larger scale
He still leaves out far more than he puts in.

We're lucky that he does. What he includes,
Almost too beautiful to contemplate,
Already hurts our hearts. Were he to fill
The gaps, the mind would have no place to rest,
No peace in the collected solitudes
Of those three fish, in how each leaf is blessed
With life. Easy to underestimate
A name like his. No substance. Too much skill.

Return of the Lost City

How far was Plato free of that 'inflamed
Community' he said we should avoid?
Sofas, incense and hookers: these he named
Among the habits not to be enjoyed,
And if you did, you ought to be ashamed.
But can't we tell, by how he sounds annoyed,
That his Republic, planned on our behalf,
Was where his own desires had the last laugh,

If only as the motor for his sense
Of discipline? Even the dreams were policed,
By the Nocturnal Council. Such immense
Powers of repression! What would be released
Without them? The Republic was intense:
The fear of relaxation never ceased.
Hence the embargo on all works of art,
However strict in form, that touched the heart.

No poetry. No poets! No, not one –
Not even Homer, if he were to be
Reborn – could be admitted, lest the sun
Set on the hard-won social harmony,
And that obscene night-life which had begun
In man's first effort at society,
Atlantis, should come flooding back, the way
The sea did, or so story-tellers say.

But Plato knew that they'd say anything:
For money or applause or just a share
Of an hetaera, they would dance and sing
And turn the whole deal into a nightmare.

The very prospect left him quivering
With anger. There is something like despair
Haunting the author of the ideal state,
A taunting voice he heard while working late:

Atlantis made you. It is what you know,
Deep down. Atlantis and its pleasures drive
Your thoughts. Atlantis never lets you go.
Atlantis is where you are most alive –
Yes, even you, you that despise it so,
When all mankind would love it to arrive
Again, the living dream you try to kill
By making perfect. But you never will.

Anniversary Serenade

You are my alcohol and nicotine,
My silver flask and cigarette machine.
You watch and scratch my back, you scrub me clean.
I mumble but you still know what I mean.
Know what I mean?
You read my thoughts, you see what I have seen.

You are my egg-flip and my ego trip,
My passion-fruit soufflé and strawberry whip.
When the dawn comes to catch you on the hip
I taste the sweet light on my fingertip.
My fingertip?
I lift it to my quivering lips and sip.

Homecoming Queen and mother of our two
Smart daughters who, thank God, take after you,
This house depends on what you say and do –
And all you do is wise and say is true.
And say is true?
True as a plumb-line or a billiard cue.

On from Byzantium to Cooch Behar
Our Messerschmitt two-seater bubble car,
Laden with foie gras and with caviare,
Follows the shining road to Shangri-La.
To Shangri-La?
With Blossom Dearie singing in the bar.

When the sun fades, the Earth will fly away.
Tell me it isn't happening today.

I have a debt of happiness to pay.
I die if you should leave, live if you stay.
Live if you stay?
Live like a king, proud as a bird of prey.

My share of Heaven and my sheer delight,
My soda fountain and my water-sprite,
My curving ribbon of a climbing kite,
You are my Starlight Roof, my summer night.
My summer night?
The flying foxes glide, the possums fight.

You are my honeydew and panther sweat,
The music library on my private jet.
Top of the bill, we fly without a net.
You are the stroke of luck I can't forget.
I can't forget?
I'm still not ready for you even yet.

You are my nicotine and alcohol,
My Stéphane Audran in a Claude Chabrol,
My sunlight through a paper parasol,
My live-in living doll and gangster's moll –
And gangster's moll?
Mine the fedora, yours the folderol.

The ring is closed. The rolling dice we cast
So long ago still roll but not so fast.
The colours fade that we nailed to the mast
We lose the future but we own the past.
We own the past?
From our first kiss, a lifetime to the last.

Double or Quits

Sydney, 2006

Only when we are under different skies
The truth strikes home of what love has become:
A compact it takes time to realise
Is better far, being less burdensome,
Than that first tempest by which we were torn.
Tonight you're there, where both of us now live,
And I am here, where both of us were born,
But there is no division we need give
A thought to, beyond localised regret:
For we will be together again soon,
And both see the one sunrise and sunset
And the face saved and the face lost by the moon –
The clouds permitting, which they seldom do
In England, but at least I'll be with you.

I'll be with you from now on to the end
If you say so. Should you choose otherwise
Then I will be a jealous loving friend
To wish you well yet prove it never dies,
Desire. Your beauty still bewilders me
Though half a century has passed. I still
Stand breathless at the grace of what I see:
More so than ever, now the dead leaves fill
The garden. A long distance will soon come.
Today, no. Nor tomorrow. But it must
Open the door into Elysium
For one of us, and me the first, I trust.
May we stay joined, as these two sonnets are –
That meet, and are apart, but just so far.

Overview

An object lesson in the speed of silence,
The condensation trail across the sky
High over London scores the Wedgwood blue
With one long streak of chalk so true and pure
It seems an angel has begun to crop-dust
The lower fields of Heaven.

Nothing is where you think it is for long.
Our granddaughter, here for a Sunday visit,
Goes through the house like a burst of friendly fire
Or a cosmic particle making its instant transit
Of a bubble chamber. A close search of my corpse
Would find the trajectory of her smile.

Convinced all lasting memories are digital,
The clump of Japanese tourists at Tower Bridge
Hold up their telephones like open notebooks.
As part of their plan, surely now near completion,
For copying the Earth,
They snap the coke-line in the stratosphere.

Our granddaughter would not sit still for that.
My wife gets pictures only of where she was.
Our elder daughter says the thing observed
Changes the observer: it works both ways.
Our younger daughter is reading *Mansfield Park*,
But the cat yawns the soft first syllable

Of Schrödinger's name. Everything happens now.
None of it hangs together except in thought,
And that, too, will pass. One ought to take
Solace from the resplendent, but it goes hard
To know the world view that you had in mind
Is fading like powdered water,
Your mark lost in the thin air it was made from.

The Nymph Calypso

Planning to leave Calypso in the lurch,
Odysseus snuck off to build a ship.
He found the right-shaped boughs of larch or birch
Or spruce, for all I know, from which to strip
The bark, and . . . but the details we can skip.
I won't pretend that I've done much research.
He had to build a ship and he knew how.
Just how he did it hardly matters now:

Enough to say he juggled rib and spar.
Calypso came to him and said, 'I see
That duty calls. Will you be going far?
You wouldn't have your mind on leaving me,
By any chance? Forget the trickery
For once, and if you're following your star
Just say so. Circe lured you with a song.
At least I wasn't stringing you along.'

'It's time,' he said. 'I'm an adventurer.
I sail in search of things. It's what I do.
I'd heard about how beautiful you were,
So lovely that I came in search of you.
But now I know you and need something new
To challenge me.' He wryly smiled at her
To show he knew he sounded like a ham.
'You wanted me. Well, this is what I am.'

'All very well,' Calypso said, 'but I
Have an investment here. You had to quit
Sometime, and I gave you a reason why.

Old studs like you need youth to love. I'm it.
I'm always eager, and you're still quite fit:
A last adventure to light up the sky.
I'll tell my tale forever, don't forget:
The greatest lover that I ever met.'

Odysseus could see the point, but still
He stood his ground, a man of destiny
Proclaiming his ungovernable will
To follow the unknown out to the sea
Beyond the sea, and solve the mystery
Of where the world went next, and not until
He had would he find rest. Calypso said,
'No wonder that you turned up here half dead.'

That night the two of them made love again.
She slapped herself against him when she came
The way she always did, but even then
She let him know she knew things weren't the same.
She cried out his polysyllabic name –
Something she'd never done for other men –
As if, this time, he was no longer there.
But though she flattered him with her despair,

Already he had made the break. His mind
Was elsewhere, on a course she could not guess.
She thought her hero had new worlds to find
Out on the edge of the blue wilderness,
But he had lied, to cause her less distress.
We needn't think of him as being kind:
He simply knew the truth would drive her mad
And make her fight with everything she had.

After he left, she let the world believe
She'd given him the boat: a likely tale
That Homer swallowed whole. Keen to deceive
Even herself, for no nymph likes to fail –
The Miss World of the Early Age of Sail
Had never yet known such a cause to grieve –
She spread the story that he'd only gone
Because she told him legends must go on.

But he was going home. There, in the end,
Lay the departure point for his last quest.
Age was a wound that time indeed would mend
But only one way, with a long, long rest.
For that, familiar territory is best.
As for Penelope, he could depend
On her care for the time he had to live.
Calypso wanted more than he could give,

And it was time to take, time to accept
The quiet bounty of domestic peace.
After he killed the suitors who had kept
His wife glued to the loom, she spread the fleece
Of their first blanket and they found release
Together as they once had. Though she wept
For their lost years, she gave him her embrace,
And he looked down into her ageing face

And saw Calypso. What the nymph would be,
Given the gift of time, was there made plain,
Yet still more beautiful. Penelope,
Because she knew that we grow old in pain
And learn to laugh or else we go insane,
Had life unknown to immortality,

Which never gets the point. 'Well, quite the boy,'
She murmured. 'And now tell me about Troy.'

Later the poets said he met his fate
In the Atlantic, or perhaps he went
Around the Horn and reached the Golden Gate.
Space vehicles named after him were sent
Into infinity. His testament,
However, and what truly made him great,
Was in the untold story of the day
He died, and, more or less, had this to say:

'Penelope, in case you ever hear
The nymph Calypso loved me, it was so:
And she tried everything to keep me near
But finally she had to let me go
Because she knew I loved you. Now you know,
And I can move on, having made that clear.'
And so he did, while she knelt by his side,
Not knowing, as he sailed on the last tide,

That just this once he almost hadn't lied.

The Magic Wheel

An ode in the manner of Theocritus

O magic wheel, draw hither to my house the man I love.
I dreamed of you as dreaming that, and now
The boxed-in balcony of my hotel room high above
Grand Harbour is a sauna. See the prow
Of that small boat cut silk. Out in the sea
No waves, and there below not even ripples turning light
To glitter: just a glow spread evenly
On flawless water spills into the skyline that last night
Was a jewelled silhouette from right to left and left to right.

Behold, the sea is silent, and silent are the winds.
The not yet risen sun edges the sky
With petal-juice of the Homeric rose as day begins.
I am alone, but with you till I die,
Now we have met again after six years.
Last night we danced on limestone in the open-air café.
I saw one woman sitting there near tears,
Aware that she would never look like you or dance that way –
A blessing, like the blessings that have brought you home to stay.

O magic wheel, draw hither to my house the man I love.
I dreamed of you as dreaming that, until
I saw you wave in welcome from your window high above,
And up the slick hard steps designed to kill,
Like all Valletta staircases bar none,
I went, as if I still had strength, to find your open door
And you, and your tremendous little son,

And your husband, the great dancer, whom I had not met before,
And I met his kindly eyes and knew you dreamed of me no more.

Behold, the sea is silent, and silent are the winds.
Stirred by the ceiling fan, the heat of noon
Refuses to grow cooler as it very slowly spins,
But I take its rearrangement as a boon,
As if it were the gradual work of time,
Which leaves things as they are but changes us and picks the hour
To make us see resentment is a crime.
A loving memory forgets and true regret yields power:
Trust in the long slow aqueduct and not the water tower.

O magic wheel, draw hither to my house the man I love.
I dreamed of you as dreaming that. Tonight
My dream was gone, but flowering in the darkness high above
The *festa*, rockets set the rain alight,
The soft, sweet rain. With you and your young men,
I walked the shining streets and all was right and nothing wrong
As the joy of our first moment lived again.
In the ruins of the opera house a lizard one inch long
Is the small but vibrant echo of an interrupted song.

Bethink thee of my love and whence it comes, O holy Moon.
I dreamed of you as dreaming that, and now
I know you never did. Another day: the afternoon
Burns white as only here the sun knows how,
But a fever is broken when I sweat –
For my delight in your contentment proves that in the past
My love must have been true, as it is yet:
The magic wheel has turned to show what fades and what holds fast.
Dream this when I am gone: that he was glad for me at last.

Portrait of Man Writing

While you paint me, I marvel at your skin.
The miracle of being twenty-four
Is there like a first blush as you touch in
The blemishes that make my face a war
I'm losing against time. So you begin,
By lending inwardness to an outline,
Your life in art as I am ending mine.

Try not to miss the story my mouth tells,
Even unmoving, of how once I had
The knack for capering in cap and bells,
And had to make an effort to seem sad.
These eyes that look as crusty as dry wells
Despite the glue they seep, once keenly shone.
Give them at least a glimmer of what's gone.

I know these silent prayers fall on deaf ears:
You've got integrity like a disease.
Bound to record the damage of the years,
You aim to tell the truth, and not to please.
And so this other man slowly appears
Who is not me as I would wish to be,
But is the me that I try not to see.

Suppose while you paint me I wrote of you
With the same fidelity: people would say
That not a line could possibly be true.
Nobody's lips in real life glow that way.
Silk eyelashes! Is this what he's come to?
Your portrait, put in words, sounds like a lie,
Minus the facts a glance would verify.

But do we credit beauty even when
It's there in front of us? It stops the heart.
The mortal clockwork has to start again,
Ticking towards the day we fall apart,
Before we see now all we won't have then.
Let's break for lunch. What progress have we made?
Ah yes. That's me exactly, I'm afraid.

Status Quo Vadis

As any good poem is always ending,
The fence looks best when it first needs mending.
Weathered, it hints it will fall to pieces –
One day, not yet, but the chance increases
With each nail rusting and grey plank bending.
It's not a wonder if it never ceases.

In beauty's bloom you can see time burning:
A lesson learned while your guts are churning.
Her soft, sweet cheek shows the clear blood flowing
Towards the day when her looks are going
Solely to prove there is no returning
The way they came. There's a trade wind blowing.

We know all this yet we love forever.
Build her a fence and she'll think you're clever.
Write her a poem that's just beginning
From start to finish. You'll wind up winning
Her heart, perhaps, but be sure you'll never
Hold on to the rainbow the top sets spinning.

What top? The tin one that starts to shiver
Already, and soon will clatter. The river
Of colour dries up and your mother's calling
Your name while the ball hasn't finished falling,
And you miss the catch and you don't forgive her.
You went out smiling but you go home bawling.

Weep all you like. Earn your bread from weeping.
Write reams explaining there is no keeping
The toys on loan, and proclaim their seeming
Eternal glory is just the dreaming
We do pretending that we aren't sleeping –
Your tears are stinging? They're diamonds gleaming.

Think of it that way and reap the splendour
That flares reflected in the chromium fender
Of the Chrysler parked in the concrete crescent.
The surge is endless, the sigh incessant.
A revelation can only tender
Sincere regrets from the evanescent.

Remember this when it floods your senses
With streams of light and the glare condenses
Into a star. It's a star that chills you.
Don't fool yourself that the blaze fulfils you
And builds your bridges and mends your fences
Merely because of the way it thrills you –

The breath of life is what finally kills you.

Meteor IV at Cowes, 1917

Sydney in spring. Tonight you dine alone.
Walk up the Argyle Cut to Argyle Place
And turn left at the end. In there you'll find
Fish at the Rocks: not just a fish-and-chip joint
But a serious restaurant, with tablecloths
And proper glassware. On the walls, a row
Of photographs, all bought as a job lot
By a decorator with a thoughtful eye:
Big portraits of the racing yachts at Cowes
In the last years before the First World War.
Luxurious in black and white as deep as sepia,
The photographs are framed in the house style
Of Beken, the smart firm that held the franchise
And must have had a fast boat of its own
To catch those vivid poses out at sea:
Swell heaving in the foreground, sky for backdrop,
Crew lying back on tilting teak or hauling
On white sheets like the stage-hands of a classic
Rope-house theatre shifting brilliant scenery –
Fresh snowfields, arctic cliffs, wash-day of titans.
What stuns you now is the aesthetic yield:
A mere game made completely beautiful
By time, the winnower, whose memory
Has taken out all but the lasting outline,
The telling detail, the essential shadow.
But nothing beats the lovely, schooner-rigged
Meteor IV, so perfectly proportioned
She doesn't show her size until you count
The human hieroglyphs carved on her deck
As she heels over. Twenty-six young men

Are present and correct below her towers
Of canvas. At the topmost point, the apex
Of what was once a noble way of life
Unquestioned as the antlers in the hunting lodge,
The Habsburg eagle flies. They let her run,
Led by the foresail tight as a balloon,
Full clip across the wind, under the silver sun,
Believing they can feel this thrill for ever –
And death, though it must come, will not come soon.

The Carnival

You can't persuade the carnival to stay.
Wish all you like, it has to go away.
Don't let the way it moves on get you down.
If it stayed put, how could it come to town?

How could there be the oompah and the thump
Of drums, the trick dogs barking as they jump?
The girl in pink tights and gold headache-band
Still smiling upside down in a hand stand?

These wonders get familiar by the last
Night of the run. A miracle fades fast.
You spot the pulled thread on a leotard.
Those double somersaults don't look so hard.

Can't you maintain your childish hunger? No.
They know that in advance. They have to go,
Not to return until they're something new
For anybody less blasé than you.

The carnival, the carnival. You grieve,
Knowing the day must come when it will leave.
But that was why her silver slippers shone –
Because the carnival would soon be gone.

We Being Ghosts

Too many of my friends are dead, and others wrecked
By various diseases of the intellect
Or failing body. How am I still upright?
And even I sleep half the day, cough half the night.

How did it come to this? How else but through
The course of years, and what its workings do
To wood, stone, glass and almost all the metals,
Smouldering already in the fresh rose petals.

Our energy deceived us. Blessed with the knack
To get things done, we thought to get it back
Each time we lost it, just by taking breath –
And some of us are racing yet as we face death.

Well, good to see you. Sorry I have to fly.
I'm struggling with a deadline, God knows why,
And ghosts keep interrupting. Think of me
The way I do of you. Quite often. Constantly.

from Nefertiti in the Flak Tower

Signing Ceremony

Hotel Timeo, Taormina

The lilac peak of Etna dribbles pink,
Visibly seething in the politest way.
The shallow vodka cocktails that we sink
Here on the terrace at the close of day

Are spreading numb delight as they go down.
Their syrup mirrors the way lava flows:
It's just a show, it might take over town,
Sometimes the Cyclops, from his foxhole, throws

Rocks at Ulysses. But regard the lake
Of moonlight on the water, stretching east
Almost to Italy. The love we make
Tonight might be our last, but this, at least,

Is one romantic setting, am I right?
Cypresses draped in bougainvillea,
The massed petunias, the soft, warm night,
That streak of candy floss. And you, my star,

Still walking the stone alleys with the grace
Of forty years ago. Don't laugh at me
For saying dumb things. Just look at this place.
Time was more friend to us than enemy,

And soon enough this backdrop will go dark
Again. The spill of neon cream will cool,
The crater waiting years for the next spark
Of inspiration, since the only rule

Governing history is that it goes on:
There is no rhythm of events, they just
Succeed each other. Soon, we will be gone,
And that volcano, if and when it must,

Will flood the slope with lip-gloss brought to boil
For other lovers who come here to spend
One last, late, slap-up week in sun-tan oil,
Their years together winding to an end.

With any luck, they'll see what we have seen:
Not just the picture postcard, but the splash
Of fire, and know this flowering soil has been
Made rich by an inheritance of ash.

Only because it's violent to the core
The world grows gardens. Out of earth we came,
To earth we shall return. But first, one more
Of these, delicious echoes of the flame

That drives the long life all should have, yet few
Are granted as we were. It wasn't fair?
Of course it wasn't. But which of us knew,
To start with, that the other would be there,

One step away, for all the time it took
To come this far and see a mountain cry
Hot tears, as if our names, signed in the book
Of marriage, were still burning in the sky?

Monja Blanca

The wild White Nun, rarest and loveliest
Of all her kind, takes form in the green shade
Deep in the forest. Streams of filtered light
Are tapped, distilled, and lavishly expressed
As petals. Her sweet hunger is displayed
By the labellum, set for bees in flight
To land on. In her well, the viscin gleams:
Mesmeric nectar, sticky stuff of dreams.

This orchid's sexual commerce is confined
To flowers of her own class, and nothing less.
And yet for humans she sends so sublime
A sensual signal that it melts the mind.
The hunters brave a poisoned wilderness
To capture just a few blooms at a time,
And even they, least sensitive of men,
Will stand to look, and sigh, and look again,

Dying of love for what does not love them.
Transported to the world, her wiles inspire
The same frustration in rich connoisseurs
Who pay the price for nourishing the stem
To keep the bloom fresh, as if their desire
To live forever lived again through hers:
But in a day she fades, though every fold
Be duplicated in fine shades of gold.

Only where she was born, and only for
One creature, will she give up everything
Simply because she is adored; and he

Must sacrifice himself. The Minotaur,
Ugly, exhausted, has no gifts to bring
Except his grief. She opens utterly
To show how she can match his tears of pain.
He drinks her in, and she him, like the rain.

He sees her, then, at her most beautiful,
And he would say so, could she give him speech:
But he must end his life there, near his prize,
Having been chosen, half man and half bull,
To find the heaven that we never reach
Though seeking it forever. Nothing buys
Or keeps a revelation that was meant
For eyes not ours and once seen is soon spent:

For all our sakes she should be left alone,
Guarded by legends of how men went mad
Merely from tasting her, of monsters who
Died from her kiss. May this forbidden zone
Be drawn for all time. If she ever had
A hope to live, it lies in what we do
To curb the longing she arouses. Let
Her be. We are not ready for her yet,

Because we have a mind to make her ours,
And she belongs to nobody's idea
Of the divine but hers. But that we know,
Or would, if it were not among her powers
Always across the miles to bring us near
To where she thrives on shadows. By her glow
We measure darkness; by her splendour, all
That is to come, or gone beyond recall.

Stage Door Rocket Science

In the early evening, before I go on in Taunton,
I'm outside the stage door for a last gasp.
Two spires, one Norman, share the summer sky
With a pale frayed tissue wisp of cirrostratus
And the moon, chipped like the milky-white glass marble
I kept separate for a whole week and then ruined
By using as a taw.

I have never been here before,
So where does this strong visual echo come from?
Concentrate. Smoke harder. And then I get it:
Cape Kennedy, the rocket park in the boondocks.
A Redstone and a Jupiter stuck up
Through clear blue air with a cloud scrap just like this one,
And the moon in the same phase.

The rockets, posing for the tourist's gaze,
Were the small-time ancestors of Saturn V,
But so were these spires. It's a longer story
Than the thirty years I just felt shrink to nothing.
Time to go in, get rigged with the lapel mike –
Its furry bobble like a soft black marble –
And feel the lectern shaking while I set
Course for the Sea of Shadows.

A Perfect Market

ou plutost les chanter

Recite your lines aloud, Ronsard advised,
Or, even better, sing them. Common speech
Held all the rhythmic measures that he prized
In poetry. He had much more to teach,
But first he taught that. Several poets paid
Him heed. The odd one even made the grade,
Building a pretty castle on the beach.

But on the whole it's useless to point out
That making the thing musical is part
Of pinning down what you are on about.
The voice leads to the craft, the craft to art:
All this is patent to the gifted few
Who know, before they can, what they must do
To make the mind a spokesman for the heart.

As for the million others, they are blessed:
This is their age. Their slap-dash in demand
From all who would take fright were thought expressed
In ways that showed a hint of being planned,
They may say anything, in any way.
Why not? Why shouldn't they? Why wouldn't they?
Nothing to study, nothing to understand.

And yet it could be that their flight from rhyme
And reason is a technically precise
Response to the confusion of a time
When nothing, said once, merits hearing twice.

It isn't that their deafness fails to match
The chaos. It's the only thing they catch.
No form, no pattern. Just the rolling dice

Of idle talk. Always a blight before,
It finds a place today, fulfils a need:
As those who cannot write increase the store
Of verses fit for those who cannot read,
For those who can do both the field is clear
To meet and trade their wares, the only fear
That mutual benefit might look like greed.

It isn't, though. It's just the interchange
Of showpiece and attention that has been
There since the cave men took pains to arrange
Pictures of deer and bison to be seen
To best advantage in the flickering light.
Our luck is to sell tickets on the night
Only to those who might know what we mean,

And they are drawn to us by love of sound.
In the first instance, it is how we sing
That brings them in. No mystery more profound
Than how a melody soars from a string
Of syllables, and yet this much we know:
Ronsard was right to emphasise it so,
Even in his day. Now, it's everything:

The language falls apart before our eyes,
But what it once was echoes in our ears
As poetry, whose gathered force defies
Even the drift of our declining years.
A single lilting line, a single turn
Of phrase: these always proved, at last we learn,
Life cries for joy though it must end in tears.

Australia Felix

Was it twenty years ago I met that couple
In the Melbourne Botanical Gardens?
In those days you would often see the couples –
Well-dressed and softly spoken, arm in arm –
Of new Australians who had made a life
A long way from the wreckage of their homelands,
But this pair were exceptionally spruce,
Though easily the age that I am now.
They were reserved, but I was curious.
Two Poles, she from an Auschwitz labour camp,
He crippled by the walk home from Siberia,
They met in Krakow, married, and came here
On a migrant ship that docked at Woolloomooloo –
Which must have seemed a long way from Lwow,
Though the old name was in the new name somewhere.
Knowing my face from TV, the man told me
My jokes against the local intellectuals
Concerned about Australia's vassal status
In a Western world controlled by the US
Were falling on deaf ears. "They've no idea,"
He said. She nodded in agreement, graceful
Like my mother, who would certainly have liked her.
"We walk here every day," she said. "So peaceful."
He nodded while he watched the currawongs.
Her first fiancé perished at Katyn,
The year my father sailed to Singapore.

Oval Room, Wallace Collection

Created purely for the court's delight,
Pictures by Boucher and by Fragonard
Still work their charm no matter how we might
Remind ourselves how frivolous they are.

Surprised by Vulcan, Venus doesn't care
A fig, and Mars is merely given pause.
The reason for the cuckold's angry stare
Might be that her sweet cleft is draped with gauze.

Boucher does more of that when, held in thrall
By naked ladies, Cupid doesn't seem
To grasp that he himself could have them all
If he were older. This is just a dream,

Even when Fragonard's girl in the swing
Splays her long legs, kicks off one velvet shoe,
Knowing that boy down there sees everything.
He can't believe such miracles are true,

And here they're really not. In this whole room
All images save one are sex made tame
By prettiness, the pranks of youth in bloom,
Winsomely keen to join a harmless game.

But Boucher's Pompadour is on her own.
Her poise commands us to include her out:
Such swinging scenes are a forbidden zone.
The kind of woman men go mad about,

Even in company her solitude
Was strictly kept. She never spilled a thing,
And what she might have looked like in the nude
No man alive could know except the king.

Always my visits here are made complete
By her, the stately counterpoint to these
Cavorting revellers. Aloof, discreet,
She guards the greatest of the mysteries:

How sensual pleasure feels. It can't be seen,
So all this other stuff was just a way
To take the edge off how much love could mean
To win and lose, back then. Just like today.

Against Gregariousness

Facing the wind, the hovering stormy petrels
Tap-dance on the water.
They pluck the tuna hatchlings
As Pavlova, had she been in a tearing hurry,
Might once have picked up pearls
From a broken necklace.

Yellowfin drive the turbine of sardines
Up near the surface so the diving shearwaters
Can fly down through the bubbles and get at them.
Birds from above and big fish from below
Rip at the pack until it comes apart
Like Poland, with survivors in single figures.

The krill, as singletons almost not there
But *en masse* like a cloud of diamond dust
Against the sunlit flood of their ballroom ceiling,
Are scooped up by the basking shark's dragline
Or sucked in through the whale's drapes of baleen –
A galaxy absorbed into a boudoir.

Make your bones in a shark family if you can.
If not, be tricky to locate for sheer
Translucence, a slick blip that will become –
Beyond the daisycutter beaks and jaws –
A lobster fortified with jutting eaves
Of glazed tile, like the castle at Nagoya
Hoisted around by jacks and cranes, an awkward
Mouthful like a crushed car. That being done,
Crawl backwards down a hole and don't come out.

Numismatics

Merely a planchet waiting to be struck,
The poem shapes up, but is not a coin
Until, by craft, and then again by luck,
He fashions clean devices fit to join
A scrupulous design that he would like
To look mint fresh and not like a soft strike –

It must be hard. "It must be hard," they say.
But no, it isn't, not when you know how.
Except he doesn't. He just knows the way
To scratch and scrape until the coin says "Now",
Boasting its lustrous proof against the sleaze
Of verdigris, that cankerous disease.

The scholar rediscovers the doubloon
Inside the encrustations we call Time.
The critic says it might shine like the moon
But pales in value next to a thin dime.
The poet only knows that he can't cheat
At any point, or else it's counterfeit.

He must be definite yet open to
The second thought. He mustn't make a mark
That falls short of the palpably brand new
Whose play of light pays tribute to the dark –
One solid, spinning, singing little disc
Perhaps not worth much, but still worth the risk.

Nefertiti in the Flak Tower

If there was one thing Egyptian Queens were used to
It was getting walled up inside a million tons
Of solid rock. Nefertiti had a taste of that
Before the painted head by which we know her –
That neck, that pretty hat, those film-star features,
The Louise Brooks of the Upper and Lower Kingdoms –
Emerged to start a tour of the museums
That finished in Berlin, almost for keeps.
It could have been the end, but for the flak tower:
With all the other treasures, she was brought there
And sat the war out barely shivering,
Deep in an armoured store-room built by slaves –
That old scenario again. During a raid
The guns sent up eight thousand shells a minute,
Some of them big enough to turn a whole
B-17 into a falling junk-yard,
But the mass concussion, spread through so much concrete,
Was just a rumbling tremble. In each tower
At least ten thousand quaking people sheltered,
Their papers having proved them Aryan.
When the war stopped, the towers fought one more day
Because the Russians couldn't shoot a hole
To get in. Finally they sent an envoy.
The great Queen was brought out and rode in state
Back to her little plinth and clean glass case.
In Berlin in the spring, I cross the bridge
To the *Museumsinsel* just to see her
And dote on her while she gives me that look,
The look that says: "You've seen one tomb, you've seen
Them all." For five long years the flak towers stood

Fighting the enemy armies in the sky
Whose flying chariots were as the locusts:
An age, but less than no time to Nefertiti,
Who looks as if she never heard a thing.

Spectre of the Rose

Goethe and Ulrike von Levetzow in Marienbad

You see this rose? This rose is not just you,
Crisp in the softness it makes visible,
With all its petals nourished by the dew
That wet its leaves last night and pumped it full
Of crimson lake before the rising sun
Reached down and opened it to be as one
Slow-motion cyclone of sheer loveliness,
Lush yet precise, contained in its excess,
A sumptuous promise to be always new,
Superbly poised as you when you undress:

This rose is also me, condemned to die.
The laws by which its nest of shells will fade
From the circumference inwards, it lives by
And follows to the end. So deep a grade
Of red is bought with borrowed time. The power
Of photosynthesis in plant or flower
That wrecks what has been built works even here,
Captured in such a jewel that it comes near
To matching you. You put it in the shade
I feel advancing with each precious hour.

Below it on the stem, regard the thorns
Meant to protect its frailty while it grew.
Doomed from the moment when the thoughtless dawn's
Fatal initiative brought it to view,
It came here to this vase, and here it glows

For us, and it is yours and mine, this rose,
But it is also you and I. Two lives
United only for a time, it thrives –
Spreading its perfumed beauty as you do –
For just a while, and while it stays it goes:

Perfect too late for me, too soon for you.

The Same River Twice

Surely you see now that you gave your name
To the easy option. Nobody disagrees
About the infinitely shifting texture
Of the world. A malefactor loves the haze
Of boiling chance that blurs the total picture,
The fog you stand in up to your stiff knees,
Looking so wise, as if you'd solved the structure
Of all causality, when you, in fact,
Left out the thing we needed most to know –
That our character will leave us free to act
In contradiction to its steady flow
Only through our regretting that the river,
Though never still, is still the same as ever.
No man steps out of it, not even once.

On A Thin Gold Chain

Opals have storms in them, the legend goes:
They brim with water held in place by force
To stir the dawn, to liquefy the rose,
To make the sky flow. They are cursed, of course:
Great beauty often is. But they are blessed
As well, so long as she herself gives light
Who wears them. Shoulders bare, you were the guest
At the garden table on a summer night
Whose face lent splendour to the candle flame
While that slight trinket echoing your eyes
Swam in its colours. What a long, long game
We've played. Quick now, before somebody dies:
Have you still got that pendant? Can I see?
And have you kept it dark to punish me?

And Then They Dream of Love

"Were you not more than just a pretty face
And perfect figure," he thought, kissing one
While clamped against the other, "this embrace
Would not be so intense." But she was done
For now with doubts and fears. Her state of grace
Had come upon her like the rising sun.
He bathed in daybreak, loving its suddenness,
The way she shook, her look of sheer distress
That meant the opposite, and everything.

Back in the world, her limbs still trembling,
She said it all again, and this time he
Expressed himself in words as best he could –
"You must know you mean more than this to me" –
Merely to find himself misunderstood.
"You mean you don't get lost in ecstasy
The way I do?" she said. "I want to be
All that you need of this." He said, "You said
I only cared what you were like in bed."
And so their bickering began again

About what you mean now and I meant then.
Only so long could they go on that way
Before they parted, worn out by their knack
For petty quarrels even when they lay
Replete. The things they said before came back
To plague them. If it matters what you say
It can't last. Best to take another tack,
And meet for just this, very late at night.
Would she do that? No. He would. She was right.

Beachmaster

Scanning the face of a crestfallen wave
He sees his life collapsing to a close,
A foaming comber racing to its grave.
But after that one, there are all of those:

The ranks of the unbroken, the young men
Completely green, queuing to take their turn
To die so that the sea might live again.
That much it took him all his life to learn.

Propped on her elbow in the burning sand,
The latest Miss Australia views it all
As one vast courtship. With a loving hand
She strokes her thigh as one by one they fall,

Those high walls in the water. Look at her,
But shade your sad glance carefully, old man –
For she will never see you as you were,
A long way out, before the end began.

Continental Silentia

Neat name for the machine
On which the lists were done:
Quietly ordered violence.
Feathers by the ton.

The whisper of a tempest,
The ghost of a parade:
Pan-European silence,
A pop-gun fusillade,

A muted rat-tat-tat,
The excuse already ripe:
We knew nothing of all that.
All we did was type,

And corrections in those days
Had to be done with x's.
You couldn't just erase
And start again: wrong sexes,

Wrong spellings . . . it took ages.
Just to get it right
Meant black spots in the pages:
Blurs of a foggy night.

Unspoken and unsung,
Those names that didn't matter.
Sonderbehandlung.
Just written, pitter-patter.

Continental Silentia
For all those in absentia
Respectable dementia
Sub rosa eloquentia

List, oh list
The rest is silence

Put to silence

Zum schweigen gebracht

Typewriter
Firelighter

Tap tap

Language Lessons

She knew the last words of Eurydice
In every syllable, both short and long.
Correcting his misuse of quantity,
She proved the plangent lilt of Virgil's song
Depended on precision, while his hand,
Light as a mayfly coming in to land,
Caressed her cheek to taste the melody
Of such sweet skin, smooth as a silk sarong.

Give her the palm for speaking well, he thought,
But has she ever melted as she should
With no holds barred, or wept the way she ought?
His scraps of Greek, it seemed, were not much good.
He said the words for rosy-fingered dawn
And when she set him straight with laughing scorn
He spoke a tongue she barely understood,
Contesting her with kisses long and short.

In such a way they traded expertise
Until the day came it took half the night.
She gradually improved his memories
And he set loose her longing for delight.
The passion underneath the verse technique
She saw in its full force, and learned to speak –
Strictly, as always, but in ecstasies.
So finally, for both, the sound was right,

A compound language fashioned out of sighs
And poetry recited line by line.
Few lovers and few scholars realise
The force with which those separate things combine
When classic metres are at last revealed
As reservoirs where rhythms lie concealed
That sprang from heartbeats just like yours and mine,
Pent breath, and what we cry with flashing eyes.

In that regard they made a pretty pair:
He with his otherwise unhurried touch,
She with her prim and finely balanced air,
When they lay down together, came to such
An ending they were like a poem caught
In the last singing phrase of what it sought
To start with: to contain what means too much
Left lying loose. In something like despair,

Though it was joy, they would forget they knew
What anybody else had ever said
Of love, and simply murmur the poor few
Abstract endearments suitable for bed
Until they slept, and dreamed they'd never met
And none of this sheer bliss had happened yet.
One woke the other – which was which? – in dread:
Ah, Orpheus, what has lost us, me and you?

Alas, what is this madness? Out of sight
Like smoke mixed with thin air I seem to fly.
Although her form, when he switched on the light,
Was still there, he had heard her spirit die.
To bring it back, he swore that he would go
To hell for her. It would be always so,
For he would live forever and defy
The halls of Dis and the gigantic night.

Having heard this from him, she smiled again,
And in his arms came back to life as one
Returning to the mortal world of men,
Their ticking clocks, the race that they must run.
Believing in their love: that was the task
That these two faced. It seemed too much to ask,
So moved were they when all was said and done –
Knowing that it would stop, but never when.

Silent Sky

Peter Porter b. Brisbane 1929, d. London 2010

The sky is silent. All the planes must keep
Clear of the fine volcanic ash that drifts
Eastward from Iceland like a bad idea.
In your apartment building without lifts,
Not well myself, I find it a bit steep
To climb so many stairs but know I must
If I would see you still alive, still here.
The word is out from those you love and trust –
Time is so short that from your clever pen
No line of verse might ever start again.

Your poems were the condensation trails
Of a bright mind's steady rush of soaring power,
Which still you show. Though plainly you are weak
In body, you can still talk by the hour.
Indeed we talk for two, but my will fails
Before the task of wishing you goodbye.
There's all our usual stuff of which to speak:
Pictures and poems, things that never die,
And then there's history, which in the end
No one survives, not even your best friend.

No one like you to talk about Mozart
Bad-mouthing Haydn: how the older man
Forgave the coming boy. No one like you
To bring it all alive, the mortal span
Of humans who create immortal art:
Your favourite theme. I ought to tell you now

That I will miss you. But I miss my cue,
Unless it's tact, not funk, that tells me how
To look convinced this visit need not be
The last at which you're here to welcome me.

If I am mealy-mouthed, though, you are not.
You say you hate to eat because it feeds
The crab that's killing you. I could well ask,
If only to find out what fear it breeds,
Whether you dread your death now that it's got
A grip the morphine can't shake. That would be
For me, however. Better to wear my mask
Of good cheer and insist Posterity
Cherishes you already while you live,
And there will be more time, and more to give.

Ten weeks? Ten poems? Scarcely, it transpires,
Ten days. The planes can fly again. The phones
That never stopped are saying you are gone.
We try to give thanks that you made old bones,
But still I see the beach at Troy, the fires
For fallen heroes. This is an event
Proving for all the great work that lives on
A great life dies, and leaves an empty tent –
An aching void to measure our time by
As overwhelming as a silent sky.

Special Needs

In the clear light of a cloudy summer morning
A stricken one, holding his father's hand,
Comes by me on the Quay where I sit writing.
His father spots me looking up, and I don't want
To look as if I wished I hadn't, so
Instead of turning straight back to my books
I look around, thus making it a general thing
That I do every so often –
To watch the ferries, to check out the crowd.
The father's eyes try not to say, "Two seconds
Is what you've had of looking at my boy.
Try half a lifetime." Yes, the boy is bad:
So bad he holds one arm up while he walks
As if to ward off further blows from heaven.
His face reflects the pain at work behind it,
But he can't tell us what it is:
He can only moan its secret name.
The Nazis, like the Spartans, would have killed him,
But where are the Spartans and the Nazis now?
And really a sense of duty set in early,
Or at least a sense of how God's ways were strange:
After the death of Alexander
The idiot boy Philip was co-regent
To the throne of a whole empire,
And lasted in the role for quite a while
Before his inevitable murder,
Which he earned because of somebody's ambition,
And not because he couldn't clean his room.
They're gone. I can look down again, two thoughts
Contesting in my head:

"It's so unfair, I don't know what to do"
Is one. The other is the one that hurts:
"Don't be a fool. It's nothing to do with you."
A lady wants a book signed.
I add "Best wishes" –
All I will do today of being kind –
And when I hand it back to her, the sun
Comes out behind her. I hold up one arm.

Pennies for the Shark

Taronga Park Aquarium once had,
When I was very young, a basement pool
Inside a mocked-up sandstone cave. A sad
Collection of big fish would, as a rule,
Just steam around it slowly till the bell
Rang for their feeding time. They didn't eat
Each other, which was strange, but just as well:
They'd had more than their fair share of defeat.

The giant rays, like blankets on patrol,
Deferred to one thing only, the Grey Nurse:
The lone shark, coloured between coke and coal,
Whose very outline spelled death like a hearse,
She was the reason that the pennies lay
So thick on the pool's floor. People would chuck
One down. It slid off, if it hit a ray,
But if it hit the shark it sometimes stuck.

As I recall, the coins in the shark's back
Were flush or even countersunk like screws.
New coins would glint but old ones turning black
Still made their little circle. The real news,
However, was about the ones that hit
The pectoral fins and stayed put: battle scars
In a fighter's wings, or code meant to transmit
Some foreign curse, like messages from Mars,

336

To pay the shark back for the pain she might
Have caused had she been free to roam at will
And find fish hiding in the reef at night,
Or humans in the surf. Licensed to kill,
She was a draw because she was a threat,
And would have shown you, had you fallen in,
The last thing she was likely to forget
Was how to deal with your white, gleaming skin.

No doubt they cleaned the pool out once a week
And picked bad pennies gently from the beast.
For what she said, she didn't need to speak,
And every year her pulling power increased.
She had to be looked after. You might think
That by the standards of today her life
Was torture, but the way she didn't blink
Told us the *femme fatale* lived by the knife.

Nevertheless I sympathised. Aware
In some vague way that nature suffered through
This notion that an animal could bear
Its prison if the roof was painted blue,
I tossed half-hearted pennies from the rail
Suspecting that she might be sick of things,
That shark, in slow pursuit of her own tail,
Pock-marked with pictures of the British kings.

Butterfly Needles

Having grown old enough to see the trellis buckle
Like an embroidered dress
Beneath so many decades weighed in honeysuckle,
The old man's idleness
Is honoured by this house as he sits late.
Until the fruit bats come he is content to wait.

Here in England, this is a different garden from that other,
Back at the start.
Here you could kick and scream and call out for your mother
Until you broke her heart
And nothing quite the same would come except the butterflies,
And even they with different squadron markings. Expert eyes

Say butterflies at dusk grow dorsal portals for receiving
Needles, or maybe pins.
That sounds to me like Nabokov relieving
The burden of his sins.
Forget about it. Just give me that old nasturtium scent
I breathed when young, and would again, now I am spent.

The nasturtiums, into which my silver Spitfire crashing
Made a banshee noise
But climbed back to my fingertips with wingtips flashing:
None of the other boys
Had anything as good, which made my fighting talk sought-after,
A first taste of the poisoned flower whose cordial is laughter.

Take it easy, mister. Sniff the real estate you're ruling:
You, the last one here.
A butterfly died once and now the whole damned planet's cooling
At the wrong time of the year.
Stand up too quickly and you hear the headsman chuckle
And the words "Sleep well" are far too near the knuckle,
And for your next trick, you will disappear.

Nimrod

Some marched, some sailed, some flew to join the war,
And not a few were brought home on their shields.
My heart is with those voiceless ones. They were
The harvest of the broken-hearted fields,
And I drew fortune from their bitter lack
Of any luck. Silent, my father stands
Before me now, as if he had come back,
While this lament, whose beauty never ends,
Not even with its final grandeur, casts
Its nets of melody to hold me still
Beneath his empty eyes. How long it lasts,
That spell, though it is just a little while.
Then he is gone again. The world returns:
Babylon, where the Tower of Babel burns.

Culture Clash

Beside the uniquely hideous GLC building
On a nasty September day
With a chill in the air and rain just starting to spit,
The Japanese couple, only this minute married,
Have come to be photographed,
The Thames in the background looking as deadly dull
As ditchwater by Dickens. Bill Sykes
Was lucky to get himself hanged
Half a mile downriver from here.
When the sun goes in, it makes falling out of a window
Seem like the thing to do. But just look
At the bride. No, not at the groom, whose suit
Would be a black-tie outfit if not in white
With trimmings a duck-egg blue, the shirt all frills
Like Tommy Steele playing Liberace's houseboy.
I mean look at her. Inside that three-tier cake
Of a dress is a model for Utamaro.
Do they have another ceremony at home
With all the traditional rigour?
And is it a *gaijin* flaunting his arrogance
To wish her lifted out of this concrete mess
And taken home by JAL to the rooms of paper,
The laths of wood and the properly arranged flowers,
With *kimono* and her hair pinned up to frame
The fresh snow of her beauty?
Look at the line of her cheek as once the painter
Would have looked at it in the Floating World
When he spoke to her with the reverence of a duke
To the Lady Murasaki.
Ah, Butterfly, you have failed to understand.
You must not come to us. We must come to you.

Fashion Statement

I see it now, the truth of what we were
Back then when we were young and Sydney shone
Like a classic silver milkshake canister
Trapping the sunlight in a cyclotron
Of dented brilliance. In our student kit
We were dandies. We just didn't look like it.

This year I almost died. Propped up in bed
I went back to that time and saw them all,
Even the ones who are already dead.
In the cloisters, encamped on the stone wall
Outside the library staircase, we cracked wise
As pretty girls went by, their shining eyes

Lit up, we fancied, by the flash word-play
Of drawling fops who didn't look the part.
But that was what our dress-sense had to say:
Farewell to choking collars. Hail the start
Of dressing down to suit the heat and light.
It took thought, though. You had to get it right.

We wore the first T-shirts. The desert boots,
The lightweight army surplus khaki drills –
These were our standard gear, the business suits
Of young men with no business. How it fills
My mind with longing now, the memory
Of lurking off with endless energy

To read the poets – seldom on the course –
To write a poem – never quite resolved –
To be removed from Manning House by force –
It was where the women were – to be involved
Completely – never fear what might befall –
In the task of doing nothing much at all.

For some, that task became their whole career,
But even they lived better for the style
We forged then over reservoirs of beer
With leave to sit around and talk awhile –
Well, talk forever. So the time slid by
Into a lifetime. Who can wonder why?

And as for those who burned to make a mark,
We made it with the tongue we mastered where
It felt like daylight even after dark,
So soothing was the heat, so sweet the air:
The perfect atmosphere for epigrams
To flaunt their filigree like toast-rack trams.

To see the harbour glittering in the sun
Like fields of diamonds and the squall arrive
Across the water sudden as a gun
Was bound to bring the optic nerve alive
Searching for words, and we who wrote them down
Might not have looked it, but we owned the town.

For nothing rules like easy eloquence
Tied to the facts yet taking off at will
Into the heady realms of common sense
Condensed and energised by verbal skill:
It has no need to check before a glass
The swerve of a frock coat around its arse.

Already ugly and with worse to come
Yet lovely in its setting past belief,
The city got into our speech. Though some
Were burdened by their gift and came to grief,
And some found fortune, but as restless men,
We were dandies. We just didn't see it then.

Paper Flower Maiden

Screwed up in every sense, she occupied
The smallest space that she could organise:
The country mouse of all church mice. Inside,
Her soul, whose only outlet was her eyes,
Was dying of compression sickness. Then
She met him, the most confident of men.

Her agonies of manifold self-doubt
Were foreign to him utterly. One touch
From him, and she began to open out
Like a chrysanthemum. This is too much,
She told herself: I'll use up all the air.
He kissed her mouth and she was everywhere,

A tide of petals that filled up the hall
And climbed the stairs. She screamed to be put back
The way she was. He, trapped against a wall,
Struggled for breath till everything went black.
He woke to find her gone. The trail of scent
She left behind her everywhere she went

Led him towards her but he never quite
Caught up with her, until he realised
She was the flower garden which, at night,
He roamed in, half entranced, half traumatised
By how the beauty he'd set loose had no
Need of him now, yet would not let him go.

On Reading Hakluyt at High Altitude

High in the stratosphere, I speed toward
Australia's share of history's cruelty,
Reading of caravels with priests aboard
Who landed on Ormuz to hack a tree
Into the deadly stakes that served the sword
Of Christ the Merciful, his soldiery,
And captured Christians died, though, truth to tell,
Our Great Queen likewise would have marked for hell

All sailors who were not True Protestants
Had they been less intent to spread her name
World wide, in script light-footed as a dance
To us, but back in those days smoke and flame
Wreathed every letter. Be it high romance
Or merest greed, unless they're both the same,
That drove the ships of old, they crashed and burned
Or fed the fishes when they overturned.

The Portuguese, the Spaniards and the Dutch,
And all the times the English almost made
A landfall on our land-mass – it's too much
Drowning to think about, a sad parade
That leaves you with a throat too dry to clutch,
Sensing the flesh dissolved, and bone decayed –
But really we should shift our starting date
To further in the past. It's far too late

The way it is, and serves the fond idea
The cloudland of our gentle indigenes
Was wrecked when we decided to come here
To exercise our new-found ways and means:
Just name the day and Lo! We would appear
Out of the surf like Hollywood marines
Sprinting ashore in roughly half the time
It takes to find a rhyme or plan a crime.

But it took centuries for men to find
The means of even failing on the waves;
It took the murderous patterns in the mind
That made a mockery of Jesus Saves;
Above all it took industry, the kind
That limes the sea lanes with a million graves.
The quick did not usurp the slow, the quick
Had just grown slightly slower to get sick.

Visit the flight deck? Asked, I always do
Not just because the toy trains never die
As thrill-providers, but because it's true
That how we sailed is still there when we fly,
In the controls. All that Magellan knew
Is in those panels, carried eight miles high
By turbo-fans whose climb to power began
With just the wind, and just the mind of man.

How unimaginable the past seems.
When read about in detail! All that pain
With little gained or even less, the schemes
To get rich quick turned rotten by the rain –
Or ruined by the lack of it. All dreams:
Except the few that worked gave us this plane
We fly in now, our voyage just begun –
To catch the giant sling swung by the sun.

The Buzz

Grown old, you long still for what young love does.
It gives the world a liquid light injection,
A sun bath even in the night. The buzz
Blurs brain-cells by infecting everything
With lust. A girl bright as an egret's wing
Will cleave unto an oaf and see perfection,
And as for him, don't ask. He thinks her thighs
Open on heaven and his hands have eyes.

Time will sort all that out, but what a loss!
Sweet reason is our name for sour reflection,
The pause for thought that kills the fairy floss.
With luck, there will be two of you to trade
Tales of the star-burst that could never fade,
But did, and give a voice to introspection:
Which is love too, though not quite the young kind
We comfort ourselves now by calling blind.

But there is nothing young love fails to see
Except the future. Bodies and their connection
Are all creation, shorn of history.
These are the only humans who exist.
Whoever thought to kiss or to be kissed
Or hit the sack from every known direction
Except them? Visions radiantly true
Don't change with age. Those that have had them do.

Dreams Before Sleeping

The idea is to set the mind adrift
And sleep comes. Mozart, exquisitely dressed,
Walks carefully to work between soft piles
Of fresh horse-dung. Nice work. Why was my gift –
It's sixty years now and I'm still obsessed –
Hidden behind the tree? I cried for miles.
No one could find it. Find the tiger's face.
It's in the tree: i.e. the strangest place.

But gifts were presents then. In fact, for short,
We called them pressies, which was just as long,
But sounded better. Mallarmé thought "night"
A stronger word than *nuit*. Nice word. The fort
Defied the tide but faded like a song
When the wave's edge embraced it at last light.
Which song? Time, time, it is the strangest thing.
The Waves. The Sea, the Sea. Awake and Sing.

Wrong emphasis, for music leads to sex.
Your young man must be stroking you awake
Somewhere about now, in another time.
Strange thing. Range Rover. Ducks de Luxe. Lex rex.
The cherry blossoms fall into the lake.
The carp cruise undisturbed. Lemon and lime
And bitters is a drink for drinkers. Just.
I who was iron burn in silence. Rust.

What would you do to please me, were you here?
The *tarte Tatin* is melting the ice cream.
One sip would murder sleep, but so does this.

Left to itself, the raft floats nowhere near
Oblivion, or even a real dream.
Strange word, nice question. Real? Real as a kiss,
Which never lasts, but proves we didn't waste
The time we spent in longing for its taste.

Seek sleep and lose it. Fight it and it comes.
I knew that, but it's too late now. The bird
Sings with its wings. The turtle storms ashore.
Pigs fly. Would that translate to talking drums?
Nice if they didn't understand a word
Each other said, but drowned in metaphor –
As we do when we search within, and find
Mere traces of the peace we had in mind.

Forget about it. Just get up and write.
But when you try to catch that cavalcade,
Too much coherence muscles in. Nice thought.
Let's hear it, heartbreak. Happiness writes white.
Be grateful for the bed of nails you made
And now must lie in, trading, as you ought,
Sleep for the pictures that will leave you keen
To draft a memo about what they mean.

You will grow weary doing so. Your eyes
Are fighting to stay open. When they fail
You barely make it back to where you lay.
What do you see? Little to memorise.
A lawn shines green again through melting hail.
Deep in its tree, a tiger turns away.
Nice try, but it was doomed, that strange request
To gaze into the furnace and find rest.

Incident in the Gandhi Bookshop Café, Avenida Corrientes

They were all dying for her,
But they died bravely, they died well.
It was well done.
I was proud to join them.
We all went over the waterfall together.
We fell together.
The world fell together.
For a sacred moment it was all one,
And then she was gone.

Briefly she had sat there
Making notes to mark her progress
Through the labyrinths of Borges –
Something in her manner
Discouraged offers of help –
And then she looked at her watch.
Did she have a lover somewhere
Or perhaps a tango class?
Imagine being the maestro
Against whom she leans
In a tensile *puente*.

Deep breasted, long legged,
Silk skinned,
She was the kind of beauty
Who makes every poet
Wish he were a painter,
So as to say:
"Take off your clothes:
I need the essence of you."

Old poets who try that
Get themselves arrested,
Whereas painters never fail,
Until the day they drop,
To score with the girl of fine family
And the perfect behind.

Having paid her bill,
She stood up and was swept away
On a wave of sighs
As we all shared the light in our eyes,
Our hearts bleeding,
Before going back to the books
We were writing and reading –
Back to the usual macho shit
Which is all there is
When you get down to it,

Out of the cloud
Into which the angel
Disappears,
Having blessed us once
With the holy presence
Of her good looks:

Eternity compressed
Into one sweet minute.
She was out of this world
And we are in it.

Now we must begin again.
Poor us. Poor men.
The waterfall:
It was our tears.

The Falcon Growing Old

The falcon wears its erudition lightly
As it angles down towards its master's glove.
Student of thermals written by the desert,
It scarcely moves a muscle as it rides
A silent avalanche back to the wrist
Where it will stand in wait like a hooded hostage.

A lifetime's learning renders youthful effort
Less necessary, which is fortunate.
The chase and first-strike kill it once could wing
Have grown beyond it, so some morning soon
This bird will have its neck wrung without warning
And one of its progeny will take its place.

Thinking these things, the ageing writer makes
Sketches for poems, notes for paragraphs.
Bound for the darkness, does he see himself
Balanced and forceful like the poised assassin
Whose mere trajectory attracts all eyes
Except the victim's? Habit can die hard,

But still the chance remains he simply likes it,
Catching the shifting air the way a falcon
Spreads on a secret wave, the outpaced earth
Left looking powerless. This sentence here,
Weighed down by literal meaning as it is,
Might only need that loose clause to take off,

Air-launched from a position in the sky
For a long glide with just its wing-tip feathers
Correcting for the wobble in the lisp
Of sliding nothingness, the whispering road
That leads you to a dead-heat with your shadow
At the orange-blossom trellis in the oasis.

Vertical Envelopment

Taking the piss out of my catheter,
The near-full plastic bag bulks on my calf
As I drag my I.V. tower through Addenbrooke's
Like an Airborne soldier heading for D-Day
Down the longest corridor in England.
Each man his own mule. Look at all this stuff.
Pipes, tubes, air bottles. Some of us have wheels.
Humping our gear, we're bare-arsed warriors
Dressed to strike fear into the enemy,
But someone fires a flare. Mission aborted.
On the airfield, the chattering Dakotas
Have fallen silent. Jump postponed again.
Stay as you are. Keep your equipment on.
When cloud and wind are OK in the drop zone
We hit the sky and leap into the dark.
Meanwhile just hunker down and get some sleep.
Look on the bright side. Everyone's still here.
The longest corridor is full of us,
Men of the Airborne going back to bed
For just one more drawn-out *Walpurgisnacht*.
Our urinary tracts hung up to drain
Throw amber highlights on the bare white wall
Until another dawn. The sky looks clear.
Dakotas cough when they start up, repeat
Themselves like women gossiping. But wait,
Where are the women? What do they go through?
They fly there by Lysander and get caught
Like Violette Szabo. Out there on their own.
Best not to think of it, stick with the guys
And shoot the bull about your CLL

Leukaemia that might hold off for years,
The hacking rattle of COPD
Which sounds as if it might star Dennis Franz
As Andy Sipowicz, but it turns out
To be the bug they once called emphysema.
The way I smoked, thank Christ it wasn't cancer:
I caught one break at least. It's dawn again.
The sky looks clear. The kit bag full of piss
Is heavy on your leg. Your name-tags itch,
The cannula inside your elbow dangles,
The patches for electrodes decorate
Your chest like Nicorettes. When you go down
Into the dark you'll see it sliced with flak
Just as the bumping CAT Scan bangs and crackles,
As the MRI inscribes the night with fire.
My outfit one by one in the green light,
Out of the door and down into the dark
They go, and not much later in the year
I'm watching Peter jump. The flak comes up
And pulls him in. But no green light for me.
I'm home in the Dakota and the same
Long corridor leads back to bed. More stuff
To hump: omeprazole and doxycycline
Pills for my lungs. The medics give me leave
To be there for my daughter's New York show.
I step ashore and wake up in Mount Sinai,
Felled by the blood clot I brought off the boat.
For ten full days and nights I lie and watch
The Gulf spill oil on CNN, which is
An oil-spill anyway, and back in England
I add syringes to my weaponry.
Bruises from Clexane like Kandinsky abstracts
Blotch me with blue and yellow and bright pink,

A waistline from the Lenbach Haus in Munich.
The women of my family watch the clock
To make sure I shoot up at the right time:
All in the timing and a simple plan.
Normandy showed, and Arnhem showed again,
The Airborne tactic was a death-trap. Crete
Fell to the German sky troops but their losses
Were too great and they never jumped again.
At Cassino and in the Hürtgen Forest
The *Fallschirmjäger* were brought in by truck.
Up in the air like white blooms on a pond
We're asking for it. Borneo was waiting
For the Aussies to jump into if the Yanks
Held back the bomb. The jump postponed,
You see them now in the long corridor,
My countrymen, their incipient melanomas
Cut out and sewn up, scars like bullet holes.
You want to see mine? In the final hours
At Dien Bien Phu fresh paratroops went in
Through tracer veils as if about to land
Slap in the middle of *SS Das Reich*.
They're here again. They must have been patched up:
Not one less handsome than Alain Delon
In *Purple Noon*, but barely half his age.
The Hitch is with them and I hear him speak
Exactly as he looked the day we met:
The automatic flak came bubbling up
Like champers, dear boy. Overrated stuff.
I watch him standing there in the green light.
It switches off. Has he come home with us?
I can't see. I just see the corridor
And my white room. Another night alive
To lie awake and rue the blasphemy

By which I take their deaths as mine, the young
Soldiers of long ago, in the first years
Of my full span, who went down through the dark
With no lives to look back on. Their poor mothers.
Where are the women? Nurse, my bag is broken.
Sorry, it's everywhere. She mops, I cough,
She brings the nebulizer and I sit
Exhaling fog. Dakotas starting up
Make whirlpools in the ground mist. Too much luck,
Just to have lived so long when I unfold
And shuffle forward to go out and down
The steep, dark, helter-skelter laundry chute
Into that swamp of blinking crocodiles
Men call Shit Creek. Come, let us kiss and part.

Book Review

Dante Alighieri: Monarchia
Edited by Prue Shaw for the Società Dantesca Italiana, 2009

More valuable than all of mine, your book
Is neatly kept like everything you do:
So clearly worth the twenty years it took,
It sparkles. Fonts well chosen, margins true,
Its every creamy page exhales the sense
Of learned judgment, tact and permanence.

If Dante waited seven centuries
To see his Latin tract receive such care
He can't complain, though being hard to please
No doubt he did while he was lying there
Still exiled in Ravenna, still annoyed
That so much effort has to be employed

In re-establishing what he first wrote.
But what could he expect? He worked by hand,
And other hands, on skins of sheep and goat,
Made copies, and those went to every land
In Europe, and were copied once again,
And soon for every error there were ten.

Tracing the manuscripts back to the first
Few spin-offs is as good as you can get.
Often you don't get that, and at the worst
A copy's copy's copy's the best bet,
And so the scholar must compare, contrast,
And from the past deduce a deeper past.

It takes far more than sweat. It takes a mind
That can connect with the great poet's heart,
Knowing his sweet new style was spare, refined,
Tough, difficult, precise in every part,
And therefore apt to be fudged in its gist
By scribes half qualified and some half pissed.

Such minds are rare, and often in disguise
They come into the world. My only role
In your brave saga is that I was wise
Enough to see the brilliant scholar's soul
Shine through her beauty in the lecture hall
Even before we met. I guessed it all.

How could that be? Well, here is how it can:
You took notes at the same speed that I ate,
With an eye for truth unknown to mortal man,
Especially this man. It was my fate
To fish the surface but my luck to see
You hungered for a deeper clarity.

I saw you flower in Florence. That was where
The bigwigs spotted you and marked your card.
The sage Contini knew you were a rare
Natural philologist worth his regard,
And while you learned, you taught me. From the way
You read me Dante I foretold today.

Today, so far from our first years, I bless
My judgment, which in any other case
Is something we both know I don't possess,
But one thing I did know. I knew my place.
I knew yours was the true gift that would bring
Our house the honours that mean everything:

The honour of our daughters raised to treat
All people with your scrupulous respect,
The honour of your laughter and the sweet
Self-abnegation of an intellect
That never vaunts itself though well it might,
And this above all, lovely in my sight –

Pursued through busy days in precious hours,
Pored over word by word and line by line
Year after year with concentrated powers
Of selfless duty to the grand design
Of someone long dead who was well aware
That dreams of peace on earth must court despair –

The honour of the necessary task
Done well, not just for show, and done for keeps.
Could I have helped you more? Don't even ask.
I can hear Dante, grunting as he sleeps:
"You are the weakling and you always were.
If you would sing for glory, sing of her."

Whitman and the Moth

Van Wyck Brooks tells us Whitman in old age
Sat by a pond in nothing but his hat,
Crowding his final notebooks page by page
With names of trees, birds, bugs and things like that.

The war could never break him, though he'd seen
Horrors in hospitals to chill the soul.
But now, preserved, the Union had turned mean:
Evangelising greed was in control.

Good reason to despair, yet grief was purged
By tracing how creation reigned supreme.
A pupa cracked, a butterfly emerged:
America, still unfolding from its dream.

Sometimes he rose and waded in the pond,
Soothing his aching feet in the sweet mud.
A moth he knew, of which he had grown fond,
Perched on his hand as if to draw his blood.

But they were joined by what each couldn't do,
The meeting point where great art comes to pass –
Whitman, who danced and sang but never flew,
The moth, which had not written *Leaves of Grass*,

Composed a picture of the interchange
Between the mind and all that it transcends
Yet must stay near. No, there was nothing strange
In how he put his hand out to make friends

With such a fragile creature, soft as dust.
Feeling the pond cool as the light grew dim,
He blessed new life, though it had only just
Arrived in time to see the end of him.

The Later Yeats

Where he sought symbols, we, for him, must seek
A metaphor, lest mere praise should fall short
Of how the poems of his last years set
Our standards for the speech that brings the real
To integrated order dearly bought,
Catching the way complexity would speak
If it had one voice. This, he makes us feel,
Is where all deeper meanings are well met,
Contained in a majestic vessel made
Out of the sea it sails on, yet so strong
We never, watching it our whole lives long,
Doubt its solidity. All else may fade,
But this stands out as if it had been sent
To prove it can have no equivalent.

Even his first things were wind-driven boats.
A coracle would have its speed enhanced
By some queen elf who stood with gauze shift spread,
Materialising from the twilight mist.
Slim dhows, as his romantic urge advanced,
Sliced through the East. A little navy floats
In his early pages. Sleek sloops joined the list
When more substantial things asked to be said.
His wild-swan racing schooners heeled and ran
Cargo from Athens, Bethlehem and Rome,
Or the body of an Irish airman home
Across the gale. The full soul of a man
Was on display: sound craft of trim outline
Criss-crossed the billows. All of his design,

These would have been enough to make him great:
The caravels that reached Byzantium
Alone proved him unmatched. Then, at the heart
Of this flotilla, as if light were haze,
Something appeared to strike the viewer dumb:
A huge three-decker fighting ship of state.
Acres of air caught in her tiered arrays
Of raw silk, she made clear, in every part,
All of her million parts were cleanly wrought
To fit together with no need of nails.
From gun-decks upward to top-gallant sails
She was one artefact, a cloud drawn taut
By force, so far beyond its builder's mind
It felt for him, and saw where he was blind.

Tea-clipper-tall but at the waterline
Three times the width, she had the looks to quell
Resistance instantly by show of might:
Empires would knuckle under. Ireland
Itself would kneel to see her breast the swell
With such bulk. But develop and refine
This image as we may, and as we planned –
Down to the shining brass, sheets chalky white,
Glazed lanterns, mullioned windows, oaken rails –
It will not serve the turn without a sense
Of brute strength tempered by benevolence.
The monarch reigns supreme because her sails,
From cinquecento chapel walls low down
On up through salon panels to her crown

Of screens, woodcuts and painted fans, are all
Unchallenged masterpieces. Her curved hull
Was moulded by the cave walls of Lascaux
And stamped with its motifs. But what we hear,
Not what we see, confirms the miracle
And makes the metaphor. We're held in thrall
By music. Music lush, music austere,
All music ever heartfelt, holds the flow
Of splendour in one place. Not thought alone –
Thought least of all, because it was his fate
To grow more infantile as it grew late –
Could build this thing, nor was it cut and sewn
Or hewn solely by touch, or sealed by skill.
A feat of the self-sacrificing will,

The peaceful man-of-war is here to prove
Any attempt to emulate her air
Of grandeur invites ridicule, unless
We, too, pour everything into the task
Of building something that will still be there
When we are gone. And that means all we love
And more, as Yeats knew when he wore a mask
To quell the self, thinking its pettiness
Could be faced down. It can't, but it can be
Tapped and diverted to an empty space
Where something permanent can take its place,
Shaped for the voyage to eternity
Out of our tears of weakness at the way
The thing we mean means more than we can say.

Worse than absurd, then – witless, in the end –
To trace him through his visionary schemes
And systems, or pay grave attention to
Those last affairs, boosted by monkey glands,
His patient wife scorned as a dotard's dreams
If more unreal. No scholarship can mend
The error of not seeing all demands
For human truth are vain. Few things are true
About the life except the work. Yeats found
His final glory when his jade and gold
Were joined by rag and bones to sink and fold
Into the flux of images and sound
That formed a magic ship to win the war
Against time, which is just a metaphor

For the battle to make sense of growing old,
And bless the ebb tide. It is outward bound,
Fit for the launch of what we have to give
The future, though that be a paltry thing.
Our house is flooded and our books are drowned,
The embers of our passion are stone cold,
We count the minutes we have left to live,
Yet even now it is of love we sing,
And for a paragon we have the vast
Swan-songs of Yeats that brought his depths to light.
Among school children or on All Souls' Night,
Humble or proud, he saved the best for last
And gave it to the waves – but no. There is
No ship. Just words, and all of them are his.

Habitués

Some older people like the ship so much
They pay again and go wherever it goes –
Which means that for a large part of the year
They just steam back and forth across the Atlantic –
Until they die, while other older people
Are there for one performance after another
Of *The Sound of Music*. They know every word.
"How" they smile wryly as they sing along,
"Do you solve a problem like Maria?" If
They conk out before the interval, are they
Removed? Surely the mark of the habitués
Is that they're dead already. When I noticed
That my club was full of men who had become
Stuffed armchairs and oak tables for school food
I resigned to save my skin. They liked the place
Too much. They thought the ship's Entertainment
Officer was entertaining. They were dewy-eyed
Instead of loud with scorn when Liesl's suitor
Expressed in terms of chaste and tender love
His youthful urge to get into her pants.
Dull death, the minimum of information –
Where entropy, to steal a phrase from S. J.
Perelman, fills every nook of Granny –
Will come when it will come, but while we're waiting
Beware the lapse into familiar comfort,
All outlines softened. In that cloud lies proof
Your life was lost on you, though I suppose
It isn't only easier but better
To echo an ecstatic singing nun –
Transfigured like Bernini's St Teresa

At the mere prospect of an edelweiss –
Than to puzzle out the dialogue of, say,
Act I, Scene IV of *Cymbeline*, which no one
Has remotely, since the day that it was written,
Enjoyed or even partly understood.
And are there no more thrills? In the fjord
The wrinklies crowd the rail to hear their voices
Come back from walls of ice. Couples hold hands.
So quick to guess their last heat is long gone,
How sure are we the failing is not ours,
Our cold contempt a portent of the void
Which is the closed heart and begins within us?
It doesn't always take time to go nowhere.

Castle in the Air

We never built our grand house on the edge
Of the Pacific, close to where we first
Drew breath, but high up in the cliffs, a ledge
Glassed in, with balconies where we would be
Enthralled to watch it hit the rocks and burst –
The ocean that still flows through you and me
Like blood, though many years have passed since we
Sailed separately away to keep our pledge

Of seeing what the world was like. Since then
We've been together and done pretty well:
You by your scholarship, I by my pen,
Both earned a living and our two careers
Paid for a house and garden we could sell
For just enough to spend our final years
Out there where the last landscape disappears
Eastward above the waves, and once again

We would be home. We've talked about that view
So often we can watch the seagulls fly
Below us by the thousand. There's the clue
Perhaps, to what we might do for the best:
Merely imagine it. The place to die
Is where you find your feet and come to rest.
Here, all we built is by our lost youth blessed.
This is your gift to me, and mine to you:

Front windows on a trimly English park,
A back yard we can bask in, but not burn
As we loll in our liner chairs. The bark
Stays on the trees, no wood-pile is a lair

For funnelwebs. Small prospect of return
Once you're accustomed to the change of air,
The calm of being here instead of there –
The slow but steady way that it grows dark.

Sleep late then, while I do my meds and dress
For the creaking mile that keeps my legs alive.
In hospital I'd lie there and obsess
About the beauty of this house, and still
I love it. But I feel the waves arrive
Like earthquakes as I walk, and not until
I'm gone for good will I forget the thrill –
Nor will the urge to start again grow less

As always in my dreams I spread my chart
In the great room of the grand house on the cliffs
And plot my course. Once more I will depart
Alone, to none beholden, full of fight
To quell the decapods and hippogryphs,
Take maidens here and there as is my right,
And voyage even to eternal night
As the hero does, made strong by his cold heart.

A Spray of Jasmine

Political developments in South East Asia, 2010

The day of her release, Suu Kyi wound flowers
Into the hair behind her head: a spray
Of jasmine. She looked lovely doing so,
Something a man my age can safely say,
For she is no child. Who knows if her powers
Extend to the real world? We have to go
On what we see, the people's thirst for her.
Today no junta general would look good
With floral attributes, or hear his name
Made music by the crowds, and if it were,
The reason would be drearily the same
As always, and too readily understood:
The crowds would be afraid. Her graceful calm
Means gentleness, as long as we recall
That Comrade Duch, who also has his poise
And clean-cut looks, for all he lacks her charm,
To most of us meant nothing much at all
When separating children from their toys
In his quiet way. Brought to the killing tree
And smashed to death, they saw a face to trust.
As cool as ever, all humility,
He now denies his guilt. Because we must –
Led by the hand of history as we are
Into the prison where the innocent
Die of their agony so very far
From all our thoughts, no matter how well meant –
We give our hearts to her for being there.
Such beauty has to be benevolent:
Look at her face, the flowers in her hair.

Madagascar Full-Tilt Boogie

The lemur that bit a piece out of my daughter
When she was a student here
By now is dead and gone,
But the island still has lemurs of every size.
A lemur not much bigger than a cicada
Swallows the cicada
As you just might park a Humvee in your hallway.
The cicada gets tons of time, on its way down,
To think "Sod this for a game of soldiers."
Larger lemurs, aloft in the spiny forest,
After feet-first triple-jumps through the parched air,
Land on a booby-trapped branch without their pads
Being even slightly punctured.
It must be done by quick adjustments,
Unless the spines go in and out and leave
No wounds. But then where would be the point,
If that's the phrase we want, of so many needles
Even being there? It would be as if, at Anzio,
Schu-mines had popped up only to serve coffee.
In this dried mud nothing pops up at all
Until it rains, and hey! It's mating day.
A million brown frogs magically appear.
Then half the brown frogs suddenly turn yellow
To indicate their wholesale macho readiness
For a no-holds-barred mass fucking.
Brown females politely yawn while their admirers,
Having dished out Nature's usual idea of passion
In less time than it takes to blow your nose,
Go back to being brown
Like the population of Rio after Mardi Gras.

You can't leave out the dressing-up factor.
The chameleon, proceeding along a branch
Like the second act of *The Family Reunion*,
Reminds us of the bad year T. S. Eliot
Wore green powder on his face
When greeting guests for dinner.
The whole damned island is chock-a-block with shape-changers.
Have you noticed that sick parrot over there
Is wearing John Galliano's face before last?
We should cut the poor bastard some slack.
Hitler, after all, started out as a dress designer
And never went near anti-Semitism
Until the critical failure
Of his first couture collection . . .
Don't look now, but in the third fork from the top
Of the tree behind you is a lemur
Doing a fair imitation of Coco Chanel.
A bit too cute perhaps,
Like Audrey Tautou in the same role.
She's coming down. She wants someone to pat her.

Bubbler

A lifetime onward, I know now the bubbler
In the school playground said things in my ear
As I soaked up the coolness with pursed lips.
"Bellerophon, framed by rejected Antea,
Has slain the Chimaera."

I was too young to know these whispering
Refreshments were the classic voice of time
Drenching the world. But it got into me
Somehow, and when I wiped my mouth and chin
My lips were tingling with the urge to speak.

The bubblers, a generation later
Fed girls of Asian origin with the rush
Of ancient love-talk as they stood tiptoe,
Their cheeks awash. "The coolness of the night:
It penetrates my screen of sheer brushed silk
And chills my pillow, making cold the jade."

Remember the brass guard to stop your kiss
Short of the dribbling bulb?
Yes, and I remember Aphrodite
Fresh from the bath, as the maths star Pam Yao Ming –
Who married an insurance man in Cabramatta –
Remembers the Shang Dynasty.

A Bracelet for Geoffrey Hill

A standard day's haul from the burial mound:
Quartz cat's eye cuff-links for a chain-mail shirt,
A Stalin button and an Iron Cross.
Small treasures liberated from their dirt.

Elsewhere in Mercia, a king prepared
For death took off his belt and doe-skin shoes,
Unzipped his lap-top, cleared security
And in the lounge sat back to watch the news

Until his flight was called. The galaxies
That showed up in the Hubble Deep Field frame
On long exposure shine like pick 'n' mix
Sweets in their coloured shapes, no two the same.

Thus thrives the densely wrought. The cloth departs
And leaves the cinch more complex on its own:
An all-star inscape spinning precious wheels
In lattices of bronze, gold, pearl and bone.

Subrius Flavus, Tribune, last to die
When the plot to topple Nero came to naught,
Knelt by the grave that had been dug for him
And saw it was too shallow and too short.

Ne hoc quidem ex disciplina. So
He speaks in Tacitus. "No discipline
Even in this." When stripping a Bren gun
Brush clean the butt-plate for the firing pin.

Coherent multiplicity takes force
For which the reader must be made to care
By how it sounds, or else it's just white noise.
The symphony that lovely women wear

Next to the skin gains weight when taken off
And folded flat with tissues in between.
From tight arrangements we deduce the role
That each part plays, if not what it must mean.

We only know that here the heat contained
Speaks volumes about what was seen and felt
And still astonishes, more now than then –
Before the buckle came loose from the belt.

The word-lord, fresh in from America,
Lectures in Oxford. He knows everything.
Note-taking Helen shivers at the thought
She'll be outlived by her engagement ring.

The Shadow Knows

See how the shadow of my former self
Moves through the kitchen, putting plates away.
The dishwasher yields up its treasure trove
Of future shards from long-ago today.
The blue-ringed soup bowls go home to their shelf.

I get home often now, as shadows are
Inclined to do, because they are so weak.
Now that my work is done, the peace I love
Is here for me, and you can hear me speak
More clearly now than I spoke from afar.

I am the shadow and the widower
Because the innocent you were I slew,
But you are here, and real, and far above
My level of attainment. It is you
Who brings me back to love what we once were.

Grief Has Its Time

"Grief has its time," said Johnson, well aware
It was himself he spoke for. Others must
Be granted full rights to a long despair
Fuelled by the ruination of their trust

In a fair world. A child born deadly sick
Or vanished: psychic wounds that never heal
Ensure that wit, though it once more be quick,
Will not be merry. Pain too deep, too real.

Free of such burdens, I pursue my course
Supposing myself blessed with the light touch,
A blithesome ease my principal resource.
Sometimes on stage I even say as much,

Or did, till one night in the signing queue
An ancient lady touched my wrist and said
I'd made her smile the way he used to do
When hearts were won by how a young man read

Aloud, and decent girls were led astray
By sweet speech. "Can you put his name with mine?
Before the war, before he went away,
We used to read together." Last in line

She had all my attention, so I wrote
The name she gave me, which I won't write here,
And wondered how I'd come to strike the note
She'd clearly heard in poems that were mere

Performances beside the hurt she'd known:
Things written for my peace and my delight.
"Be certain, sir, we take a deeper tone
Than we believe. Enough now for tonight."

Out in the street he spurned my proffered arm:
His cobbled features caught the link-boy's flame.
"The love of God can get no lasting harm
From fear of death. The two things are the same."

Yet all the way home he pursued the point
As if the argument about God's will
Within him made him ache in every joint
Until he reached the truth and could be still.

Utmost concision, even in a rage;
Guarding the helpless from experiment;
Stalwart against the follies of the age;
The depth of subtlety made eloquent –

These were the qualities of Johnson's mind
Even the King felt bound to venerate,
Who entered through the library wall to find
The rumpled, mumbling sage, alone and great.

Vision of Jean Arthur and the Distant Mountains

Look back and you can almost pick the minute
When the last power and spring of youth withdrew,
And you began to walk, not run,
Searching ahead for places to sit down.
Really it's been the one long day since then,
But gradually invaded by this peace
By which you are looked after. The light ebbs
As it does before the heavens open,
And the air fills with this strange comfort,
As if there were a soft and loving voice
Putting sweet emphasis on just one word
To mark the moment of your growing old.
Shane,
You can't just stand there in the *rain*.
You'll catch your death of cold.

The Light As It Grows Dark

The light as it grows dark holds all the verve
That you were ever thrilled or dazzled by,
But holds it folded thick, stacked in reserve.
More for your memory than for your eye
It brings back pictures that your every nerve
Once revelled in while scarcely caring why.

You care now. Time has come, and there will be
No light at all soon, so look hard at this:
Behold the concentrated panoply
Just here in this small garden's emphasis
On colour drained of visibility.
In daylight, such wealth might be what you miss.

The flowers are growing dark, but they will live,
And so will you, at least a little while.
Good reason you should do your best to give
All your attention now. It's not your style,
I'm well aware, to be contemplative:
The thought of chasing shadows makes you smile.

And yet I swear to you each figment had
Full meaning once. The images are here
That made your day when you would run half-mad
For too much good luck. Now they reappear
So fragmentarily you find it sad.
But really it's all there, so have no fear:

The light as it grows dark has come for you
To comfort you. It is the sweet embrace
Of what your history was bound to do:
Close in, and in due time to take your place.
You can't believe it, but it's nothing new:
Your life has turned to look you in the face.

Plate Tectonics

In the Great Rift, the wildebeest wheel and run,
Spooked by a pride of lions which would kill,
In any thousand of them, only one
Or two were they to walk or just stand still.
They can't see that, nor can we see the tide
Of land go slowly out on either side,
As Africa and Asia come apart
Inexorably like a broken heart.

We measure everything by our brief lives
And pity most a life cut shorter yet.
Granddaughters get smacked if they play with knives,
Or should be, to make sure they don't forget.
So think the old folk, by their years made wise,
Believing what they've seen before their eyes,
And knowing what time is, and where it goes.
Deep on the ocean floor, the lava flows.

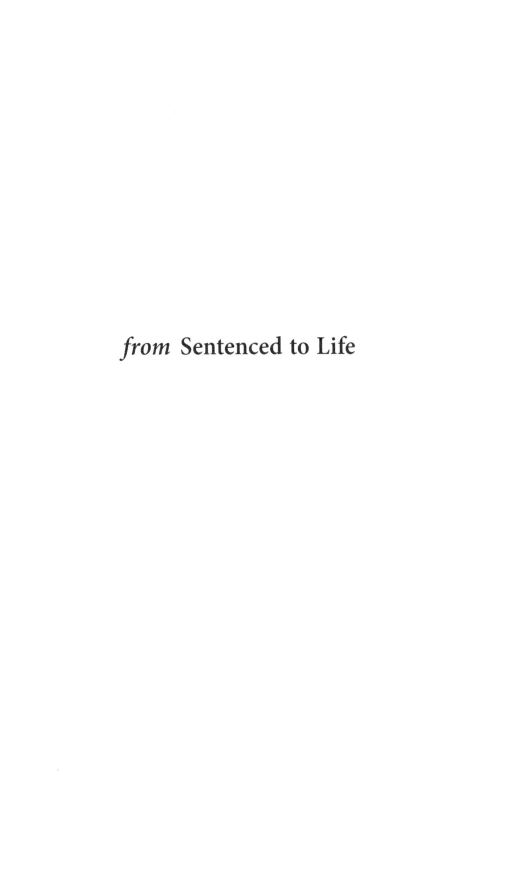

from Sentenced to Life

To Prue

If you're the dreamer, I'm your dream, but when
You wish to wake I am your wish, and grow
As mighty as all mastery, and then
As silent as a star
Ablaze above the city that we know
As Time: so very strange, so very far.

Sentenced to Life

Sentenced to life, I sleep face-up as though
Ice-bound, lest I should cough the night away,
And when I walk the mile to town, I show
The right technique for wading through deep clay.
A sad man, sorrier than he can say.

But surely not so guilty he should die
Each day from knowing that his race is run:
My sin was to be faithless. I would lie
As if I could be true to everyone
At once, and all the damage that was done

Was in the name of love, or so I thought.
I might have met my death believing this,
But no, there was a lesson to be taught.
Now, not just old, but ill, with much amiss,
I see things with a whole new emphasis.

My daughter's garden has a goldfish pool
With six fish, each a little finger long.
I stand and watch them following their rule
Of never touching, never going wrong:
Trajectories as perfect as plain song.

Once, I would not have noticed; nor have known
The name for Japanese anemones,
So pale, so frail. But now I catch the tone
Of leaves. No birds can touch down in the trees
Without my seeing them. I count the bees.

Even my memories are clearly seen:
Whence comes the answer if I'm told I must
Be aching for my homeland. Had I been
Dulled in the brain to match my lungs of dust
There'd be no recollection I could trust.

Yet I, despite my guilt, despite my grief,
Watch the Pacific sunset, heaven sent,
In glowing colours and in sharp relief,
Painting the white clouds when the day is spent,
As if it were my will and testament –

As if my first impressions were my last,
And time had only made them more defined,
Now I am weak. The sky is overcast
Here in the English autumn, but my mind
Basks in the light I never left behind.

Driftwood Houses

The *ne plus ultra* of our lying down,
Skeleton riders see the planet peeled
Into their helmets by a knife of light.
Just so, I stare into the racing field
Of ice as I lie on my side and fight
To cough up muck. This bumpy slide downhill
Leads from my bed to where I'm bound to drown
At this rate. I get up and take a walk,
Lean on the balustrade and breathe my fill
At last. The wooden stairs down to the hall
Stop shaking. Enough said. To hear me talk
You'd think I found my fate sad. Hardly that:
All that has happened is I've hit the wall.
Disintegration is appropriate,

As once, on our French beach, I built, each year,
Among the rocks below the esplanade,
Houses from driftwood for our girls to roof
With towels so they could hide there in the shade
With ice creams that would melt more slowly. Proof
That nothing built can be forever here
Lay in the way those frail and crooked frames
Were undone by a storm-enhanced high tide
And vanished. It was time, and anyhow
Our daughters were not short of other games
Which were all theirs, and not geared to my pride.
And here they come. They're gathering shells again.
And you in your straw hat, I see you now,
As I lie restless yet most blessed of men.

Landfall

Hard to believe, now, that I once was free
From pills in heaps, blood tests, X-rays and scans.
No pipes or tubes. At perfect liberty,
I stained my diary with travel plans.

The ticket paid for at the other end,
I packed a hold-all and went anywhere
They asked me. One on whom you could depend
To show up, I would cross the world by air

And come down neatly in some crowded hall.
I stood for a full hour to give my spiel.
Here, I might talk back to a nuisance call,
And that's my flight of eloquence. Unreal:

But those years in the clear, how real were they,
When all the sirens in the signing queue
Who clutched their hearts at what I had to say
Were just dreams, even when the dream came true?

I called it health but never stopped to think
It might have been a kind of weightlessness,
That footloose feeling always on the brink
Of breakdown: the false freedom of excess.

Rarely at home in those days, I'm home now,
Where few will look at me with shining eyes.
Perhaps none ever did, and that was how
The fantasy of young strength that now dies

Expressed itself. The face that smiled at mine
Out of the looking glass was seeing things.
Today I am restored by my decline
And by the harsh awakening it brings.

I was born weak and always have been weak.
I came home and was taken into care.
A cot-case, but at long last I can speak:
I am here now, who was hardly even there.

Early to Bed

Old age is not my problem. Bad health, yes.
If I were well again, I'd walk for miles,
My name a synonym for tirelessness.
On Friday nights I'd go out on the tiles:

I'd go to tango joints and stand up straight
While women leaned against me trustingly,
I'd push them backward at a stately rate
With steps of eloquence and intricacy.

Alone in the café, my favourite place,
I'd sit up late to carve a verse like this.
I couldn't do it at my usual pace
But weight of manner would add emphasis.

The grand old man. Do I dare play that part?
Perhaps I am too frail. I don't know how
To say exactly what is in my heart,
Except I feel that I am nowhere now.

But I have tempted providence too long:
It gives me life enough, and little pain.
I should be grateful for this simple song,
No matter how it goes against the grain

To spend the best part of a winter's day
Filing away at some reluctant rhyme
And go to bed with so much still to say
On how I came to have so little time.

My Home

Grasping at straws, I bless another day
Of having felt not much less than all right.
I wrote a paragraph and put some more
Books in a box for books to throw away.
Such were my deeds. Now, short of breath and sore
From all that effort, I prepare for night,
Which occupies the windows as I climb
The stairs. A step up and I stand, each time,

Posed like the statue of a man in pain,
Although I'm really not: just weak and slow.
This is the measure of my dying years:
The sad skirl of a piper in the rain
Who plays 'My Home'. If I seem close to tears
It's for my sins, not sickness. Soon the snow
Will finish readying the ground for spring.
The cold, if not the warmth that it will bring,

Is made, each day, so clearly manifest
I thank my lucky stars for second sight.
The children of our street head off for school
Most mornings, stronger for their hours of rest.
Plump in their coloured coats they prove a rule
By moving brilliantly through soft white light:
We fade away, but vivid in our eyes
A world is born again that never dies.

Holding Court

Retreating from the world, all I can do
Is build a new world, one demanding less
Acute assessments. Too deaf to keep pace
With conversation, I don't try to guess
At meanings, or unpack a stroke of wit,
But just send silent signals with my face
That claim I've not succumbed to loneliness
And might be ready to come in on cue.
People still turn towards me where I sit.

I used to notice everything, and spoke
A language full of details that I'd seen,
And people were amused; but now I see
Only a little way. What can they mean,
My phrases? They come drifting like the mist
I look through if someone appears to be
Smiling in my direction. Have they been?
This was the time when I most liked to smoke.
My watch-band feels too loose around my wrist.

My body, sensitive in every way
Save one, can still proceed from chair to chair,
But in my mind the fires are dying fast.
Breathe through a scarf. Steer clear of the cold air.
Think less of love and all that you have lost.
You have no future so forget the past.
Let this be no occasion for despair.
Cherish the prison of your waning day.
Remember liberty, and what it cost.

Be pleased that things are simple now, at least,
As certitude succeeds bewilderment.
The storm blew out and this is the dead calm.
The pain is going where the passion went.
Few things will move you now to lose your head
And you can cause, or be caused, little harm.
Tonight you leave your audience content:
You were the ghost they wanted at the feast,
Though none of them recalls a word you said.

Procedure for Disposal

It may not come to this, but if I should
Fail to survive this year of feebleness
Which irks me so and may have killed for good
Whatever gift I had for quick success –
For I could talk an hour alone on stage
And mostly make it up along the way,
But now when I compose a single page
Of double-spaced it takes me half the day –
If I, that is, should finally succumb
To these infirmities I'm slow to learn
The names of lest my brain be rendered numb
With boredom even as I toss and turn,
Then send my ashes home, where they can fall
In their own sweet time from the harbour wall.

Manly Ferry

Too frail to fly, I may not see again
The harbour that I crossed on the *South Steyne*
When I was still in short pants. All the boys
Would gather at the rail that ran around
The open engine-room. The oil, the noise
Of rocking beams and plunging rods: it beat
Even the view out from the hurdling deck
Into the ocean. The machinery
Was so alive, so beautiful, so neat.

Years later the old ferries disappeared,
Except for the *South Steyne*, which looked intact
Where she was parked at Pyrmont, though a fire
Had gutted her. I loved her two-faced grace:
Twin funnels, and each end of her a prow,
She sailed into a mirror and back out,
Even while dead inside and standing still:
Her livery of green and gold wore well
Through years of weather as she went nowhere
Except on that long voyage in my mind
Where complicated workings clicked and throbbed
And everything moved forward at full strength.

And then, while I was elsewhere, she was gone:
And now I, too, await my vanishing,
Which, unlike hers, will be for good. She went
Away to be refitted. In her new
Career as a floating restaurant
She seems set for as long as oysters grow
With chilled white Cloudy Bay to wash them down:

A brilliant inner city ornament.
But is it better to be always there
Than out of it, and just a fading name?
For me, her life was when the engine turned.
Soon now my path across the swell will end.
If I can't work, let me be broken up.

Tempe Dump

I always thought the showdown would be sudden,
Convulsive as a bushfire triple-jumping
A roadway where some idiot Green council
Had forbidden the felling of gum trees,
And so, with no firebreaks to check its course,
The fire rides on like the army of Attila
To look for houses where the English Garden
Is banned, and there is only the Australian garden,
With eucalypts that overhang the eaves
And shed bark to ensure the racing flames
Will send the place up like a napalm strike.

Instead, it's Tempe Dump. When we were small
My gang went there exploring. Piston rings
Lay round in heaps, shiny among the junk
Which didn't shine at all, just gave forth wisps
Of smoke. The dump was smouldering underneath
But had no end in view. This is the fire
Within me, though I harbour noble thoughts
Of forests under phosphorous attack
And in an hour left black, in fields of ash –
Not this long meltdown with its leaking heat,
Its drips of acid, pools of alkali:
This slow burn of what should be finished with
But waits for the clean sweep that never comes.

Living Doll

An *Aufstehpuppe* is a stand-up guy.
You knock him over, he gets up again:
Constantly smiling, never asking why
The world went sideways for a while back then.

I have an *Aufstehpuppe* on the shelf
Under the mirror in my living room:
I wish I were reminded of myself
Merrily dipping in and out of doom.

The truth, alas, is I've been knocked askew
For quite a while now and I can't get back
To find the easy balance I once knew.
Until the day when everything goes black

I'll spend more time than he does on my side
Wishing the sparkle of his painted eyes
Was shared by mine. I envy him his pride:
That simple strength he seems to realise.

My *Aufstehpuppe* was a crude antique
When first I met him. Soon he might descend
Further into our family, there to speak
Of how we are defeated in the end,

But still begin again in the new lives
Which sort our junk, deciding what to keep.
Let them keep this, a cheap doll that contrives
To stand straight even as I fall asleep.

Event Horizon

For years we fooled ourselves. Now we can tell
How everyone our age heads for the brink
Where they are drawn into the unplumbed well,
Not to be seen again. How sad, to think
People we once loved will be with us there
And we not touch them, for it is nowhere.

Never to taste again her pretty mouth!
It's been forever, though, since last we kissed.
Shadows evaporate as they go south,
Torn, by whatever longings still persist,
Into a tattered wisp, a streak of air,
And then not even that. They get nowhere.

But once inside, you will have no regrets.
You go where no one will remember you.
You go below the sun when the sun sets,
And there is nobody you ever knew
Still visible, nor even the most rare
Hint of a face to humanise nowhere.

Are you to welcome this? It welcomes you.
The only blessing of the void to come
Is that you can relax. Nothing to do,
No cruel dreams of subtracting from your sum
Of follies. About those, at last, you care:
But soon you need not, as you go nowhere.

Into the singularity we fly
After a stretch of time in which we leave
Our lives behind yet know that we will die
At any moment now. A pause to grieve,
Burned by the starlight of our lives laid bare,
And then no sound, no sight, no thought. Nowhere.

What is it worth, then, this insane last phase
When everything about you goes downhill?
This much: you get to see the cosmos blaze
And feel its grandeur, even against your will,
As it reminds you, just by being there,
That it is here we live or else nowhere.

Nature Programme

The female panda is on heat
For about five minutes a year
And the male, no sprinter at the best of times,
Hardly ever gets there
Before she cools off again.

In the South Island of New Zealand
There is a rainforest
With penguins in it.
They trot along the dangerous trails
Towards the booming ocean

Where albatross chicks in training
For their very first take-off
Are snatched by tiger sharks
Cruising in water
No deeper than your thighs.

Doomed to the atrophy of lust,
Lurching with their flippers out,
Dragged under as they strain for flight,
They could be you:
Wonder of nature that you were.

Managing Anger

On screen, the actor smashes down the phone.
He wrecks the thing because he can't get through.
He plays it stagey even when alone.
If you were there, he might be wrecking you.

Actors believe they have to show, not tell,
Any annoyance that the script dictates,
Therefore it's not enough for them to yell:
They must pull down a cupboard full of plates.

An actor wrecks a room. The actress who
Is playing wife to him does not protest.
Perhaps she doesn't have enough to do
All day, and thinks his outburst for the best.

For God forbid that actors bottle up
Their subterranean feelings so that we
Can't see them. We must watch the coffee cup
Reduced to smithereens, the shelf swept free

Of all its crockery. Another take
Requires the whole set to be dressed again
With all the gubbins that he got to break
The first time. Aren't they weary, now and then,

The poor crew, setting up the stuff once more
That some big baby trashes in a rage,
And all that fury faked? False to the core,
The screen experience gives us a gauge

For our real lives, where we go on for years
Not even mentioning some simple fact
That brings us to the aching point of tears –
Lest people think that it might be an act.

Echo Point

I am the echo of the man you knew.
Launched from the look-out to the other side
Of this blue valley, my voice calls to you
All on its own, and more direct for that.
My line of sweet talk you could not abide
Came from the real man. It will all be gone –
Like glitter back to the magician's hat –
Soon now, and only sad scraps will remain.
His body that betrayed you has gone on
To do the same for him. Like veils of rain,
He is the cloud that his tears travel through.

When the cloud lifts, he will be gone indeed.
Hearing his cry, you'll see the ghost gums break
Into clear air, as all the past is freed
From false hopes. No, I nowhere lie awake
To feel this happen, but I know it will.
At the last breath, my throat was full of song;
The proof, for a short while, is with you still.
Though snapped at sharply by the whipbird's call,
It has not stopped. It lingers for your sake:
Almost as if I were not gone for long –
And what you hear will not fade as I fall.

Too Much Light

My cataracts invest the bright spring day
With extra glory, with a glow that stings.
The shimmering shields above the college gates –
Heraldic remnants of the queens and kings –
Flaunt liquid paint here at the end of things
When my vitality at last abates,
And all these forms bleed, spread and make a blur
Of what, to second sight, they are and were.

And now I slowly pace, a stricken beast,
Across a lawn which must be half immersed
In crocuses and daffodils, but I
Can only see for sure the colours burst
And coalesce as if they were the first
Flowers I ever saw. Thus, should I die,
I'll go back through the gate I entered when
My eyes were stunned, as now they are again.

My Latest Fever

My latest fever clad me in cold sweat
And there I was, in hospital again,
Drenched, and expecting an attack of bugs
As devastating as the first few hours
Of *Barbarossa*, with the Russian air force
Caught on the ground and soldiers by the thousand
Herded away to starve, while Stalin still
Believed it couldn't happen. But instead
The assault turned out to be as deadly dull
As a bunch of ancient members of the Garrick
Emerging from their hutch below the stairs
To bore me from all angles as I prayed
For sleep, which only came in fits and starts.
Night after night was like that. Every day
Was like the night before, a hit parade
Of jazzed-up sequences from action movies.
While liquid drugs were pumped into my wrist,
My temperature stayed sky-high. On the screen
Deep in my head, heroes repaired themselves.
In *Rambo First Blood*, Sly Stallone sewed up
His own arm. Then Mark Wahlberg, star of *Shooter*,
Assisted by Kate Mara, operated
To dig the bullets from his body. Teeth
Were gritted in both cases. No one grits
Like Sly: it looks like a piano sneering.
Better, however, to be proof against
All damage, as in *Salt*, where Angelina
Jumps from a bridge onto a speeding truck
And then from that truck to another truck.
In North Korea, tortured for years on end,

She comes out with a split lip. All this mayhem
Raged in my brain with not a cliché scamped.
I saw the heroes march in line towards me
In slo-mo, with a wall of flame behind them,
And thought, as I have often thought, 'This is
The pits. How can I make it stop?' It stopped.
On the eleventh day, my temperature
Dived off the bridge like Catherine Zeta-Jones
From the Petronas Towers in Kuala Lumpur.
I had no vision of the final battle.
The drugs, in pill form now, drove back the bugs
Into the holes from which they had attacked.
It might have been a scene from *Starship Troopers*:
But no, I had returned to the real world.
They sent me home to sleep in a dry bed
Where I felt better than I had for months.
No need to make a drama of my rescue:
Having been saved was like a lease of life,
The thing itself, undimmed by images –
A thrill a minute simply for being so.

The Emperor's Last Words

An army that never leaves its defences
Is bound to be defeated, said Napoleon,
Who left them, and was defeated.
And thus I gather my remaining senses
For the walk, or limp, to town
Where I have a haircut and visit
The Oxfam bookshop near the bridge.

Only a day out of Addenbrooke's
Where another bout of pneumonia
Damned near nailed me,
I walk slowly now, sitting on low brick walls.
But the haircut is successful,
Completing my resemblance to Buzz Aldrin
On the surface of Jupiter,

And in the bookshop I get, for my niece,
The Penguin Book of English Verse
(John Hayward's excellent anthology)
And the old, neat, thin-paper OUP edition
Of the Louise and Aylmer Maude translation
Of *War and Peace*, so handy for the pocket.

Still in her teens, already reading everything,
She wants to be a writer, and when she visits me
She gets a useful lesson
On how a writer can end up.
But things could have been worse:
I could have been married to Laura Riding,
Whose collected poems I purchase for myself.
Have fifteen years of death improved her verses?

No, still stridently incomprehensible, befitting
The way she won an argument with Robert Graves
By throwing herself backwards from a window:
A token, no doubt, of an artistic commitment
The purity of whose achievements was proved
By being intelligible to nobody at all
Except her fellow fruit-cakes.

Well, she sure left her defences.
Almost everyone wants to be a writer.
My niece, however, has got the knack:
That feeling for a sentence, you can't mistake it.
The only question is how far you will go,
Even walking ever so slowly,
Away from your fortress. All the way to Russia?

But Tolstoy, himself an awful husband,
Waits to make a midget of your memory.
You escaped from Elba
But not from St Helena.
Had you stayed in Corsica
None of this would have happened.
But you left, and now every nut ward in the world
Has one of you at least.

The Maudes were married more than fifty years.
In two days' time, the Tour de France
Will go past here
Where I now sit to gather strength
For my retreat from this hot sun.
It's time to go. High time to go. High time.
France, army, head of the army, Josephine.

Bugsy Siegel's Flying Eye

In Havana, at the Hotel Nacional,
Lucky Luciano, or so the story goes,
Persuaded a reluctant Meyer Lansky
That Bugsy Siegel, who had squandered the mob's money
On taking years to finish the Flamingo
And might even have skimmed from the invested capital,
Would need to have his venture in Las Vegas
Brought to a sudden end.

But the execution happened in LA
With Bugsy unwisely sitting near a window.
The first bullet took out his right eye
And flung it far away across the carpet
Into the tiled dining area.
He should have known that something bad would happen
Because when he got home he had smelled flowers
And when there are no flowers in the house
But you still smell them, it means death.

After the window shattered, the smell of jasmine
Seeped through the house, but that was no premonition,
Because Bugsy was already dead.
Scholars still ask the question why
He never guessed that he would soon get hit,
Even after closing down his dream-land
For yet another re-design. He was
An artist among gangsters. The others weren't.

When I got to Vegas, the original Flamingo
Had been torn down, with a garden on the site,
But in Havana, at the Nacional,
I met the waiter who had built a long career
Out of once having slept with Ava Gardner,
And I sat to drink mojitos where Meyer Lansky
And Lucky Luciano might once have done the same
While they pondered what to do about Bugsy.
Maybe they did. It was mob business
So nothing got written down. Nobody can be sure
Of anything except that flying eye.

Only the Immortal Need Apply

'I am as the demon of the tumult'
Gabriele d'Annunzio, quoted by Lucy Hughes-Hallett in *The Pike*

In Paris, at Diaghilev's *Cleopatra* –
Decor by Bakst, choreography by Fokine,
Ida Rubinstein in the title role –
D'Annunzio and his powerful halitosis
Sat beside Robert de Montesquiou,
The model for Proust's Baron de Charlus.

Rubinstein, who could not dance a step,
Merely stood there looking beautiful
Or adopted the occasional Egyptian pose,
While d'Annunzio laid his plans.

Backstage in her crowded dressing-room
The Nile-nymph recovered from her exertions
By lying back in her couch.
D'Annunzio was six inches shorter than she was
But her posture put him within range.

He fell to his knees and kissed her lovely legs
Upward from toes to crotch.
As he plunged his face into the *tarte tatin*,
Barrès and Rostand bowed their heads in awe
And Montesquiou adjusted his moustache.

Later on a man in the street was arrested
And charged with not being famous.
He remains nameless to this day.

Plot Points

On the rafting ice
The afterbirth of seals
Leaves stains like pink blancmange.
Glyco proteins in the fish
Keep them from freezing.

M13 in Hercules
Is a globular star cluster –
A glitterball that my mother
Could have danced the Charleston under.
She had lovely hands.

Renoir, choosing models, always looked
At their hands first.
After the war, at Lodz,
On a tour of the concentration camp,
Rubinstein said 'I was born here.'

In Melanesia, the House of Memories
Contains the treasures of the tribe.
The Somme chalk was good for tunnels.
When the barrage broke them,
The parapet bags spat white.

At Kokoda, the treetop phosphorescence
Turned the night to Christmas.
The Aussies in Tobruk
Brushed dust from bully beef.
In the dry valleys of Antarctica
Dust is raised by the katabatic wind.

With the *Wehrmacht* stalled in front of Moscow,
Even the grease froze. The 88s
Were jammed by their own shells.
Rasputitsa was the mud
Of spring thaw and autumn rain.

On a hard day in the Alhambra
The Sultan sent an apple
To the virgin of his choice.
The logo on your MacBook
Is an echo of the manner
In which Alan Turing killed himself.

In the battle for Berlin
The last panzers were overrun
Before they reached the start-line.
A dead hippo in the *Tiergarten*
Had an unexploded mortar bomb
Sticking out of its side.

While you were reading this
Millions of stars moved closer
Towards their own extinction
So many years ago –
But let's believe our eyes:
They say it's all here now.

Asma Unpacks Her Pretty Clothes

Wherever her main residence is now,
Asma unpacks her pretty clothes.
It takes forever: so much silk and cashmere
To be unpeeled from clinging leaves of tissue
By her ladies. With her perfect hands, she helps.

Out there in Syria, the torturers
Arrive by bus at every change of shift
While victims dangle from their cracking wrists.
Beaten with iron bars, young people pray
To die soon. This is the Middle Ages
Brought back to living death. Her husband's doing,
The screams will never reach her where she is.

Asma's uncovered hair had promised progress
For all her nation's women. They believed her.
We who looked on believed the promise too,
But now, as she unpacks her pretty clothes,
The dream at home dissolves in agony.

Bashar, her husband, does as he sees fit
To cripple every enemy with pain.
We sort of knew, but he had seemed so modern
With Asma alongside him. His big talk
About destroying Israel: standard stuff.
A culture-changing wife offset all that.

She did, she did. I doted as *Vogue* did
On her sheer style. Dear God, it fooled me too,
So now my blood is curdled by the shrieks
Of people mad with grief. My own wrists hurt

As Asma, with her lustrous fingertips –
She must have thought such things could never happen –
Unpacks her pretty clothes.

Nina Kogan's Geometrical Heaven

Two of her little pictures grace my walls:
Suprematism in a special sense,
With all the usual bits and pieces flying
Through space, but carrying a pastel-tinged
Delicacy to lighten the strict forms
Of that hard school and blow them all sky-high,
Splinters and stoppers from the bombing of
An angel's boudoir. When Malevich told
His pupils that their personalities
Should be suppressed, the maestro little knew
The state would soon require exactly that.
But Nina, trying as she might, could not
Rein in her individuality,
And so she made these things that I own now
And gaze at, wondering at her sad fate.
She could have got away, but wished instead
Her gift devoted to Utopia.
She painted trams, designed official posters:
Alive until the siege of Leningrad
And then gone. Given any luck, she starved:
But the purges were still rolling, and I fear
The NKVD had her on a list,
And what she faced, there at the very end,
Was the white cold. Were there an afterlife,
We might meet up, and I could tell her then
Her sumptuous fragments still went flying on
In my last hours, when I, in a warm house,
Lay on my couch to watch them coming close,
Her proofs that any vision of eternity
Is with us in the world, and beautiful

Because a mind has found the way things fit
Purely by touch. That being said, however,
I should record that out of any five
Pictures by Kogan, at least six are fakes.

Star System

The stars in their magnificent array
Look down upon the Earth, their cynosure,
Or so it seems. They are too far away,
In fact, to see a thing; hence they look pure
To us. They lack the textures of our globe,
So only we, from cameras carried high,
Enjoy the beauty of the swirling robe
That wraps us up, the interplay of sky
And cloud, as if a Wedgwood plate of blue
And white should melt, and then, its surface stirred
With spoons, a treasure too good to be true,
Be placed, and hover like a hummingbird,
Drawing all eyes, though ours alone, to feast
On splendour as it turns west from the East.

There was a time when some of our young men
Walked plumply on the moon and saw Earth rise,
As stunning as the sun. The years since then
Have aged them. Now and then somebody dies.
It's like a clock, for those of us who saw
The Saturn rockets going up as if
Mankind had energy to burn. The law
Is different for one man. Time is a cliff
You come to in the dark. Though you might fall
As easily as on a feather bed,
It is a sad farewell. You loved it all.
You dream that you might keep it in your head.
But memories, where can you take them to?
Take one last look at them. They end with you.

And still the Earth revolves, and still the blaze
Of stars maintains a show of vigilance.
It should, for long ago, in olden days,
We came from there. By luck, by fate, by chance,
All of the elements that form the world
Were sent by cataclysms deep in space,
And from their combination life unfurled
And stood up straight, and wore a human face.
I still can't pass a mirror. Like a boy,
I check my looks, and now I see the shell
Of what I was. So why, then, this strange joy?
Perhaps an old man dying would do well
To smile as he rejoins the cosmic dust
Life comes from, for resign himself he must.

Change of Domicile

Installed in my last house, I face the thought
That fairly soon there will be one house more,
Lacking the pictures and the books that here
Surround me with abundant evidence
I spent a lifetime pampering my mind.
The new place will be of a different sort,
Dark and austere, and I will have to find
My way along its unforthcoming walls.
Help is at hand here should I fall, but there
There will be no one to turn on the lights
For me, and I will know I am not blind
Only by glimpses when the empty halls
Lead me to empty rooms, in which the nights
Succeed each other with no day between.

I may not see my tattered Chinese screen
Again, but I shall have time to reflect
That what I miss was just the bric-a-brac
I kept with me to blunt my solitude,
Part of my brave face when my life was wrecked
By my gift for deceit. Truth clears away
So many souvenirs. The shelves come clean.
In the last, the truly last house there will be
No treasured smithereens to take me back
To when things hung together. I'll conclude
The way that I began so long ago:
With nothingness, but know it fit for me
This time around, now I am brought so low,
Yet ready to move soon. When, I can't say.

Rounded with a Sleep

The sun seems in control, the tide is out:
Out to the sandbar shimmers the lagoon.
The little children sprint, squat, squeal and shout.
These shallows will be here until the moon
Contrives to reassert its influence,
And anyway, by then it will be dark.
Old now and sick, I ponder the immense
Ocean upon which I will soon embark:
As if held in abeyance by dry land
It waits for me beyond that strip of sand.

It won't wait long. Just for the moment, though,
There's time to question if my present state
Of bathing in this flawless afterglow
Is something I deserve. I left it late
To come back to my family. Here they are,
Camped on their towels and putting down their books
To watch my granddaughter, a natural star,
Cartwheel and belly-flop. The whole scene looks
As if I thought it up to soothe my soul.
But in Arcadia, Death plays a role:

A leading role, and suddenly I wake
To realise that I've been sound asleep
Here at my desk. I just wish the mistake
Were rare, and not so frequent I could weep.
The setting alters, but the show's the same:
One long finale, soaked through with regret,
Somehow designed to expiate self-blame.
But still there is no end, at least not yet:
No cure, that is, for these last years of grief
As I repent and yet find no relief.

My legs are sore, and it has gone midnight.
I've had my last of lounging on the beach
To see the sweet oncoming sunset light
Touching the water with a blush of peach,
Smoothing the surface like a ballroom floor
As all my loved ones pack up from their day
And head back up the cliff path. This for sure:
Even the memories will be washed away,
If not by waves, by rain, which I see fall,
Drenching the flagstones and the garden wall.

My double doors are largely glass. I stand
Often to contemplate the neat back yard
My elder daughter with her artist's hand
Designed for me. This winter was less hard
Than its three predecessors were. The snow
Failed to arrive this time, but rain, for me,
Will also do to register time's flow.
The rain, the snow, the inexorable sea:
I get the point. I'll climb the stairs to bed,
Perhaps to dream I'm somewhere else instead.

All day tomorrow I have tests and scans,
And everything that happens will be real.
My blood might say I should make no more plans,
And when it does so, that will be the deal.
But until then I love to speak with you
Each day we meet. Sometimes we even touch
Across the sad gulf that I brought us to.
Just for a time, so little means so much:
More than I'm worth, I know, as I know how
My death is something I must live with now.

Elementary Sonnet

Tired out from getting up and getting dressed
I lie down for a while to get some rest,
And so begins another day of not
Achieving much except to dent the cot
For just the depth appropriate to my weight –
Which is no chasm, in my present state.
By rights my feet should barely touch the floor
And yet my legs are heavy metal. More
And more I sit down to write less and less,
Taking a half hour's break from helplessness
To craft a single stanza meant to give
Thanks for the heartbeat which still lets me live:
A consolation even now, so late –
When soon my poor bed will be smooth and straight.

Leçons de ténèbres

But are they lessons, all these things I learn
Through being so far gone in my decline?
The wages of experience I earn
Would service well a younger life than mine.
I should have been more kind. It is my fate
To find this out, but find it out too late.

The mirror holds the ruins of my face
Roughly together, thus reminding me
I should have played it straight in every case,
Not just when forced to. Far too casually
I broke faith when it suited me, and here
I am alone, and now the end is near.

All of my life I put my labour first.
I made my mark, but left no time between
The things achieved, so, at my heedless worst,
With no life, there was nothing I could mean.
But now I have slowed down. I breathe the air
As if there were not much more of it there

And write these poems, which are funeral songs
That have been taught to me by vanished time:
Not only to enumerate my wrongs
But to pay homage to the late sublime
That comes with seeing how the years have brought
A fitting end, if not the one I sought.

Winter Plums

Two winter plum trees grow beside my door.
Throughout the cold months they had little pink
Flowers all over them as if they wore
Nightdresses, and their branches, black as ink
By sunset, looked as if a Japanese
Painter, while painting air, had painted these

Two winter plum trees. Summer now at last
Has warmed their leaves and all the blooms are gone.
A year that I might not have had has passed.
Bare branches are my signal to go on,
But soon the brave flowers of the winter plums
Will flare again, and I must take what comes:

Two winter plum trees that will outlive me.
Thriving with colour even in the snow,
They'll snatch a triumph from adversity.
All right for them, but can the same be so
For someone who, seeing their buds remade
From nothing, will be less pleased than afraid?

Spring Snow Dancer

Snow into April. Frost night after night.
Out on the Welsh farms the lambs die unborn.
The chill air hurts my lungs, but from the light
It could be spring. Bitter as it is bright,
The last trick of the cold is a false dawn.

I breathed, grew up, and now I learn to be
Glad for my long life as it melts away,
Yet still regales me with so much to see
Of how we live in continuity
And die in it. Take what I saw today:

My granddaughter, as quick as I could glance,
Did ballet steps across the kitchen floor,
And this time I was breathless at the chance
By which I'd lived to see our dear lamb dance –
Though soon I will not see her any more.

Mysterious Arrival of the Dew

Tell me about the dew. Some say it falls
But does it fall in fact? And if it fall
Then where does it fall from? And why, in falling,
Does it not obscure the moon?

Dew on the hibiscus, dew on the cobweb,
Dew on the broken leaf,
The world's supply of diamond earrings
Tossed from a car window.

Some intergalactic hoodlum sugar-daddy
Is trying to get girls.
Goethe had a name for these flattering droplets:
Shiver-pearls. Grab a handful.

Statistics say dew doesn't fall at all:
Going nowhere near the moon,
It just gathers on any susceptible surface
When the temperature is right.

There is talk in every arid country
Of collecting it by the truck-load,
But the schemes get forgotten in the sun
As soon as it sucks up those trillion baubles.

Tell me about the dew. Is it a case
Of falling back the better to advance,
By the same veil, shawl or glittering pashmina
As last time out? But darling, it's to die for.

Cabin Baggage

My niece is heading here to stay with us.
Before she leaves home she takes careful stock
Of what she might not know again for years.
The berries (so she writes) have been brought in,
But she'll be gone before the peaches come.
On days of burning sun, the air is tinged
With salt and eucalyptus. 'Why am I
Leaving all this behind? I feel a fool.'
But I can tell from how she writes things down
The distance will assist her memories
To take full form. She travels to stay still.
I wish I'd been that smart before I left.
Instead, I have to dig deep for a trace
Of how the beach was red hot underfoot,
The green gold of the Christmas beetle's wing.

Transit Visa

He had not thought that it would be his task
To gauge the force of the oncoming wave
Of night; to cast aside his jester's mask,
Guessing it was not Ali Baba's cave
That would engulf him, but an emptiness
Devoid of treasure heaped to serve his dreams;
His best hope, to be set free from distress.
No guiding light, not even moonlight beams,
Will lead him forward to find life refined
Into a fit reward or punishment:
No soul can well continue when the mind
Fades with the body. All his store is spent
Of pride, or guilt, or anything that might
Have steeled him for the non-stop outbound flight

Were it to lead somewhere, but it does not.
That much becomes clear as the sky grows dark.
He hears the rattle of his childhood cot,
The rain that fills the creek that floods the park:
But these are memories. The way ahead
Will send no messages that can be kept.
One doesn't even get to meet the dead.
You planned to see the bed where Dido slept?
No chance. It didn't last the course. Back then
They forged the myths that feed our poetry
Not for our sake, but theirs, to soothe them when
Life was so frightful that death had to be
A better place, a holiday from fear.
But now we know that paradise is here,

As is the underworld. To no new dawn
He gets him gone, nor yet a starry hour
Of silence. He goes back to being born
And then beyond that, though he feels the power
Of all creation when he lifts a book,
Or when a loved face smiles at his new joke,
Which could well be his last: but now just look
At how the air, before he turns to smoke,
Is glowing in the window. If the glass
Were brighter it would melt. That radiance
Is not a way of saying this will pass:
It says this will remain. No play of chance
From now on includes you. The world you quit
Is staying here, so say goodbye to it.

Japanese Maple

Your death, near now, is of an easy sort.
So slow a fading out brings no real pain.
Breath growing short
Is just uncomfortable. You feel the drain
Of energy, but thought and sight remain:

Enhanced, in fact. When did you ever see
So much sweet beauty as when fine rain falls
On that small tree
And saturates your brick back-garden walls,
So many Amber Rooms and mirror halls?

Ever more lavish as the dusk descends
This glistening illuminates the air.
It never ends.
Whenever the rain comes it will be there,
Beyond my time, but now I take my share.

My daughter's choice, the maple tree is new.
Come autumn and its leaves will turn to flame.
What I must do
Is live to see that. That will end the game
For me, though life continues all the same:

Filling the double doors to bathe my eyes,
A final flood of colours will live on
As my mind dies,
Burned by my vision of a world that shone
So brightly at the last, and then was gone.

Balcony Scene

Old as the hills and riddled with ill health,
I talk the talk but cannot walk the walk
Save at the pace of drying paint. My wealth
Of stamina is spent. Think of the hawk,
Nailed to its perch by lack of strength, that learns
To sing the lark's song. What else can it do,
While dreaming of the day its power returns?
It is with all my heart I write to you.

My heart alone is what it always was.
The ultrasound shows nothing wrong with it,
And if we smile at that, then it's because
We both know that its physical remit
Was only half the task the poor thing faced.
My heart had spiritual duties too,
And failed at all of them. Worse than a waste
Was how I hurt myself through hurting you.

Or so he says, you think. I know your fear
That my repentance comes too easily.
But to discuss this, let me lure you here,
To sit with me on my stone balcony.
A hint of winter cools the air, but still
It shines like summer. Here I can renew
My wooing, as a cunning stranger will.
His role reversed, your suitor waits for you.

The maple tree, the autumn crocuses –
They think it's spring, and that their lives are long –
Lend colour to the green and grey. This is
A setting too fine for a life gone wrong.
It needs your laughter. Let me do my best
To earn that much, though you not find me true,
Or good, or fair, or fit for any test.
You think that I don't know my debt to you?

High overhead, a pair of swallows fly,
Programmed for Africa, but just for now
They seem sent solely to enchant the eye
Here in this refuge I acquired somehow
Beyond my merit. Now a sudden wave
Of extra sunlight sharpens all the view.
There is a man here you might care to save
From too much solitude. He calls for you.

Here two opposing forces will collide –
Your proper anger and my shamed regret –
With all the weight of justice on your side.
But once we gladly spoke and still might yet.
Come, then, and do not hesitate to say
Art thou not Romeo, and a Montague?
Be wary, but don't brush these words away,
For they are all yours. I wrote this for you.

Sunset Hails a Rising

O lente, lente currite noctis equi!
Marlowe, after Ovid

La mer, la mer, toujours recommencée.
Valéry

Dying by inches, I can hear the sound
Of all the fine words for the flow of things
The poets and philosophers have used
To mark the path into the killing ground.
Perhaps their one aim was to give words wings,
Or even just to keep themselves amused,
With no thought that they might not be around
To see the rising sun:
But still they found a measure for our plight
As we prepare to leave the world of men.
Run slowly, slowly, horses of the night.
The sea, the sea, always begun again.

In English of due tact, the great lines gain
More than they lose. The grandeur that they keep
From being born in other tongues than ours
Suggests we will have time to taste the rain
As we are drawn into the dreamless sleep
That lasts so long. No supernatural powers
Need be invoked by us to help explain
How we will see the world
Dissolve into the mutability
That feeds the future with our fading past:
The sea, the always self-renewing sea.
The horses of the night that run so fast.

Selected Song Lyrics

Prefatory Note

This selection from the song lyrics I have written for the music of Pete Atkin adds up to less than half of the total in existence. I have left out all the love songs. (There was a time when that sentence would have started me writing another one.) Many of them I am quite proud of and I hope there is none without its turn of phrase. But they are all written within the courtly love tradition; and are thus mainly more about the loss of love than its acquisition; and so, without the music to help them sound universal, they give the exact effect of a single, lonely man crying repeatedly into his beer.

Other strong candidates for exclusion were those lyrics, mainly from early on, which needed too much help to get started from phrases unwittingly lent by Ronsard, Nerval, Laforgue, Apollinaire, Leopardi, Rilke, W. B. Yeats or T. S. Eliot. Some of the lyrics I have included do indeed contain literary allusions, but the allusions are not the driving force. When listened to, such anacreontic borrowings can add to the texture without insisting on separate notice. But on the page, if they come too thick and fast, they can look like a misplaced claim to erudition. In the nineteenth century, Thomas Moore, for the publication of his collected lyrics along with his poems, would unapologetically gloss his Latin and Greek borrowings with learned footnotes, to a total length that often exceeded that of the lyric itself. Still feeling obliged to prove his kinship with learned colleagues, he failed to realize that when his lyrics were sung in the salons, they silenced not only the audience but the competition. With the living laurels already his, he went on striving for the bronze simulacrum, never publishing even the slightest lyric about a shy damsel of Dublin without appending some supererogatory rigmarole about an intransigent priestess on the island of Hypnos. Today the practice would look absurd, not because the lyrical tradition is less robust but because it is much more so. If Dorothy Fields could draw a perfect lyric from what she heard on the sidewalk or in the subway, we can expect no points for flagging the help we got from Dante.

As for the lyrics that have been included, the first criterion was that they should have enough poetic content to be of interest when read. But they would be true poems only if they could altogether do without their common organizing principle, which was music. Deprived of that, they are something else. I hope they are not something less, but some readers might decide they can be safely skipped. Other readers, however, might be encouraged to seek them out in recorded form. If that happened, I could give myself credit for a cunning plan.

The Master of the Revels

Allow me to present myself, my ladies
And gentlemen of this exalted age
Before my creatures take the stage
For I am the Master of the Revels
In what appertains to mirth I am a sage

I work myself to death for each production
And though the world's great wits are all on file
I have not been known to smile
For I am the Master of the Revels
And mastery demands a certain style

In my office hang the blueprints
Of the first exploding handshake
And the charted trajectories of custard pies
For Harlequin ten different kinds of heartbreak
For Columbine the colour of her eyes

Some other windows darken in the evening
And never before morning show a light
But for me there is no night
For I am the Master of the Revels
The caller-up and caster-in of devils
And I am here for your instruction and delight

The Ice-cream Man

This afternoon the ice-cream man
Has driven his magnetic van
From Angkor Wat or Isfahan
To park down by the meadows

The captain of a pirate ship
He struggles hard to keep his grip
With cannonades of strawberry whip
Delivered through the windows

A battered Bedford Dormobile
Done over pink for eye appeal
With rainbow discs on every wheel
It makes a magic wagon

A mass of metal glorified
Sesame thrown open wide
And this amazing man inside
Fantastic as a dragon

It must be standing on tiptoe
And reaching up to trade your dough
For scoops of technicolor snow
That makes the man look royal

To me he looks a normal bloke
With a second line in lukewarm Coke
Busting for a decent smoke
To break the round of toil

I guess I've got a jaundiced eye
The children never spot the lie
They're queueing up and reaching high
For something that tastes lovely

Neapolitan wafers make the day
The king is in his castle gay
And they're behind him all the way
Below me they're above me

Who'd guess from how they make a meal
With darting tongue and teeth of steel
From a mess of frigid cochineal
That they were born to sorrow

Gone to dust the age of kings
Lost the taste for simple things
If only time would give me wings
I'd double back tomorrow

Stranger in Town

I never will remember how that stranger came to town
He walked in without a swagger, got a job and settled down
The place would have seemed the same without him
And now I can't recall a thing about him

He didn't wear a poncho or a gun with a filed sight
And he wasn't passing through like a freight train in the night
He rarely wore a Stetson with a shadowy big brim
And I still can't be sure if he was him

From Kansas to Wyoming, from Contention to Cheyenne
His name meant less than nothing and it didn't scare a man
So folks didn't worship him or fear him
And I can't remember ever going near him

He didn't tote a shotgun with the barrels both sawn off
So people didn't hit the deck or dive behind a trough
He walked the street in silence, ignored on every side
And it's doubtful if he could even ride

I never could remember how that stranger met his death
He was absolutely senile and with his dying breath
He forgot to ask his womenfolk to kiss him
And afterwards they didn't even miss him

Nothing Left to Say

The breakers from the sea that kept me sane
Were clean and lucid all along the line
Like shavings tumbled upward from the plane
That leave with ease the surface of the pine
When the carpenter is planing with the grain
It's nothing
Nothing but a dream of mine

    And I have come to nothing in a way
    That leaves me with nothing left to say

Half a lifetime bending with the breeze
To buy the stuff I don't know how to use
A deck of credit cards, a bunch of keys
A station I achieved but didn't choose
The screws are on and no one beats the squeeze
It's nothing
Nothing I can't bear to lose

    And I have come to nothing in a way
    That leaves me with nothing left to say

The sea I dreamed of closes like a vice
Parading waves are frozen into place
Their veils of vapour scattering like rice
And far below, the ultimate disgrace
A mermaid crushed to death inside the ice
It's nothing
Nothing but a frightened face

    And I have come to nothing in a way
    That leaves me with nothing left to say

National Steel

Shining in the window a guitar that wasn't wood
Was looking like a silver coin from when they still were good
The man who kept the music shop was pleased to let me play
Although the price was twenty times what I could ever pay

    Pick it up and feel the weight and weigh the feel
    That thing is an authentic National Steel

A lacy grille across the front and etchings on the back
But the welding sealed a box not even Bukka White could crack
I tuned it to an open chord, picked up the nickel slide
And bottlenecked a blues that sounded cold yet seemed to glide

    The National Steel weaves a singing shroud
    Just as sure as men in winter breathe a cloud

Scrapper Blackwell, Blind Boy Fuller and Blind Blake
Son House or any name you care to take
And from many a sad railroad, mine or mill
Lonnie Johnson's bitter tears are in there still

    Be certain, said the man, of who you are
    There are dead men still alive in that guitar

Back there the next morning half demented by desire
For that storybook assemblage of heavy plate and wire
I sold half the things I valued but I'll never count the cost
While I can pick a note like broken bracken in the frost

    And I hear those fabled names becoming real
    Every time I feel the weight or weigh the feel
    Of the vanished years inside my National Steel

I See the Joker

Mornings now I breakfast in the tower
Then travel thirty floors to the garage
My sons are with me even underground
With nothing but our gun-cars all around
From anything but nuclear attack
That place is safe, but when I cut the pack I see the Joker
I cut the pack and see the Joker

The forecourt is crawling with our boys
A heavy weapon rides in every car
My Cadillac's a safe-deposit box
With plastic armour in the top and sides
Solid like a strongroom in Fort Knox
And all along the parkway into town
We're covered for a mile front and back
By Family cars, but when I cut the pack I see the Joker
I cut the pack and see the Joker

Who is this guy and why does he want me?
This city has been ours since Christ knows when
At first from booze and girls and junk, and then
Legitimate, from rents and industry
The Chief of Police is ours to buy and sell
The DA and the Mayor are ours as well
There's no one left to fight, the enemy
Are dead and gone, or just some juicehead black
Loose with a knife, but when I cut the pack I see the Joker
I cut the pack and see the Joker

The cops are checking each incoming flight
For solo hitmen with an urge to die
No one gets in here by day or night
Without I don't know who they are and why
I'm in the clear, at barely fifty-five
One of the most respected men alive
Some blubber here and there, but nothing slack
I'm right on top, but when I cut the pack I see the Joker
I cut the pack and see the Joker

We do the journey different every day
Today we hit the garment district first
Then double back and take the boulevard
And as we drive I don't know which is worst
To know he'll come but not to know the way
To know he'll make a play but not know how
Is he somewhere out there setting up the gun?
Is this headache from his crosshairs on my brow?
There's no way, not a crevice, not a crack
That he can reach me, but when I cut the pack I see the Joker
I cut the pack and see the Joker

Sessionman's Blues

I've got the sessionman's blues
I played on three albums today
I paid a sessionman's dues
I played what they told me to play
Then I climbed in my Rover three-litre and motored away

    I've got the sessionman's blues
    The squattin' in a booth alone blues

I've got the sessionman's blues
But I get the dots right from the start
I drink a sessionman's booze
But my tenor blows what's on the chart
A single run through and I've got the whole solo by heart

    I've got the sessionman's blues
    The squattin' in a booth alone
    Isolated microphone blues

I've got the sessionman's blues
I'm booked up a lifetime ahead
I get a sessionman's news
The voice on the blower just said
They want me to work on the afternoon after I'm dead

    I've got the sessionman's blues
    The squattin' in a booth alone
    Isolated microphone
    Doublin' on baritone blues

My Egoist

The garden was in bloom, my egoist
The light was right, the show was very brave
You simply had to shy your hat away and rave
Because the colours looked so gay

The garden was your home, my egoist
You grew blasé, you asked 'What else is new?'
Or perhaps it crushed your spirit, it was all for you
And the surroundings were too plush

The garden felt your loss, my egoist
And what it gained were others not your kind
At first the heavy-handed came and finally the blind
Until nothing looked the same

The garden is alone, my egoist
They've all flown on, the butterflies of day
And nothing now takes flight above this sad display
Except the butterflies of night

Song for Rita

A tribute to Kris Kristofferson

The way my arms around you touch the centre of my being
As I step inside the marshland of your mind
Makes me weak inside my senses like a dog hit by a diesel
And more alone than Milton goin' blind

And I know I need to lose you if I ever want to find you
'Cause the poet's way is finished from the start
And I feel a palpitation kinda flutter in my forehead
As I think the problem over in my heart

    Yes I guess I'll always never know the question to your answer
    If I can't be doin' wrong by feelin' right
    But I'm really lookin' forward to how you'll be lookin' backward
    When I'm walkin' with you sideways through the night

I can keep this kind of writin' goin' more or less forever
But I can't undo destruction when it's gone
I can only think of you and what you cost me in hotel bills
As I settle down to dream of movin' on

If I've never longed to love you less than now you'll know the reason
Is because my whole desire is to sing
And everything I'm sayin' is the mirror of your beauty
As it hovers like a vulture on the wing

    Yes I guess I'll always never know the question to your answer
    If I can't be doin' wrong by feelin' right
    But I'm really lookin' forward to how you'll be lookin' backward
    When I'm walkin' with you sideways through the night

Senior Citizens

You've seen the way they get around
With nothing beyond burdens left to lose
The drying spine that bends them near the ground
The way their ankles fold over their shoes
They've had their day and half of the day after
And all the shares they ever held in laughter
Are now just so many old engravings
Their sands have run out long before their savings
And the fun ran out so long before the sands
They've lost touch with the touch of other hands
That once came to caress and then to help
A single tumble means a broken hip
The hair grows thinner on the scalp
And thicker on the upper lip
And who is there to care, or left to please?

It's so easy when we're young
For me to wield a silver tongue
And cleverly place you among
The girls the boys have always sung

It's so simple when it's you
For me to coax from my guitar
The usual on how fine you are
Like this calm night, like that bright star

And the rest would follow on
The rest would follow on

And there'll be time to try it all
I'm sure the thrill will never pall
The sand will take so long to fall
The neck so slim, the glass so tall

Shadow and the Widower

As we left each other on our final night
And I walked away with all the love remaining
A classic whisper near the station wall
I could just hear without straining
Asked if I was scared to realize this was all
Disappointed there was only this much in it
The perfume and suppliance of a minute?
It was him – the Shadow and the Widower

There's that all right, I said, and so much more
An hour of life inside a world of dying
A wider limit set to one's regard
The kinder forms of lying
And beyond all that the privilege of a memory scarred
In prettier ways than most, perhaps than any
Such a fate must seem desirable to many
Even you, the Shadow and the Widower

The classic laughter echoed near the wall
A strip torn from a three-sheet stirred and fluttered
The whisper said, Well don't that just beat all
What this oracle hath uttered?
A straight-up scalp-collector I could understand
All those lineaments of gratified desire
But he's handing me that old refining fire
This to me, the Shadow and the Widower

The whisper moved with me into the light
Where the access tunnel ran beneath the tracks
The wind searched for a way back to the night
But no romance, no lonely alto sax
Just litter and the notes left for the blacks
The graffiti stopped your pulse like heart attacks

To perdition with that rarefied regret
Those half-remembered ladies swathed in yearning
Said the whisper just an inch behind my head
The world is burning
And the tales of love fit for the guiltless dead
Will have little in them of the airs and graces
With which your tender soul goes through its paces
Commit that to your fragrant memory
And while you're doing that, remember me
The Shadow and the Widower

Payday Evening

Of late I try to kill my payday evenings
In many an unrecommended spot
Curiosity accounting for a little
Loneliness accounting for a lot

The girls who pull the handles force their laughter
The casual conversation's not the best
Indifference accounting for a little
Unhappiness accounting for the rest

And the gardens of the heyday in Versailles
And Pompadour's theatre in the stairs
Should be created in my magic eye
From a jukebox and a stack of canvas chairs

But somehow we have failed to come through
The styles are gone to seed, no more parades
There seems to be no talk of me and you
No breath of scandal in these sad arcades

Concerning us there are no fables
No brilliant poems airily discarded
Just liquid circles on Formica tables
A silence perhaps too closely guarded

Outside a junkie tries to sell his girl
Her face has just begun to come apart
Look hard and you can see the edges curl
Speed has got her beaten at the start

And what care these two for a broken heart?

The lady's calling Time and she is right
My time has come to find a better way
A surer way to navigate at night
The poetic age has had its day

In midnight voices softer than a dove's
We shall talk superbly of our lost loves

Screen-freak

You've got to help me, doc, I see things in the night
The tatters of my brain are bleached with flashing light
Just the way Orion's sword is pumping stars in flight
My mind's eye's skies are glittering and white

The Lady in the Dark has shot the Lady from Shanghai
The Thin Man and the Quiet Man are comin' through the rye
At Red Line Seven Thousand there's No Highway in the sky
The villains are the deepest but they plumb refuse to die

    Dance, Ginger, dance
    The caftan of the caliph turns to powder at your glance

The Ambersons have spiked the punch and livened up the ball
Cagney's getting big and Sydney Greenstreet's getting small
The Creature from the Black Lagoon left puddles in the hall
And Wee Willie Winkie is the most evil of them all

Strangers on a Wagon Train have crashed the China Gate
The Portrait of Jennie has decided not to wait
The Flying Leathernecks arrived a half a reel too late
The Broadcast wasn't big enough and Ziegfeld wasn't great

    Dance, Ginger, dance
    The caftan of the caliph turns to powder at your glance
    This one for Funny Face and Fancy Pants

The love of Martha Ivers caused the death of Jesse James
Kitty Foyle guessed it though she didn't link their names
I've seen the plywood cities meet their doom because of dames
Atlantis down in bubbles and Atlanta up in flames

And I've seen the Maltese Falcon falling moulting to the street
He was caught by Queen Christina who was Following the Fleet
And Scarface found the Sleep was even Bigger than the Heat
When he hit the Yellow Brick Road to where the Grapes of Wrath
    are sweet

    Dance, Ginger, dance
    The caftan of the caliph turns to powder at your glance
    This one for Funny Face and Fancy Pants
    A buck and wing might fix the Broken Lance
    And break my trance

The Double Agent

Your manifest perfections never cease
To drive the day-long terrors out of mind
They are the lights the darkness hides behind
Allowing satisfaction its increase
Beyond the petty boundaries designed
To keep us well aware the world's unkind
And still your eyes proclaim a reign of peace

A ruined man falls sideways far away
And too far gone to see my lady's hair
Supposing he was here or she was there
My lover's mouth has not a word to say
To stanch the flow or slow him on his way
It sends a smile to me across the air
And still I feel that fortune smiles today

Between the breaking of your morning bread
And the final pretty speeches of the night
A million destinies drop out of sight
A million people get it in the head
You join the silks and perfumes of your bed
Like a long delightful insult to the dead
And still your breast is where I'd lay my head

Forgive, forget the rest of what I said
And still your breast is where I'd lay my head

A King at Nightfall

The ring hangs on a string inside your shirt
You wedge the stable door
You eat your beans and bunk down in the straw
A king at nightfall

    You're going to have to learn to live with this
    As you work or beg your way towards the border
    And shade your face to miss
    The multiplying eyes of the new order

You spun the crown away into a ditch
And saw the water close
The army that you fed now feeds the crows
A king at nightfall

    You're going to have to watch your manners now
    And never let your face show what you're missing
    Don't wait for them to bow
    Stick out your hand for shaking, not for kissing

Tomorrow's men who trace you from the field
Will be in it for the bread
There'll be a price on your anointed head
A king at nightfall

    You're going to have to learn how quick to run
    And that means slowly, watching all the angles
    Don't try to use that gun
    Stay very loose and cool and out of tangles

You reach to brush your collar free of straw
And then you feel the string
There's light enough for one look at the ring
And it's lovely but it doesn't mean a thing
A king at nightfall
A king at nightfall

Apparition in Las Vegas

When the King of Rock and Roll sang in the desert
He didn't seem to age like other men
To Vegas came the ladies with pink rinses
Agog to see the dreamboat sail again

To Vegas came the shipwrecked and the broken
Their long regrets, their searing midnight rages
Their disappointment seldom left unspoken
In marriages that turned to rows of cages
He wrote and bound the book of which their early
    aspirations were the pages

When the King of Rock and Roll sang in the desert
With a ring of confidence around his smile
He sparkled like the frosting on a drumkit
He was supple as the serpent of the Nile

To Vegas came the ladies with pink rinses
With all their ills and all their soured karma
With all their pills and all their tics and winces
To feel again the liberating drama
Of a shining silver buckskin suit against a solid purple
    cyclorama

When the King of Rock and Roll sang in the desert
He broke no hearts that hadn't burst before
To Vegas came the ladies with pink rinses
It was they and never he that knew the score
And knowing that they only loved him more

To Vegas came the debris of an era
For the promise that no longer could deceive them
Their eyes grew misty as their sight grew clearer
With a drum roll the past began to leave them
And it all drew further from them as the spotlight caught
    the King and brought him nearer

Be Careful When They Offer You the Moon

Be careful when they offer you the moon
It gives a cold light
It was only ever made to light the night
You can freeze your fingers handling the moon

Be careful when they offer you the moon
It's built for dead souls
It's a colourless and dusty ball of holes
You can break an ankle dancing on the moon

When you take the moon you kiss the world goodbye
For a chance to lord it over loneliness
And a quarter-million miles down the sky
They'll watch you shining more but weighing less

So be careful when they offer you the moon
It's only dream stuff
It's a Tin Pan Alley prop held up by bluff
And nobody breathes easy on the moon
Nobody breathes easy on the moon
Count to ten when they offer you the moon

Touch Has a Memory

Touch has a memory
Better than the other senses
Hearing and sight fight free
Touching has no defences
Textures come back to you real as can be
Touch has a memory

Fine eyes are wide at night
Eyelashes show that nicely
Seeing forgets the sight
Touch recollects precisely
Eyelids are modest yet blink at a kiss
Touching takes note of this

When in a later day
Little of the vision lingers
Memory slips away
Every way but through the fingers
Textures come back to you real as can be
Making you feel
Time doesn't heal
And touch has a memory

Frangipani Was Her Flower

Frangipani was her flower
And amethyst her birthday stone
The fairest blossom of the bower
She wasn't born to be alone
And now she was terribly alone

A Ford Cortina was the car
Eleven thirty-five the hour
The squeak of gravel in the drive
Left the damsel in the tower
Pondering her vanished power

Always, everything had gone so well
Her dolls had been the best
She was better than the rest
Always, everything had gone so well
The world at her behest
Had fed her from the breast

Always, everything had gone so well
She was married all in white
To a lad serenely trite
Always, everything had gone so well
And on her wedding night
Things had more or less gone right

By fairest fortune she was kissed
Frangipani was her bloom
A silver spoon was in her fist
Upon emerging from the womb
Tonight she wrecked the room

The Rider to the World's End

From a phrase by Lex Banning

You simply mustn't blame yourself – the days were perfect
And so were exactly what I was born to spoil
For I am the Rider to the World's End
Bound across the cinder causeway
From the furnace to the quarry
Through the fields of oil

And I left you with the sign of the Rider to the World's End
It was not the mark of Zorro
Written sharply on your forehead with a blade
Just a way of not turning up tomorrow
And of phone calls never made

My time with you seemed ready-made to last for always
And so was predestined to be over in a flash
For I am the Rider to the World's End
Bound across the fields of oil
Through the broken-bottle forest
To the plains of ash

And I left you with the sign of the Rider to the World's End
It was not the ace of diamonds
Or the death's head of the Phantom on your jaw
Just a suddenly relaxing set of knuckles
Never rapped against a door

You were more thoughtful for and fond of me than I was
And so were precisely what I can never trust
For I am the Rider to the World's End
Bound across the plains of ashes
To the molten metal valleys
In the hills of dust

No Dice

I tried hard to be useful, but no dice
With no spit left I couldn't soften leather
With these old hands I couldn't even sew
So yesterday they left me on the ice
I could barely lift my head to watch them go
The sky was white, my eyes grew full of snow
And whatever reached me first, bears or the weather
I just don't know
Yesterday was oh so long ago – so very long ago

I saw across our path through the lagoon
Thick shrubberies of hail collide and quarrel
Sudden trees of shellburst hump and blow
Our LVT turned through the reef too soon
The front went down, we all got set to go
But the whole routine was just too friggin' slow
What kind of splinters hit me, steel or coral
I just don't know
Yesterday was oh so long ago – so very long ago

We hit the secret trails towards thin air
Aware we'd never live to tell the story
And at the last deep lake before the snow
We rigged the slings, chipped out the water-stair
Swung out the holy gold and let it go
It sank so far it didn't even glow
And if the priests died too to share our glory
I just don't know
Yesterday was oh so long ago – so very long ago

Yesterday we finished with the ditch
We stacked our spades and knelt in groups of seven
Our hands were wired by an NCO
With a fluent-from-long-practice loop and hitch
No dice – there was nothing left to throw
A bump against your neck and down you go
And if I kept my peace or cried to heaven
I just don't know
Yesterday was oh so long ago – so very long ago

Yesterday from midnight until dawn
I lay remembering my lost endeavour
The love song that would capture how things flow
The one song that refuses to be born
For I have tried a thousand times or so
To link the ways men die with how they grow
But no dice, and if I'll do it ever
I just don't know
Yesterday was oh so long ago

Driving through Mythical America

Four students in the usual light of day
Set out to speak their minds about the war
Unaware that Eddie Prue was on the way
Things had to snap before they knew the score

They were driving through mythical America

    A Rooney–Garland show was in the barn
    Fields was at the Pussycat Cafe
    No one had even heard of Herman Kahn
    And Jersey Joe was eager for the fray

Four students had to take it in their stride
And couldn't feel the road beneath the wheels
Of the car they didn't know they rode inside
Across the set and through the cardboard hills

They were driving through mythical America

    They sold their Studebaker Golden Hawk
    And bought a Nash Ambassador Saloon
    Bogart said 'Even the dead can talk'
    And suddenly the coats were all raccoon

Four students never knew that this was it
There isn't much a target needs to know
Already Babyface had made the hit
And Rosebud was upended in the snow

They were driving through mythical America

Gatsby floated broken in the pool
The Kansas City Seven found a groove
Barrymore and Lombard played the fool
And Cheetah slowly taught John Wayne to move

Four students watched the soldiers load and aim
And never tumbled they were on the spot
Moose Malloy pulled ten years on a frame
The dough was phoney and the car was hot

They were driving through mythical America

Henry Ford paid seven bucks a day
Rockwell did the covers on the *Post*
FDR set up the TVA
And the stars rode silver trains from coast to coast

Four students blinked at ordinary skies
But the sunlight came from thousands of motels
A highway through the night was in their eyes
And waiting at the roadblock Orson Welles

They were driving through mythical America

Four students never guessed that they were through
Their history had them covered like a gun
It hit them like a bolt out of the blue
Too quick to grasp and far too late to run

They crashed and died together in the sun

They were driving through mythical America

Thief in the Night

A guitar is a thief in the night
That robs you of sleep through the wall
A guitar is a thin box of light
Throwing reflections that rise and fall
It reminds you of Memphis or maybe Majorca
Big Bill Broonzy or Garcia Lorca
A truck going north or a cab to the Festival Hall

And the man who plays the guitar for life
Tests his thumbs on a slender knife
Forever caresses a frigid wife
His fingers travel on strings and frets
Like a gambler's moving to cover bets
Remembering what his brain forgets
While his brain remembers the fears and debts

Long fingernails that tap a brittle rhythm on a glass
Around his neck a ribbon with a little silver hook
Like some military order second class
You can read him like an open book

From the hands that spend their lives creating tension
From the wrists that have a lean and hungry
Eyes that have a mean and angry look
A guitar is a thief in the night
That robs you of sleep through the wall
A guitar is a thin box of light
Throwing reflections that rise and fall
A guitar reminds you of death and taxes
Charlie Christian outplaying the saxes
The beginners' call and the very last call of all

Practical Man

Last night I drank with a practical man
Who seemed to think he knew me well
He had no debts and he had no troubles
All night long he kept setting up doubles
And he asked me 'What have you got to sell?'

'I'll see you right' said the practical man
'A boy like you should be living high
All you do is get up and be funny
And I'll turn the laughs into folding money
Can you name me anything that can't buy?'

'So you deal in dreams' said the practical man
'So does that mean you should be so coy?
I fixed one chap a show on telly
Who limped like Byron and talked like Shelley
Through a ten-part epic on the fall of Troy'

'I'll tell you what' said the practical man
As he tapped the ash from a purple fag
'Let's head uptown for a meal somewhere
You can sing me something while we're driving there
There's a grand piano in the back of my Jag'

So I sang my song to the practical man
It sounded bad but she couldn't hear
And the silent lights of town went streaming
As if the car was a turtle dreaming
The night was sad and she was nowhere near

'It's a great idea' said the practical man
As they brought in waiters on flaming swords
'You love this chick and it's really magic
But she won't play ball – that's kind of tragic
Now how do we get this concept on the boards?'

'I see it like this' said the practical man
As he chose a trout from the restaurant pool
'We change it round so she's going frantic
To win the love of the last romantic
And you're the one, her wild creative fool'

So I thought it all over as the practical man
Watched them slaughter the fatted calf
I saw again her regretful smile
Sweet to look at though it meant denial
It was bound to hurt but I had to laugh

And that's when I told the practical man
As he drank champagne from the Holy Grail
There are some ideas you can't play round with
Can't let go of and you can't give ground with
'Cause when you die they're what you're found with
There are just some songs that are not for sale

Cottonmouth

Cottonmouth had such a way of saying things
Phrases used to fly like they were wearing wings
Never had to weigh a word
Said the first thing that occurred
And round your head the stuff he said went running rings

Cottonmouth, what a brain
Absolutely insane

Cottonmouth would tell the girls he sighed for them
He talked of all the lonely nights he cried for them
Afterwards they told their men
I just saw Cottonmouth again
That guy's a scream, and never guessed he died for them

Cottonmouth, what a brain
Absolutely insane

Cottonmouth packed up one day and did a fade
Turned edgeways on and vanished like a razor blade
Considering how people here
Are downright simple and sincere
It could have been the smartest move he ever made

Beware of the Beautiful Stranger

On the midsummer fairground alive with the sound
And the lights of the Wurlitzer merry-go-round
The midway was crowded and I was the man
Who coughed up a quid in the dark caravan
To the gypsy who warned him of danger
'Beware of the beautiful stranger'

'You got that for nothing' I said with a sigh
As the queen's head went up to her critical eye
'The lady in question is known to me now
And I'd like to beware but the problem is how
Do you think I was born in a manger?
I'm in love with the beautiful stranger'

The gypsy (called Lee as all soothsayers are)
Bent low to her globular fragment of star
'This woman will utterly screw up your life
She will tempt you from home, from your children and wife
She's a devil and nothing will change her
Get away from the beautiful stranger'

'That ball needs a re-gun' I said, shelling out
'The future you see there has all come about
Does it show you the girl as she happens to be
A Venus made flesh in a shell full of sea?
Does it show you the shape of my danger?
Can you show me the beautiful stranger?'

'I don't run a cinema here, little man
But lean over close and tune in if you can
You breathe on the glass, give a rub with your sleeve
Slip me your wallet, sit tight and believe
And the powers-that-be will arrange a
Pre-release of the beautiful stranger'

In the heart of the glass I saw galaxies born
The eye of the storm and the light of the dawn
And then with a click came a form and a face
That stunned me not only through candour and grace
But because she was really a stranger
A total and beautiful stranger

'Hello there' she said with her hand to her brow
'I'm the one you'll meet after the one you know now
There's no room inside here to show you us all
But behind me the queue stretches right down the hall
For the damned there is always a stranger
There is always a beautiful stranger'

'That's your lot' said Miss Lee as she turned on the light
'These earrings are hell and I'm through for the night
If they'd put up a booster not far from this pitch
I could screen you your life to the very last twitch
But I can't even get the Lone Ranger
One last word from the beautiful stranger'

'You live in a dream and the dream is a cage'
Said the girl 'And the bars nestle closer with age
Your shadow burned white by invisible fire
You will learn how it rankles to die of desire
As you long for the beautiful stranger'
Said the vanishing beautiful stranger

'Here's a wallet for you and five nicker for me'
Said the gypsy 'And also here's something for free
Watch your step on my foldaway stairs getting down
And go slow on the flyover back into town
There's a slight but considerable danger
Give my love to the beautiful stranger'

Have You Got a Biro I Can Borrow?

Have you got a biro I can borrow?
I'd like to write your name
On the palm of my hand, on the walls of the hall
The roof of the house, right across the land
So when the sun comes up tomorrow
It'll look to this side of the hard-bitten planet
Like a big yellow button with your name written on it

Have you got a biro I can borrow?
I'd like to write some lines
In praise of your knee, and the back of your neck
And the double-decker bus that brings you to me
So when the sun comes up tomorrow
It'll shine on a world made richer by a sonnet
And a half-dozen epics as long as the *Aeneid*

Oh give me a pen and some paper
Give me a chisel or a camera
A piano and a box of rubber bands
I need room for choreography
And a darkroom for photography
Tie the brush into my hands

Have you got a biro I can borrow?
I'd like to write your name
From the belt of Orion to the share of the Plough
The snout of the Bear to the belly of the Lion
So when the sun goes down tomorrow
There'll never be a minute
Not a moment of the night that hasn't got you in it

Laughing Boy

In all the rooms I've hung my hat, in all the towns I've been
It stuns me I'm not dead already from the shambles that I've seen
I've seen a girl hold back her hair to light a cigarette
And things like that a man like me can't easily forget

I've got the only cure for life, and the cure for life is joy
I'm a crying man that everyone calls Laughing Boy

A kid once asked me in late September for a shilling for the guy
And I looked that little operator in her wheeling-dealing eye
And I tossed a bob with deep respect in her old man's trilby hat
It seems to me that a man like me could die of things like that

I've got the only cure for life, and the cure for life is joy
I'm a crying man that everyone calls Laughing Boy

I've seen landladies who lost their lovers at the time of
    Rupert Brooke
And they pressed the flowers from Sunday rambles and then
    forgot which book
And I paid the rent thinking 'Anyway, buddy, at least you
    won't get wet'
And I tried the bed and lay there thinking 'They haven't
    got you yet'

I've got the only cure for life, and the cure for life is joy
I'm a crying man that everyone calls Laughing Boy

I've read the labels on a hundred bottles for eyes and lips and hair
And I've seen girls breathe on their fingernails and wiggle them
    in the air
And I've often wondered who the hell remembers as far back as
    last night
It seems to me that a man like me is the only one who might

I've got the only cure for life, and the cure for life is joy
I'm a crying man that everyone calls Laughing Boy

Sunlight Gate

The heroes ride out through the Sunlight Gate
And out of the sunset return
I have no idea how they spend their day
With a selfless act, or a grandstand play
But high behind them the sky will burn
In the glittering hour of return

The heroes ride out in unbroken ranks
But with gaps in their number come back
I have no idea how they lose their men
To some new threat, or the same again
But they talk a long while near the weapon stack
In the clattering hour they come back

The heroes return through the Sunset Gate
But their faces are never the same
I have no idea why their eyes go cold
And the young among them already look old
But high behind them the sky's aflame
In the flickering hour of their fame

The Faded Mansion on the Hill

When you see what can't be helped go by
With bloody murder in its eye
And the mouth of a man put on the rack
The voice of a man about to crack

When you see the litter of their lives
The stupid children, bitter wives
Your self-esteem in disarray
You do your best to climb away
From the streaming traffic of decay

Believing if you will that all these sick hate days
Are just a kind of trick fate plays
But still behind your shaded eyes
That mind-constricting thick weight stays

When on the outskirts of the town
Comes bumping cavernously down
Out of the brick gateways
From the faded mansion on the hill
The out-of-date black Cadillac
With the old man crumpled in the back
That time has not yet found the time to kill

Between the headlands to the sea the fleeing yachts of
    summer go
White as a sheet and faster than the driven snow
Like dolphins riding high and giant seabirds flying low

And square across the wind the cats and wingsails pull
    ahead
Living their day as if it almost could be said
The cemetery of home could somehow soon be left for dead

But the graveyard of tall ships is really here
Where the grass breaks up the driveway more each year
And here is all these people have
And everything they can't retrieve

The beach the poor men never reach
The shore the rich men never leave

Between the headlands from the sea the homing yachts of
    summer fill
The night with shouts and falling sails and then are still
The avenues wind up into the darkness of the hill
Where time tonight might find the time to kill

Thirty-year Man

Nobody here yet
From the spotlight that will ring her not a glimmer
Not a finger on its squeaky dimmer
I play piano in a jazz quartet
That works here late with a young girl singer

    And along from the darkened and empty tables
    By the covered-up drums and the microphone cables
    At the end of the room the piano glistens
    Like the rail at the end of the nave

    Thirty years in the racket
    A brindled crew cut and a silk-lined jacket
    And it isn't my hands that fill this place
    It's a kid's voice still reaching into space
    It's her they're driving down to hear
    And it's my bent-over back she's standing near

Nobody talks yet
From the glasses that will touch soon not a tinkle
Not a paper napkin shows a wrinkle
I play piano in a jazz quartet
That backs a winner while the big notes crinkle

    And along from the darkened and empty tables
    By the covered-up drums and the microphone cables
    At the end of the room the piano glistens
    Like the rail at the end of the nave
    And I play a few things while no one listens

Thirty years in the racket
A brindled crew cut and a silk-lined jacket
And it isn't my name that brings them in
It's a little girl just starting to begin
It's her they're piling in to see
And I'd kill that kid if she wasn't killing me

Nobody moves yet
From the tables near the bandstand not a rustle
Not a loudmouth even moves a muscle
I play piano in a jazz quartet
That backs a giver while the takers hustle

And along from the darkened and empty tables
By the covered-up drums and the microphone cables
At the end of the room the piano glistens
Like bones at the end of a cave
And I play a few things while no one listens
For an hour alone spells freedom to the slave

Carnations on the Roof

He worked setting tools for a multi-purpose punch
In a shop that made holes in steel plates
He could hear himself think through a fifty-minute lunch
Of the kids, gas and stoppages, the upkeep and the rates
While he talked about Everton and Chelsea with his mates

With gauge and micrometer, with level and with rule
While chuck and punch were pulsing like a drum
He checked the finished product like a master after school
The slugs looked like money and the cutting-oil like scum
And to talk with a machinist he made signals like the dumb

    Though he had no great gifts of personality or mind
    He was generally respected, and the proof
    Was a line of hired Humbers tagging quietly behind
    A fat Austin Princess with carnations on the roof

Forty years of metal tend to get into your skin
The surest coin you take home from your wage
The green cleaning jelly only goes to rub it in
And that glitter in the wrinkle of your knuckle shows your age
Began when the dignity of work was still the rage

He was used and discarded in a game he didn't own
But when the moment of destruction came
He showed that a working man is more than flesh and bone
The hands on his chest flared more brightly than his name
For a technicolor second as he rolled into the flame

Though he had no great gifts of personality or mind
He was generally respected, and the proof
Was a line of hired Humbers tagging quietly behind
A fat Austin Princess with carnations on the roof

The Hypertension Kid

Last night I met the Hypertension Kid
Grimly chasing shorts with halves of bitter
In a Mayfair club they call the Early Quitter
He met my eyes and hit me for a quid

'I spend fortunes in this rat-trap' said the Kid
'But the plush and flock soak up the brain's kerfuffle
And I like to see a servile barman shuffle
If sympathy's your need let's hear your bid'

'It's my lousy memory' I told the Kid
'What other men forget I still remember
The flies are still alive inside the amber
It's a garbage can with rubbish for a lid'

'Your metaphors are murder' said the Kid
'I know the mood – give in to it a little
The man who shatters is the man who's brittle
Lay off the brakes and steer into the skid

'Strained virtue warps the soul' announced the Kid
'Those forced attempts at cleanliness that linger
Like soap between your wedding ring and finger
They're residues of which you're better rid

'For evil' said the Hypertension Kid
'Is better contemplated in the deeds of others
Mass murderers and men who knife their mothers
Be glad that what you've done is all you did

'With me the problem's women' said the Kid
'Befuddled, fondled under separate covers
One and all they've gone to other lovers
As I powered down to zero from the grid

'But I love the little darlings' sighed the Kid
'The slide from grace is really more like gliding
And I've found the trick is not to stop the sliding
But to find a graceful way of staying slid

'As for the dreadful memories' said the Kid
'The waste and poison in the spirit's river
Relax your hands and let the bastards quiver
They tremble more the more you keep it hid'

We turned to leave the bar, me and the Kid
I with lightened head and lessened terror
Toward the street, and he into the mirror
My second self, the Hypertension Kid

Perfect Moments

Perfect moments have a clean design
Scoring edges that arrest the flow
Skis cut diamonds in the plump of snow
Times my life feels like a friend of mine

Perfect moments wear a single face
Variations on each other's theme
Renoir's mistresses in peach and cream
Rembrandt's mother in a ruff of lace

Perfect moments bear a single name
They're placed together though they never meet
Charlie Chaplin policing Easy Street
Charlie Parker playing 'My Old Flame'

Perfect moments should redeem the day
Their teeming richness ought to be enough
To take the sting out of the other stuff
A perfect bitch it doesn't work that way

The Road of Silk

And still his dreaming eyes are full of sails
The tree house leaves the peach tree like a bird
In time the swelling bark takes in the nails
Of those adventures nothing more is heard
Easy
Let him sleep now
Not a word

He's losing what he hardly knew was there
The lead dragoons pack up and quit the tray
The early snowfalls lift into the air
The Road of Silk rolls backward from Cathay
Easy
Let him sleep now
Come away

His fondest memories have left their mark
For just so long as lipstick on a glass
The highway scatters jewellery through the dark
The circus leaves a circle on the grass
Easy
Let him sleep now
Let it pass

The Hollow and the Fluted Night

This kind of ocean fails to reach the coast
A special famine rages at the feast
The one loved most is always present least

You are the loved one, very nearly here
Who did not feel so far away before
But now I fear our separation more

The hollow and the fluted night that weaves
The cloth combining loves divides their lives
Black velvet hills between the silver knives

The sunlight on the windowsill kowtows
And opens up the sky to further skies
For all the thousand miles to your eyes

The realization daunts the both of us
And so we draw a deep breath through a kiss
When was it ever otherwise than thus?
And what goodbyes are more alone than this?

Secret Drinker

Perching high like an old-time man of law
He travels on a bar stool to enchanted lands
And as the world before him swims and glows
The secret drinker's only sure that he is real
By the feel of his elbows and the steadily increasing
Weight of his forehead in his hands

    And behind the bar
    Like turreted and battlemented towns of long ago
    The lines of coloured bottles swim and glow
    Brilliantly as at the day of wrath
    Or the year of the comet
    But the secret drinker is far from it
    Away from it all

He can ease the present back into the past
Staring at the pastels and the prisms on the shelf
With the magic words that make the evening last
The same again and have one for yourself

    He's a connoisseur
    He can space it out with chasers, he can let it burn
    It's a trick it takes a little while to learn
    You might see the youngsters of today sniff a cork
       and they vomit
    But the secret drinker is far from it
    Away from it all

He can make the looming future lose its sting
Staving off the pressure is a bargain at the price
Of the magic words that make the angels sing
The same again, go easy on the ice

Perching high like an old-time man of law
He travels on a bar stool to enchanted lands
And as the world before him swims and glows
The secret drinker's only sure that he is real
By the feel of his elbows and the steadily increasing
Weight of his forehead in his hands that should be ceasing
To tremble by now and beginning to resemble
The hands of a man he used to know

Search and Destroy

I'm glad to say we're mopping up up here
I'm sending you today's report in clear
Security's no problem now at all
You just pick up the phone and make a call

　　We should have done all this back at the beginning
　　And never let the clowns think they were winning

We took a month to crack their second man
But when he talked the strudel hit the fan
He named eleven leaders who we shot
And then the top guy's girl who we've still got
The chick was tough and held out for a week
But spilled a bibful when we made her speak
We picked his mother up and worked on her
He came in on his own and there you were

　　We should have nailed the first ones when we found them
　　Before all the mystique built up around them

We never gave the local heat a chance
To get him on their own and make him dance
We did him in upcountry, bombed the cave
And made the whole damn mountainside his grave
The faithful talk some wishful-thinking cock
About a spook who rolls away the rock
At which point golden boy walks out alive
We're bumping them all off as they arrive

　　And that winds up this dreary exhibition
　　A total waste of time and ammunition

Tenderfoot

Beyond the border town they call Contrition
The badlands are just boulders and mesquite
A school of Spanish friars built the mission
But left because they couldn't take the heat
And further on the road to Absolution
The mesas turn to mountains capped with snow
And the way becomes a form of execution
That only hardened travellers can go

    You can tell the horseman grieves for how he sinned
    He rides a killing trail
    Reminded of his hard heart by the hail
    And of his folly by the chilling wind

By day the canyon ramparts blaze their strata
Like purple battlements he shall not pass
The sunlight sears the horseman like a martyr
The glacier's a magnifying glass
And by night the clouds black out the constellations
While veils of icicles lock up his eyes
He moves by echo through the cold formations
Walls of drift and ice-fall fall and rise

    You can tell the horseman grieves for how he sinned
    He rides a killing trail
    Reminded of his hard heart by the hail
    And of his folly by the chilling wind

He knows he made pretence of love too often
His deadly carelessness went on for years
At dawn the shields on his eyes will soften
And all of his regrets will be in tears
But far too late to go back and be gentle
Or say how clearly now it comes to mind
His pride at never being sentimental
Was just a clever way to be unkind

You can tell the horseman grieves for how he sinned
He rides a killing trail
Reminded of his hard heart by the hail
And of his folly by the chilling wind

Around him lie the stunning and the drastic
Where nothing but the utmost can be felt
The temperatures will always be fantastic
Noon will never cool nor midnight melt
A fitting climate for one so unfeeling
Who once was so indifferent to distress
He's goaded onward with his senses reeling
Without the prospect of forgetfulness

You can tell the horseman grieves for how he sinned
He rides a killing trail
Reminded of his hard heart by the hail
And of his folly by the chilling wind

The golden handshake and the lightning kisses
Were all his for the asking in the past
But the subtlety and softness that he misses
For them the horseman always moved too fast
And now at last to contemplate his error
Facing the dimensions of his loss
He journeys where the sky meets the Sierra
That every man alive must one day cross

You can tell the horseman grieves for how he sinned
He rides a killing trail
Reminded of his hard heart by the hail
And of his folly by the chilling wind

Care-charmer Sleep

I've come to think
Of what you are and everything you seem
As mine to keep
I am the sleep of which you are the dream

A state of mind
Where seeing you and thinking are the same
But there's a catch
I strike a match to set the glass aflame

And pale purple on a clear liqueur
That ring of light is all we ever were

So slight a thing
In no one's mind should ever reign supreme
I'm in deep
I am the sleep of which you are the dream

Canoe

The perfect moon was huge above the sea
The surf was easy even on the reef
We were the lucky three
Who slid in our canoe
Through the flowers on the water
And tried to read the signals in the sky

We travelled with our necklaces of shell
The moon was waning through the nights and days
And how we dreamed of home!
We couldn't find the island
Where you trade the shells for feathers
We fainted in the sun's reflected blaze

With cracking lips I turned to tell my friends
The time had come for all of us to die
'She's out a whole degree'
I told them as I floated
Checking navigation read-outs
'Re-enter at this angle and we'll fry'

The go for override came up from Earth
We took control and flew her with our hands
And how we dreamed of home!
We saw the South Pacific
As we fought to get her zeroed
Before the heat shield started hitting air

We came home in a roaring purple flame
And gave the mission back to the machines
We were the lucky three
The parachutes deployed
We were rocking like a cradle
As we drifted down in silence to the sea

I Feel Like Midnight

I feel like midnight
And whether a new day
Will ever dawn
Is just a guess

I see by starlight
The long road from the day
That I was born
To this address

And I look at where you slept
And I taste the tears you wept
And you're here again except
I feel like midnight

I feel like midnight
And you are here again
To mock me with a smile
Each time I say

I feel like midnight
And the only chance I had
To rest a while
I threw away

Give me a break
Give me the break of day –
I feel like midnight

Ready for the Road

A belt with a bull's head for a buckle
High boots that satisfy the western code
A signet ring the size of Samson's knuckle
And I'm gettin' ready for the road

I'm gettin' ready, I'll soon be good an' ready
Yes I'm gettin' ready for the road
I'm gettin' ready, yes I'll soon be good an' ready
For the road

Blue jeans that clutch me tighter than a pipe wrench
Two guns it took a forklift truck to load
I feel like I'm standin' in a slit trench
But I'm gettin' ready for the road

For the road is the home of a troubadour
And a troubadour is what I am
And I travel the trail of a troubadour
From the Empire Pool to Birmingham

But my heart belongs to Tulsa and to Tucson
For me the Alamo is à la mode
And just as soon as my horse can get its shoes on
I'll be ready for the road

I'm gettin' ready, I'll soon be good an' ready
Yes I'm gettin' ready for the road
I'm gettin' ready, yes I'll soon be good an' ready
For the road

Commercial Traveller

Home early from a meeting of the reps
He leaves the cream-bath samples in the car
A pull-along gorilla guards the steps
Confusion leads to where the children are
At the sandpit
In the garden

He wades into the kitchen through the toys
His wife leans to kiss him with a smile
And neither knows how much distance led to this
How long the while
Since on the sand spit
In the morning
The hero
Lay asleep
Until
The nymph adored him

The early dawn was baby-lotion pink
And softer than the suds of Infacare
She laved him of his brine and saw him blink
He woke to see the sunburst in her hair
And be her captive
Always

He hails the children playing in the sand
Solves the padlock on the garden shed
A giant bow should be waiting for his hand
But there instead
Lie all the implements

Of duty
For centuries
Employed
By the prisoner
On his island

He plants the hose and sets the nozzle fine
Embellishing his roses with the spray
And rainbows of a sea as dark as wine
On which he will never sail away
He will never sail away
He will never sail away

Urban Guerrilla

Automatic weapons rake the roof
Powdered concrete hangs around like spray
He huddles underneath the parapet
And knows there is no way –
This is as far as he will get

The hostages and all his friends are dead
His turn is coming soon
What was it that motherfucker said?
Better chance of conquering the moon
He holds his ringing head

    The happy endings never came
    The terrors were seldom just a dream
    Bambi was finished by the flame
    You still could hear him scream

    Snow White was rubbed out by the witch
    Mary Poppins never made the scene
    Mother Goose was just another bitch
    Full of bullshit like the Fairy Queen

The gas grenades are telling him to run
He does and something stops him like a wall
It puts him back where he has always been
His nightmares laugh to see him fall

I told you they were gonna bust your ass
Says Tom Thumb inside an upturned glass

The Eye of the Universe

I have been where time runs into time
And so partaken of the vanished glamour
Have seen Atlantis and the perfect crime
Felt eloquence replace my mental stammer
Seen every evil brought beneath the hammer
In this mood all that Faust desired is mine

I am the eye with which the universe beholds itself
And knows itself divine

I have been to see my death prepare
Inside a Packard, somnolently cruising
The sure-fire way of giving me the air
And totting up exactly what I'm losing
Found such an end not too far from my choosing
I have settled up with Charon at the Styx

I am the eye with which the universe beholds itself
And knows itself a fix

I've crossed an atlas with the Golden Horde
Seen all the Seven Cities of Cibola
Olympus was a geriatric ward
The Promised Land is just the old payola
It's all the same shellac, the same Victrola
Eternity should have more in the bag

I am the eye with which the universe beholds itself
And knows itself a drag

I have been where age runs into age
Have seen the children burned, the slaves in halters
The cutting edge is wearing off my rage
I leave them their strange gods, their reeking altars
And the way the reign of terror never falters
They were fighting for the right to count the slain

I am the eye with which the universe beholds itself
And knows itself insane

I have seen the gentle meet the savage day
In the sunlight on the spandrels of the towers
And in the moonlight very far away
The honeymoon canoe glide through the flowers
And the party left behind go on for hours
For a while things were as peaceful as they seemed

I am the eye with which the universe beholds itself
And knows itself redeemed

My Brother's Keeper

My brother lives in fear
Of the hidden cries he seems to hear
Somewhere ahead the King of Hell
Somewhere below a kitten in a well

Am I my brother's keeper?
Am I my brother's keeper?

My brother lives a lie
When his laughter splits the summer sky
Somewhere inside he skips a breath
Somewhere in there he dies the little death

Am I my brother's keeper?
Am I my brother's keeper?

Every second morning now for years
My brother has put on my brawn and brain
To wander through the universe in pain
And my happiness of yesterday
Is walked and scorned away
Before he returns to me in tears

My brother lives a life
In the narrow shadow of the knife
Somewhere behind a hill of skulls
Somewhere below a beach of dying gulls

Am I my brother's keeper?
Am I my brother's keeper?

History and Geography

The history and geography of feeling less than wonderful
    are known to me
The dates of broken bubbles and the whereabouts of every
    lost belief
And from the point of tears I see how far away across the
    of troubles
The pinnacles of happiness are halfway hidden in the clouds
    sea of grief

My common sense can tell me all it likes to count myself
    among the lucky
For pity's sake to draw a breath and take a look around me
    and compare
But all I seem to see and hear is something I'm unable to
    remember
The flowing speech that stuttered out, the pretty song that
    faded on the air

When the jet returns me half awake and half asleep to what
    I call my homeland
I look down into the midnight city through the empty inkwell
    of the sky
And in that kit of instruments laid out across a velvet-covered
    table
I know that nothing lives which doesn't hold its place more
    worthily than I

Without a home, without a name, a girl of whom to say this is
    my sister
For I am all the daughters of my father's house and all the
    brothers too
I comb the rubble of a shattered world to find the bright face
    of an angel
And say again and say again that I have written this – this is
    for you

The history and geography of feeling less than wonderful are
    known to me
When sunsets are unlovely and the dawns are coldly calculated
    light
And from the heights of arrogance across the steps that later
    I regretted
I see those angel faces flame their last and flicker out into the
    night

Femme Fatale

It isn't fear I feel, or lack of nerve
Call it just a sensible reserve
When faced with the intoxicating verve
Of anyone who dazzles me like you
The children turning flint-wheels in the mines looked pretty too
And sparks were shaken out like golden rain
And oh so very lovely were the loneliness and pain

It's not because I'm burning out or old
I hesitate to snuggle in the fold
Of body heat that really beats the cold
Though Icarus flew near the sun and fell
The chandeliers above the weeping fields looked warm as well
And flares would crumple down like fairy lights
And oh so very lovely were the long and fearful nights

It's all because you are too much for me
Too good to last, too beautiful to be
That you are doomed to be a casualty
Of the night fight on my deeps of memory
A galleon with fire below falls glowing through the sea
And every mast shall tremble like a tree
And oh so very lovely shine the blast that breaks them free

A Hill of Little Shoes

I live in the shadow of a hill
A hill of little shoes
I love but I shiver with a chill
A chill I never lose
I live, I love, but where are they?
Where are their lives, their loves? All blown away
And every little shoe is a foot that never grew
Another day

If you could find a pair and put them on the floor
Make a mark in the air like the marks beside your door
When you were growing
You'd see how tall they were

And the buckles and the laces they could do up on their own
Or almost could
With their tongue-tips barely showing
Tell you how small they were

And then you'd think of little faces looking fearfully alone
And how they stood
In their bare feet being tall for the last time
Just to be good
And that was all they were

They were like you in the same year but you grew up
They were barely even here before they suddenly weren't there
And while you got dressed for bed they did the same but they were led
Into another room instead
And they were all blown away into thin air

I live in the shadow of a hill
A hill of little shoes
I love but I shiver with a chill
A chill I never lose
And I caught that cold when I was chosen to grow old
In the shadow of a hill of little shoes

Dancing Master

As the world goes past me
I have enough to last me
As long as you come to call
And hang your coat and hat on the hook in the hall

This is the step we'll learn tonight
Turn on a dime and stay upright
Come back slowly in your own time
I'll wait for you

As the world goes past me
I have enough to last me
As long as we dance like this
And what a man's never had he will never miss

This is the way the step looks best
Keep it neat as you come to rest
And if my heart seems to skip a beat
Just wait for me

Just wait for me the way I wait for you
For all the endless hours in a week
This is the silent language lovers speak
When they mean nothing except what's true

Just wait for me the way I wait for you
To change your shoes before we say goodbye
This is the world where I will never die
Or lie awake for what I'm going through

As the world goes past me
I have enough to last me
As long as we dance like that
There's a hook in the hall and it's waiting for your coat and hat

I Have to Learn to Live Alone Again

I have to learn
To live alone again
I used to burn
To live alone again
But this is now
And that was then
And now I have to live alone again

Did you paint your bedroom gold the way you planned?
Is the same love song open on the music stand?
Not knowing things like that is part of missing you
As much as never touching you or kissing you

I cross the silver bridge and see your balcony
The vines have filled the trellis with a filigree
I had such plans to see the way your garden grew
But missing out on that is part of missing you
As much as never touching you or kissing you

I have to learn
To live alone again
I used to burn
To live alone again
But now I do
I wonder when
I'll ever learn
To live alone
Again

Winter Spring

This is the way that winter says goodbye to spring
By whispering we will not meet this year
This year I will not see you flower or hear you sing

The time is over now you could look back to me
And see the way the crocus cupped the snow
Part of the picture in your show of pageantry

The grass would not have been as green without the frost
The night prepares the splendour of the day
My hands were cold and now they're cold as cold can be
I fold them to my chest and turn away

This is the way that winter says goodbye to spring
By whispering we will not meet this year
This year I will not see you flower or hear you sing
Or taste the brilliance that you bring
To everything.

Notes

Four Poems About Porpoises

I wrote most of this suite of miniature poems in the Sunda Strait, on the ship to England. But the mention of 'Fylingdales' indicates that at least one of the poems was written after I got there. Situated in the North York Moors, Fylingdales, an American-designed Ballistic Missile Early Warning Station (BMEWS), came online in 1953, and was a key element of the NATO defence system throughout the Cold War.

The Banishment

The epigraph is from Dante, *Inferno*, Canto X, the episode featuring Dante's great political enemy Farinata degli Uberti. Standing in his grave in the burning cemetery of heretics, Farinata reminds Dante that when there was talk of destroying Florence, he, Farinata, was alone in defending her with his visor open, so that his face could be seen.

The Young Australian Rider, P. G. Burman

Largely due to the influence of my doomed friend, I knew an awful lot about competition motorcycles when I was young, and even in my old age I follow the Isle of Man TT races on television. Luckily I was able to keep most of my mugged-up technical knowledge out of the poem, but the reader might need to be told that for the post-war amateur bike-builders there was a crucial, snobbish difference between an overhead valve engine and a side-valve engine. The OHV delivered more power for the same capacity. 'One-lung three-fifty': a single cylinder engine of 350 cc swept volume. Further up the scale of desirability and power, an OHV engine with valves actuated by push-rods was outranked by an OHV engine with camshafts. The racing bikes of the factory teams had camshafts; and the British AJS company revolutionized the sport by making its 7R camshaft racing model available on the commercial market. Suffice it to say that the technical information in the poem would be enough to tell an aficionado that my friend was trying to do the whole thing on a shoe-string.

A Line and a Theme from Noam Chomsky

Though I eventually came to view Noam Chomsky's political opinions as adding up to a toxic attack on the liberal outlook he professed to support, I was immensely impressed by his first theoretical work in linguistics. As an undergraduate in Cambridge I caught a train to Oxford just to hear him expound his concept of deep grammar, and I was never more thrilled by a lecture in my life: it was better than listening to Isaiah Berlin. But I did notice a flaw in Chomsky's contention that a string of words – 'Colourless green ideas sleep furiously' was the example he concocted – could be completely meaningless. Not, I thought, if you could sufficiently widen the context.

Reflections on a Cardboard Box

Hostathion and Triazophos were two different pesticides that I somehow encountered in the form of empty cardboard boxes marked with their names. The boxes came in handy for transporting books during a move in Cambridge from one address to another, just around the corner. At one point the work got too tiring and I sat down to write this poem. God knows how I got the idea that insane barbarism was a thing of the past.

Will Those Responsible Come Forward?

The line 'Lest the Druze and the Jews or the Juze and the Drews' can't be made to work when recited. After I found this out the hard way, I took care to make every line of verse I wrote pass the test of being read aloud.

Funnelweb

Apart from a few would-be Hart Crane efforts perpetrated in my student days in Sydney, I have only ever once set out to be obscure, and this poem was the result. Obscurity, in my view, is rarely a tolerable aim in the arts, although it may sometimes have to be put up with as an incidental result; and even for mere difficulty the only justification is a striving for simplicity; so a poem like this should normally be consigned to the oblivion with which it flirted. But there are things in it that I could not have said more clearly, so I have kept it, even though there are also things that demand explanation. Most of them can be tracked down on the Web, but some might prove elusive even then. The Banzai Pipeline is a surf reef break in Hawaii, off the north coast of Oahu: a gathering place for tube-riders, it also offers an excellent chance to get killed. A running W, back in the bad old days when Hollywood stunt arrangers were allowed to hurt animals, was a ruthless device to make a horse crash at the gallop. At the time I wrote the poem, Natalia Makarova, the only runaway Soviet female dancer to make the same impact as Nureyev and Baryshnikov, was the darling of Covent Garden. The dear friend with cancer was Penny Faber, much loved by our family. In the Ni-Jo Castle in Kyoto the nightingale floors were designed to make it impossible for any assassin to approach the Shogun's sleeping quarters unheard. 'Saito' was Lt General Yoshitsugu Saito, the officer in command on the island of Saipan in June 1944. At this point in the poem the narration is taken over by a US Marine who was not only in the frightful last battle against the Japanese garrison, but also witnessed the even more horrible events the next morning, when the Japanese civilians on the island committed suicide. Analysts of the casualty figures concluded, surely correctly, that the cost of invading the Japanese home islands would be ruinously high. The next two stops on the bitter trail through Japan's inner defences were Iwo Jima and Okinawa. Both battles were so expensive in American lives that they made the use of the atomic bombs against Hiroshima and Nagasaki inevitable, but really those cities had been already doomed before the fighting stopped on Saipan. Late in the poem, the atomic bombs mentioned are the ones held at the American airfields in East Anglia: as graduate students in Cambridge we were very aware of their nearby presence at that stage of the Cold War. One of the survivors of the Tokyo fire raid on the night of 10 March 1945 later described how he had been a member of a party that had dedicated itself to saving the Emperor's portrait from the flames. In a chapel built within the confines of KZ Dachau the nuns set themselves the task of keeping perpetual vigil: on a visit in 1983 I saw them praying. The stanza that begins 'High over Saipan' records a flight south I made in the 1970s from Tokyo to Sydney, during which I saw another airliner going in the opposite direction, unspooling a condensation trail that evoked, in my mind, the B-29s on their way from Tinian in the Marianas to their target cities in Japan; although, because of the jet stream over the home islands, most of the fire raids were carried out at low level. On the raids that delivered the atomic bombs, however, the planes flew high up.

The Light Well

The epigraph is from Fidel Castro's pamphlet *History Will Absolve Me*. 'We were born in a free country given to us by our fathers, and this island will sink into the sea before we consent to be the slaves of anyone.' At the time I first visited Cuba, almost twenty years after the battle at Playa Girón (the Bay of Pigs), you could still meet the winners in Havana, and the losers in Miami.

The Artificial Horizon

The epigraph, an anonymous Latin motto, translates as 'God navigates the ship.' Even today, with all kinds of electronic instrumentation to locate the aircraft's altitude in space, pilots are grateful to have a simple mechanical instrument to tell them, in dense cloud, whether they are still the right way up.

What Happened to Auden

'Chester' was Chester Kallman, Auden's lifetime companion. At the time I wrote the poem, everyone knew who Chester was, and that he could be hard on the nerves. After Auden's death Kallman could often be found lunching late in Soho, and complaining loudly that nobody would publish his poetry. But it was unwarrantedly brusque of me to first-name him. *Salonfähig*: ready for the salon, i.e. *sortable*. There is no real equivalent in English, except perhaps 'presentable'.

Lament for French Deal

The epigraph is from Virgil, *Georgics* IV, the sublime episode in which Eurydice berates Orpheus for looking back after he has been told not to. 'For I am carried folded in gigantic night/ Holding towards you the useless hands alas no longer yours.' On Sydney Harbour the little white-and-yellow-painted ferries that ran from Circular Quay over to Luna Park and McMahon's Point were eventually withdrawn in favour of the catamarans, just as the splendid double-ended ferries that ran to Manly gave way to the less imposing but much faster hydrofoils, which in turn were replaced by the JetCats. In the course of seven decades, romance has been usurped by efficiency, but whatever kind of ferry it is, it's still more fun than the bus, and the glitter on the water is always there.

The Eternity Man

For generations, everyone in Sydney knew about the lonely madman who wrote 'Eternity'. At the turn of the millennium, the word was written in huge copperplate fire on Sydney Harbour Bridge, to the puzzlement of the entire world.

In Praise of Marjorie Jackson

Scholars of Australian slang will notice that I use the correct term, Bondi Special, in my oblique reference to the hallowed motto 'He (or she, they or it) shot through like the Bondi Special'. The popular but corrupt version is 'shot through like a Bondi tram': more immediately appreciable, perhaps, but incorrect, because an ordinary Bondi tram would have stopped at every stop, whereas it was the Special, which usually ran late at night, that went non-stop all the way from the city to the beach. In her later life Marjorie Jackson was Governor of South Australia, and when I was filming in Adelaide she kindly invited me for a tour of her official residence. Among the trophies on display, along with her collection of Olympic and Commonwealth Games gold medals, was her famous first pair of running shoes, aptly made of kangaroo skin.

Lucretius the Diver

Though I wrote the poem in Europe, the reef I had in mind was far away, where Lucretius could never have suspected that it existed. But the Great Barrier Reef is always in the mind of any Australian who has ever seen it. In recent years, when the notion of man-made Climate Change took hold, along with all its gaggle of subsidiary predictions, the supposed threat to the Barrier Reef attained world-wide currency, but not so much within Australia, where the proprietorial pride of those specialists who had given their lives to studying and caring for the Reef tended to set aside the dire warnings from distant pundits. My own response to the Reef can be read in my poem 'The Great Wrasse', nominally a tribute to my distinguished compatriot Les Murray but also a salute to the South Pacific: the geographical extravaganza into which we both were born, not long before the whole area became a battlefield.

Edwin Estlin Cummings Dead

I wrote this all-purpose E. E. Cummings pastiche when I was still a student in Sydney, and still deeply in his debt, although no longer in his thrall. Since it was designed to spoof some of the sub-Apollinaire tricks that Cummings worked on the page, it couldn't really work in performance, though I sometimes had fun trying. And I hope even this squib conveys a hint of what I really got from him: with his acute ear for phonetic balance, he could make a line go like a Bunk Johnson trumpet solo. In the decades to come I got a lot of my ideas about the forward drive of a syncopated rhythm from jazz and rock and roll. Even today, when my feet are almost too tired to tap, my work in verse is less likely to be haunted by the Elizabethan sonneteers than by the Count Basie rhythm section or the Funk Brothers, the engine room of Tamla Motown.

Richard Wilbur's Fabergé Egg Factory

A parody is nearly always a tribute as well as a critique, and this imitation was a particularly obvious case of the double role. Michael Donaghy was right to call Wilbur the greatest modern phrase-maker: any mimic of his diction is obliged to dig deep, in the hard effort to bring to him what he brought to La Fontaine. Laforgue said 'Comme ils sont beaux, les trains manqués', so my transcription is almost right. Alekhine was the Russian chess master. All the other proper names are either self-explanatory or not crucial. Their prevalence is true to one of the chief pleasures offered by Wilbur's poetry when he came back to America after the fighting in Europe: he was a walking encyclopaedia, with a knack for making erudition an enchantment.

To Martin Amis: A letter from Indianapolis

The chosen form is the Spenserian stanza, in which two master-pieces are always with us to serve as models: Spenser's *The Faerie*

Queene and Shelley's magnificent elegy for Keats, *Adonais*. For any modern exponent of the form, the chief trick is to make a virtue of its obstacle: the alexandrine at the end of each stanza. In every other respect the Spenserian stanza is a playground for variations of tempo, although Hazlitt was probably right to say that the requirement of its rhyme scheme for a fourth rhyme was a hobble even for Spenser himself. To square myself with the petrol-heads, I should say that I wrote this poem so as to sweeten a bitter assignment: I always thought that racing in the Brickyard at Indianapolis was a waste of time compared with the merest event in Formula One, which only in later years became tediously processional.

To Tom Stoppard: a letter from London

Because of the frequent use of it by Burns, the form is usually called Burnsian metre. It has often been used for light verse ever since, but perhaps most infectiously by Auden and Isherwood as an inspired choral interruption (variously called 'The Two' or 'The Witnesses') in their early verse play *The Dog Beneath the Skin*. I first encountered the poem in the late 1950s in Sydney and it had an immediate effect on the rhythmic ambitions of my own work: it was such fun to recite. You could snap your fingers.

To Craig Raine: a letter from Biarritz

Borrowed from Italy, the stanza form called *ottava rima* comes so naturally to the writer of poetry in English that other, slightly different forms are often incorporated under the same name. Thus Auden's wonderful *Letter to Lord Byron* is often described as being in *ottava rima* when it is actually in rhyme royal. But no matter: as long as there is that temptingly punchy couplet at the end of the stanza.

The Great Wrasse: for Les Murray at sixty

People who live on or near the Great Barrier Reef usually pronounce 'wrasse' as two syllables, to rhyme with 'sassy'. This verse letter is composed in blank verse paragraphs, the most demanding form of the lot for anybody who is trying to keep things tight. At the time when my family was holidaying on Lizard Island, the tourist industry's light impact on the Reef had not yet been supplemented by the intense interest of countless television crews in the forthcoming climate catastrophe which would heat the water, raise the ocean, and reduce billions of tons of coral to a ruin any time soon. In the absence of such an event – nowadays still absent, but surely only minutes away – all was peace, and I lay down to begin reflecting upon my younger days. Necessarily there were a few references to Sydney University, which Les Murray and I both attended as beneficiaries of the Menzies Government's plan to extend tertiary education even further among the less well-off. 'Frensham girls' would have been to private schools: not among the less well-off at all, but with a bewitching access to silk and cashmere. Andersonians were acolytes of the Professor of Philosophy, John Anderson: to some extent I was one of them, and still am. The quotation in italics is from Anderson's key book *Studies in Empirical Philosophy*, which is still in the shelves before me as I write this. Toorak is a plush Melbourne enclave that ranks with Belgravia in London or the Sutton Place area in New York. In Australia, during the period of economic deregulation fostered by the Hawke and Keating governments, it was a regular event for some instant billionaire to become just as instantly broke again. Kerry Packer, however, always kept his money, perhaps because he carried a lot of it around in a paper bag. He and Rupert Murdoch were the big media tycoons, but whereas Rupert Murdoch went on to become world famous, Kerry Packer was, as the Australian saying goes, world famous in Australia. When the first atomic bomb was exploded at the 'Trinity' site in New Mexico, the desert at Ground Zero turned to green glass. Ginger Meggs was a young larrikin in a famous comic strip that we all read every Sunday: always in trouble but never unforgiven for very long.

To Leonie Kramer. . . A Report on My Discipline

The sprightly decorum of *ottava rima* is meant, in this case, to be a match for my view of the subject's achievement and personality. Leonie Kramer, both as a Professor of English and later in her role as Vice Chancellor of Sydney University, was a stickler for sound academic behaviour but found it within her heart to promote me for an honorary doctorate. In her youth she turned the heads of romantically minded men, and A. D. Hope's long poem *Letter from Rome* can be thought of not only as a satirical masterpiece, but as a love song. Almost as much as Auden's *Letter to Lord Byron*, it had a lasting influence on my own verse, for the way it helped me to realize how the play of tone could be wider the more strict the form. My admiration for Alfred Polgar I later expressed in greater detail in *Cultural Amnesia*: the phrase *'an den Rand geschrieben'* (written in the margin) was his title for one of his collections of pieces. At the time I wrote the poem, Marcel Reich-Ranicki's definitive six-volume Rowohlt edition of Polgar was still coming out. Regarded even by Thomas Mann as the greatest modern exponent of German prose, Polgar was the kind of writer that Leonie would have approved of: an untrammelled thematic scope based on perfect grammar. As her little book about the poet James McAuley attests, her cultural conservatism was adventurous: more so than his, in fact.

Under the Jacarandas

The jacarandas in question stand in the small park at the left-hand end of Sydney's Circular Quay, as you approach the quondam Maritime Services Building, a sandstone-clad Art Deco heirloom rather more distinguished than most of the creations to which it nowadays plays host in its new role as the Museum of Contemporary Art. In my later years, until illness stopped me flying, I was always glad to be in Sydney in October so that I could sit writing at my favourite table outside Rossini's and occasionally look up to watch the jacarandas raining purple. If the falling petals could have made a sound as they hit the grass, it would have been the slow scattering of individual piano notes in one of Debussy's *Images*, or perhaps the linked glissandi in the haunting voice of Gurrumul. Last time I saw them, the office workers taking their lunch on the grass looked as if they were posing for a plane-load of French Impressionists.

The Victor Hugo Clematis

The rockets and the Gothas are from Proust: a rare acknowledgement in his novel that a war is going on not far out of town.

Statement from the Secretary of Defense

Saddam Hussein's regime was so horrible that I was one of the many people who saw a good case for removing him from power, although a lot of them changed their minds retroactively when things went wrong. A strong suggestion that things would go wrong even in the event of a successful invasion was provided by the bizarre press conferences of the US Secretary of Defense Donald Rumsfeld, whose choice of language might have been dictated by Gilbert and Sullivan, or George Orwell in a vicious satirical mood.

The Australian Suicide Bomber's Heavenly Reward

Conceived as a satirical fantasy, this poem would have had some claim to prescience if it had not become evident that the kind of youngster volunteering as a suicide bomber is unlikely to be put off by the disinclination of those who assign him to his mission to share his fate. I neither foresaw, nor thought it possible, that Australia would ever become a hatchery for jihadis. But it continues to be a rule of modern politics that what the satirists think they have absurdly exaggerated today will come true tomorrow.

When We Were Kids

Most of the local references in this poem can be easily figured out, but a 'connie-agate' might prove a puzzle. It was a clear-glass marble with a polychrome spiral trapped inside it, like a Mandelbrot equation spun through three dimensions in a medium of liquid crystal. I found the first one I ever owned so fascinating to look into that I couldn't look away, and was several times found sitting hypnotized.

Ramifications of Pure Beauty

The designer of the various Focke-Wulf WWII fighter aircraft, Kurt Tank, was one of the understandably unsung heroes of modern sculpture. There was never any rational reason for WWII military aircraft to be graceful, so it remains remarkable that so many of them were: aerodynamic efficiency seemed to have beauty as a consequence. The British Spitfire, however, for all its ballerina-like glamour, was left standing by the American P-47, which had the same poise and delicacy as a charging buffalo. The National Gallery in London had a Titian exhibition in 2003: as usual, too many people came to see too many paintings, so hardly anybody saw anything.

Fires Burning, Fires Burning

The title of the poem came from my memory of a round that I was obliged to join in singing at Sydney Technical High School. The last line of the chorus before the round started again was 'Come sing and be merry'. For some reason I remembered this many years later when I first read about the killing fires of WWII. Perhaps one has an irony gene. If so, one needs to remember that no impulse is easier to overindulge. People with a gift for sarcasm can make you laugh, but only once.

Naomi from Namibia

I never forgot that the patently worthy and intelligent Naomi had to go home to Africa. What she should have done, while still on Australian soil, was commit a crime. Later on there was a celebrated case of a defiantly unassimilable illegal immigrant who, after living for several years on welfare, beat his wife to death, went to prison, got himself released on the grounds that his human rights had been infringed, and was compensated to the tune of several hundred thousand dollars.

Status Quo Vadis

This immortal piece of bad Latin can be heard spoken in that enchanted movie *Strictly Ballroom*, and therefore counts as classic Australian poetry on all levels.

We Being Ghosts

The title is a quotation from Louis MacNeice: 'For we being ghosts cannot catch hold of things'. Given his background in classics, MacNeice was more probably thinking of the vainly embracing ghosts in the *Aeneid*, rather than in the *Divine Comedy*. MacNeice, like his friend Auden, had the valuable gift of being able to make a classical reference sound like a natural flourish in conversation. It's a quality that makes the poetry of the Thirties a tunnel to the ancient world.

A Perfect Market

In the epigraph, *'plutost'* is left in the old spelling as a reminder that Ronsard, though he still sounds so modern, has been dead for several hundred years. His line '*Ronsard me célébrait du temps quand j'estois belle*' was one of the first things in French that I ever learned. It was a vengeful clincher to a recriminatory poem, but he wasn't really angry with the young lady: he was angry with time itself, and today I think of him often, toiling painfully up some spiral staircase in the Tuileries Palace to see the young Hélène, and well-knowing that she would grant him nothing except grief. He gave us a language for the lyricism of the long goodbye.

Spectre of the Rose

Young Ulrike lived to be an old lady and was many times pestered by arts-page gossip-writers (the breed was already in existence) to reveal whether she and her grand old man had ever been lovers in the technical sense. She did him the honour of playing it vague, instead of issuing a downright denial. The ageing Goethe, by his proposal of marriage, had made a tremendous fool of himself over her, but he had also written one of the great lyric poems in the German language, the *Marienbad Elegy*: a tribute she was perfectly capable of appreciating.

The Same River Twice

The poem is an apostrophe to Heraclitus, rather impatient with him for making such a fuss about the obvious.

Continental Silentia

The title is the brand name of a silent typewriter. *Sonderbehandlung* (Special Treatment) was a Nazi euphemism for extermination. After the war, the survivor Victor Klemperer analysed Nazi language in a brilliant little book called *LTI* (*Lingua Tertii Imperii* – Language of the Third Reich). 'List, oh list' and 'the rest is silence' are both from *Hamlet*. *Zum schweigen gebracht*: put to silence.

Language Lessons

The learned muse was a love object from Elizabethan times all the way through to the Brownings, but she is less so nowadays, strangely enough, when a male poet has a much better chance of falling mutually in love with a scholarly female, and even of getting married to her. It remains notable that Napoleon, an erudite man with his choice among all the unmarried young females of Europe and most of the married ones as well, and who took at least twenty upmarket mistresses during his career, was happiest with Marie Walewska, who had scarcely read a book; although perhaps he thought he could get all that from Josephine. She would read him the latest novels aloud when they travelled by coach. 'Ah, Orpheus,' is Eurydice complaining to Orpheus in my previously cited favourite passage of Virgil in *Georgics* IV: 'what is this madness?' (*Quis tantus furor?*) 'Like smoke mixed with thin air' (*ceu fumus in auras commixtus tenues*). The last line of the stanza alludes to the 'gigantic night' in the same passage, and also to the *Aeneid*, Book VI, where Aeneas, in one of the scenes that had a formative effect on Dante, is guided by the Sybil of Cumae through the halls of Dis and the empty regions (*perque domos Ditis vacuas et inania regna*). Virgil's gift for the music of lamentation still sets the mark for any poet wishing to register regret. In my poem, the lovers are doomed, but at least they are soothed by Virgil's plangent melodies, though we should remember that Keats struck the same measure for his runaway couple without being able to read Latin much at all: 'These lovers fled away into the storm'. Given time, Keats would undoubtedly have picked up all he needed of a classical education, simply because his perfect ear was hungry for past example.

Nimrod

I was impressed that when the city-state's Governor Chris Patten presided over the ceremony at which Hong Kong was handed back to China, he chose Elgar's *Nimrod* as the play-out music. The Tower of Babel is in the last line because Nimrod built it.

Culture Clash

In Japanese, *gaijin* (outside person) is the word, not always used politely, for a foreign stranger. The Floating World, *Ukiyo*, was the disreputable but vivid Yoshiwara district – kabuki, geishas, etc. – of Edo, once the capital of Japan, and later, under its new name Tokyo, the capital again. From the Floating World came the woodcuts (*Ukiyo-e*) whose attention to the space between objects influenced the post-Impressionists, and hence the whole of modern art in all its forms. The Lady Murasaki (Murasaki Shikibu) wrote *The Tale of Genji*, and thus, like Jane Austen, put the feminist credentials of her nation's literature beyond dispute.

Fashion Statement

In the blessed days when the trams still ran in Sydney, the toast-rack was the ideal tram, open to the breeze and with a running board on each side, so that the conductor could swing casually along and impress the girls while he collected the fares. It made me very much want to be a tram conductor, but alas I was too late, and I only got to conduct a bus, with the disastrous outcome related in my early book *Unreliable Memoirs*.

On Reading Hakluyt at High Altitude

In the excellent first-year English course at Sydney University we were meant to read Hakluyt's *Voyages* and I made a big mistake in not doing so, because I would have been equipped to face a lot earlier the possibility that some of the best literature is composed with no literary ambitions in mind. Concrete engagement trumps abstract pretension every time, and everything in Hakluyt is strictly reportage, with specific detail the common currency. It makes an unbeatable resource for poetry. In my first manuscript of this poem I followed Hakluyt in calling the Portuguese 'Portugals' but my editor thought it looked like a misprint. The last line shows my fascination with the slingshot effect that the unmanned space vehicles get as they thread the orbits from one planet to the next.

Dreams Before Sleeping

'Time, time, it is the strangest thing' is an allusion to the Feldmarschallin's sad line in Act One of *Der Rosenkavalier* when she faces the disaster of having turned thirty: *Die Zeit, die ist ein sonderbar Ding*. 'The bird sings with its wings' is one of the mystery messages from the underworld in Cocteau's film *Orphée*, which my group of Sydney University literati all quoted from until we became unbearable even to each other.

The Falcon Growing Old

At the end of the poem, the orange-blossom trellis in the oasis is a nod to Fauré's setting of the lyric by Leconte de Lisle *Les roses d'Ispahan*. The song was exhaustively imposed on me by my voice trainer, the late and cherished Ian Adam, who had been assigned the task of teaching me to breathe from the diaphragm so that I would stop running out of puff in the TV studio at the end of a two-day rehearsal period, just when the tape was ready to roll. Thus, as so often happens, the hard laws of business led to the materials of art.

Vertical Envelopment

Some of the American critics understandably failed to realize that the real setting of this poem was not a D-day airfield in East

Anglia but Addenbrooke's Hospital in Cambridge, where I had my life saved for the first time in the year 2010, but at the price of being led to believe that my combination of ailments added up to several different kinds of curtains. The drama of the poem's storyline thus consists of waiting for the signal to jump. 'Peter' was my friend Peter Porter, who died before I started the poem, and 'the Hitch' was another friend, Christopher Hitchens, who died not long after I finished it. SS *Das Reich*: the name of one of the Panzer divisions that, against all the confident predictions of British military intelligence, just happened to be parked ready and waiting in the drop zone at Arnhem. Edgar Orriss, our barman in the Cambridge Footlights clubroom during the 1960s, had been one of the glider troops on the operation and he told me that they might just as well have landed in a POW camp. The poem's narrator is not quite right to say that after Crete the German paratroopers never jumped again. A small *Kampfgruppe* jumped into the Battle of the Bulge, but its mission was a complete failure. The bulk of the German paratroopers who fought at Bastogne arrived at the battle after travelling over land. The same applied to the US 101st and 82nd Airborne, arriving from the opposite direction, some of their veteran soldiers no doubt wondering why they were not travelling by aircraft. The short answer to the puzzle is that the airborne tactic, for all its glamour and apparent might, had proved itself too vulnerable. 'Come, let us kiss and part' is from the first line of Michael Drayton's sonnet, which begins 'Since there's no help'.

Book Review

The eminent philologist Gianfranco Contini was the star professor at the University of Florence in the 1960s. He was the main reason why Prue Shaw, my future wife, was there, along with her studious friends, all of them sedulously copying down what Contini whispered as if it were a state secret. I myself was never equipped to follow his work at the level of scholarship, but he was also a critic and curator of modern writing. He acted as a mentor to Pasolini and was a close friend of Eugenio Montale, one of my heroes among the modern poets. (Contini's little book of essays on Montale, *Una lunga fedeltà* – A Long Faithfulness – is a model of the form.) In his more scholarly work Contini's prose style was notoriously over-condensed; and my wife was careful to absorb from him every influence except that. At the time of the poem she had not yet begun to write her pellucid handbook *Reading Dante*, but it was already clear that the analytical force of her writings was a tribute to her old professor. It was a long faithfulness.

The Later Yeats

The form of this poem depends on the idea that to use whole sonnets for stanzas might be a way of paying tribute to the majesty of Yeats's final masterpieces. 'Our books are drowned' is a reference to Prospero's farewell scene in *The Tempest*.

Castle in the Air

The last stanza was meant to be a would-be heroic fantasy, with the choice of diction indicating that the boast was a pose. Nevertheless there were one or two tone-deaf critics who preferred to think that I was claiming a kind of death-bed *droit du seigneur*. In their dreams. The poem's narrator is past all that.

Bubbler

For the conferring of an honorary doctorate from Sydney University, I was asked to give an address, and while speaking with apparent fluency I was still recovering from the impact of having found that almost every graduating student sitting there politely in the Great Hall was of Asian origin. Pam Yao Ming, the maths whizz in my poem, was probably one of them.

The Shadow Knows

The line 'I am the shadow and the widower' is taken from Gérard de Nerval's desolate poem 'El Desdichado', written not long before his suicide. (Years before, I had borrowed the same desperate idea for a song lyric, to be found in the final section of this book.) As a corrective, the title is a catchline from the radio show *The Shadow*, which I listened to regularly early in my hidden career as a leader of secret night-time gangs.

Grief Has Its Time

The title expression can be found in Boswell's *Life of Samuel Johnson*, as can the story about the King emerging from a hidden door in the library. The other quotations from Johnson are my inventions. The old lady in the signing queue is not an invention, but she is a compilation. My first landlady in London, whose basement bedsit I rented during the hard winter of 1963, lost her fiancé in World War I: she had a book of Rupert Brooke poems in which she had pressed some flowers that she and her young man had picked together.

Epigraph for Sentenced to Life

The epigraph is yet another borrowing from Rilke, whose lost tomb is so often plundered that there ought to be a five-star hotel on the site. He had a tone of sex-soaked spirituality that nobody wants to own but anybody might need to rent, like morning dress. The translation is my own.

Driftwood Houses

The 'skeleton riders' lie prone on minimal toboggans that carry them at high velocity down the frozen chute with their noses an inch from the ice. Luge riders lie supine and see the sky, but they look ridiculous. Either way, it comes under the heading of the kind of sports I never dreamed of doing but which showed up in my nightmares when I was ill. Another one was weightlifting: female weightlifting.

My Home

In Kogarah I went to the local Presbyterian church and was therefore subjected to quite a lot of pipe-band music, a massed caterwaul marching and counter-marching seemingly without end. The only bearable number was the lament 'My Home', perhaps because there was only one set of pipes playing it. As I recall, it was played at the funerals of both King George VI and Winston Churchill, and on each occasion I grew wet-eyed watching.

Tempe Dump

When I was young, the name of the Sydney suburb Tempe was so closely associated with industrial waste that I later thought Keats was joking when he used the name Tempe as short-hand for Arcadia. Later still, while I was living in England, Tempe dump disappeared among the new constructions for the railway approach to Sydney Airport. *Sic transit gloria mundi.*

Managing Anger

An outstanding piece of angry male thespian shelf-clearing is accomplished by Val Kilmer in the movie *Heat*, with Ashley Judd betraying no sign of anger that she will have to clean up the ruins. She is angry, but for other reasons, one of which might be Val's fixed pout, which stays in place even when he is redistributing the crockery. The propensity of male actors to wreck the room was pioneered by Marlon Brando in the Broadway production of *A Streetcar Named Desire*. Actors who wanted to be Brando were from then on encouraged to smash up the set by directors who wanted to be Elia Kazan. No union of stage-hands ever protested:

putting the set back together got them into overtime. As usual, only the public suffered.

Too Much Light

The title was not meant as a contradiction of Goethe's supposed dying demand for more light: *'Mehr Licht! Mehr Licht!'* It's a translation of a remark in Eugenio Montale's criticism, where he contends that a work of art can suffer from too much study. Since Montale himself was a supreme student of poetry in several languages, it was a generous statement. Montale was the poet who defined the poem as 'a dream in the presence of reason', still the best definition I have ever heard.

The Emperor's Last Words

The sudden appearance of Napoleon (like his hero Julius Caesar, he was a master of quick movement) in the thoughts of a dying poet is not necessarily a mark of succumbing to a senescent mad interest in military dominance. It could equally be a sign of finally getting interested in literature. Certainly Napoleon was. He underestimated Shakespeare in the same way as he underestimated the English navy, but in all other respects he had a voracious and adventurous curiosity for history and the arts. Goethe in his old age said that the time he spent talking about tragedy with Napoleon was the high point of his life.

Bugsy Siegel's Flying Eye

The mention of Ava Gardner might seem gratuitous, but I should confess that when I was twelve years old her appearance in *Pandora and the Flying Dutchman* marked me for life, and that I was forever afterwards the Dutchman, played by James Mason as the commander of a ghost ship who was given to reciting quatrains from the Fitzgerald translation of *The Rubaiyat of Omar Khayyam* while he sailed in perpetual search of the woman who would redeem him from his anguish. Later on, when I met my future wife, it turned out that she was in perpetual search of James Mason. My mother cherished the copy of the Fitzgerald *Rubaiyat* from which she and my father had once read aloud together. She would read it to me with what I can now recall as a naturally sensitive attention to the stanza form. In the key line 'Nor all thy tears wash out a word of it' she would give the word 'tears' precisely the light but slightly lingering emphasis that it required.

Leçons de ténèbres

Though the title phrase is well known to all musicians and music lovers who have ever come across the name of Couperin, I myself encountered it in *One Art*, the treasure house of Elizabeth Bishop's collected correspondence. She used the phrase untranslated in a letter to Marianne Moore. After I fell ill and the light sometimes seemed on the point of fading, I turned to Elizabeth Bishop's poetry more and more often, and even now I still wonder how she got the effect of the sandpiper thinking bird thoughts as it walks along the beach.

Only the Immortal Need Apply

The scene at the Russian Ballet ('*Tableau! Scandale!*' as the central figure might have said) is taken from Lucy Hughes-Hallett's biography of Gabriele d'Annunzio, *The Pike*.

Mysterious Arrival of the Dew

In this poem every line of the first stanza, with the addition of only a single word, is a *trouvaille* taken from a single paragraph of one of the later novels in Patrick O'Brian's Jack Aubrey sequence. Goethe calls the dew *Zitteperlen* (shiver-pearls) in *Faust*.

Sunset Hails a Rising

The title started life as a line in a poem by Francis Webb, an Australian poet of the previous generation who spent much of his life as a mental patient. His poems rarely cohered but some of them contained fragments too beautiful to forget. In the same poem, the line from *Doctor Faustus* about the horses of the night was taken from *Ovid* by Marlowe, who left it in the Latin, changing only the word order. The line from Valéry can be found in *Le Cimetière marin*, best translated by Derek Mahon: although the two translations here, like the two translations from Marlowe's Latin, are both my own.

Notes for the Song Lyrics

Nothing Left to Say

This lyric is one of my earlier efforts and clear proof that the idea of facing the end appealed to me at the start: but only, I insist, as subject matter. Just as, in the history of song writing, there are more songs about losing love than finding it, so there are more songs about winding things up than pressing on. One of the several big changes that rock and roll made to Tin Pan Alley was that it increased the vocabulary of a life worth living.

National Steel

Pete's acquisition of an authentic National Steel guitar gave me the chance to write the lyric for a catalogue song, as it is called in the trade. In this case the catalogue was of the names of the blues singers who had played a National Steel. Lonnie Johnson was the one we both cared most about.

I See the Joker

As I recall, I started writing this lyric before the first *Godfather* movie came out, but by the time the song got into performance the audience easily recognized the references. My own formative gangster movies dated back to the time of *The Big Heat* (Lee Marvin ruins Gloria Grahame's face with hot coffee), *Murder Incorporated* with Humphrey Bogart, and the Rod Steiger version of *Al Capone*.

Sessionman's Blues

Back in the day, the sessionmen were heroes of mine. They were the musicians who could be relied upon to come into the studio, read the music, and play it correctly first time. A lot of well-known musicians were denied a reliable source of income because they couldn't do this.

Shadow and the Widower

As in my later poem 'The Shadow Knows', the shadowy widower came from Nerval's *El Desdichado*: *'Je suis le Ténébreux – le Veuf . . .'* The source of 'The perfume and suppliance of a minute' was *Hamlet*: Laertes warns his sister Ophelia that the wooing of the Prince can't be relied on. In my earlier lyrics I often took pleasure in piecing lines and phrases from Renaissance plays and poems into the scheme, counting it as a form of theft legitimized by the way it declared itself. A three-sheet was a publicity poster that was pasted up in three sections, like a cheap triptych. The 'lineaments of gratified desire' were from Blake.

Screen-freak

This one is a catalogue song *in extremis*, with the drawback that a lot of the movie references have gone hopelessly out of date. As Peter Bogdanovich once told me, it isn't only that young people don't know who Moses was when you talk about Charlton Heston starring as Moses, they don't know who Charlton Heston was. But I remain proud of my line 'Atlantis down in bubbles and Atlanta up in flames'. At least most people still know that Atlanta burns in *Gone with the Wind*. If the movie were remade today, the burning would be accomplished by CGI, but Selznick had to burn down the set. For *Broken Lance*, however, there is no eternal life. It was one of the first CinemaScope movies, and on a TV screen it looks like nothing. Only when you get to the Fred and Ginger level does immortality kick in. The caliph in the caftan was usually played by George Macready while Piper Laurie waited to be rescued by Gordon MacRae, all three of them unaware that one day even the film buffs would forget their names. Gone, gone: with the wind.

A King at Nightfall

My own considered critical opinion is that each of Eliot's *Four Quartets* is better than the others, but that 'Little Gidding' takes the prize. The nightfall king is flagged near the beginning but makes his full impact near the end, after the fabulous intermediate section which echoes the sequence in *Inferno* where Dante walks with the ghost of his old teacher Brunetto Latini. Scholarly comment largely agrees that Eliot, in his version, walks with the ghost of Yeats, but I always saw myself as the third man, listening in.

Apparition in Las Vegas

In his second last phase, before he was finally enslaved by the deadly combination of cocaine, hamburgers and bad caped costumes, Elvis Presley made marvellous music. Much of it he made in Las Vegas. None of it was quite as good as the 1968 concert, in which he sat there relatively immobile in black leather while a bunch of veteran guitarists rocked up a storm. (Preserved on video, the concert still hasn't reached YouTube at the time of this writing: you have to buy it, in one of those strange cash transactions peculiar to early capitalism.) But he would still give the Las Vegas audiences the best he could do, even when miles overweight and clad in an outfit that made him look like Abba rolled into one. Both Pete and I thought the world of him, with reservations; which, when you come to think of it, is what anyone sensible thinks of the world itself. It will be seen from the lyric that I thought I had the old people well summed up. Pete was too sensible to think the same, and in his music he was careful to give some of the heroic dignity to the pink-rinsed audience.

Touch Has a Memory

The title line is from Keats, in a mysterious, distraught and song-like love poem to an unnamed addressee. 'Touch has a memory.

Oh say, love, say/ What can I do to kill it and be free/ In my old liberty?' In that mood he was practically Leonard Cohen: all he needed was a trilby hat.

The Rider to the World's End

The title line is a tip of the hat to the late Lex Banning, a palsied poet of Sydney's Downtown Push whom I met briefly and still admire. (The very pretty Edwards & Shaw edition of his only collection *Apocalypse in Springtime* is in the bookcase before me as I compose this note.) He once wrote that a row of men fishing with rods looked like illustrations from Euclid. I spent a lot of time wondering how he thought of that. Luckily, in those days, I still had time to burn. The narrator of the lyric is cursing himself for his own unreliability. Feckless men when young often believe that a confession absolves them.

No Dice

The lyric with a multiple narrator in a multiple setting was a way for its author to be anyone and everywhere. Pete's task was to unite the multiplicity with the music, and thus suggest that there can be a coherence in chaos. The test lay in the performance. Would the audience realize, as the song unfolded, that the puzzle had a point? The evidence suggested that they enjoyed the tease, and over the years we wrote several songs with a similar approach, although always, I hope, with a different array of themes. The LVT (Landing Vehicle Tracked) was used by the American forces in the Pacific, most famously by the Marines at Tarawa. The Incas really did hide their gold in a lake.

Driving through Mythical America

This was the title track of Pete's second commercial album. The multiple narrative hinges on the traumatic event at Kent State University, where the National Guard fired on protesting students, killing four of them. Eddie Prue is the psychotic killer in Raymond Chandler's novel *The Little Sister*. Moose Malloy is the star hoodlum from another Chandler novel, *Farewell My Lovely*. Herman Kahn was a guru who pioneered the art of earning large fees from predicting what the world would be like far enough ahead so that nobody of mature years would be able to check up on what he had predicted. Lavishly supported with pie-charts and elastic statistics, his expert-sounding spiel helped to generate the thousands of futurologists who pull the same stunt now. Bogart said 'Even the dead can talk' in the film *Murder Incorporated*.

Thief in the Night

A lament half-disguised as a catalogue song, this lyric brings in the deep grief of a blues singer (Big Bill Broonzy) and also the glittering melancholy added by Charlie Christian to the Benny Goodman small groups that I so adored. I would have put Django Reinhardt into the same frame except that he gave me too much joy, and at the time I preferred to register despair. Another of my favourites was Ry Cooder, but he was too recent: there needed to be a touch of nostalgia, of looking back in hunger. Luckily Pete made the melody a rabble-rouser, and the song has always been a hit in the clubs. Backstage in the theatre, the 'beginners' call' is the intercom signal from the stage-manager that tells the actors in the first scene it's time to get to work. As Footlights performers we were both familiar with it.

Practical Man

Although it is true that we ended up taking out an injunction against our first agent, we would both have liked to meet a Practical Man who really was practical. The music business in those days was too much of a jungle to navigate unguided. It will be noticed that the Practical Man in the song is cultivated as well as rich. But from my angle he was all too practical; although it was the merest posturing on my part to write a line like 'There are just some songs that are not for sale'. We would have dearly liked to sell some songs, if only to keep eating: but the music business in those days was all against it, because we had started writing songs to be sung by other people at the exact moment in history when the singers had started writing their own songs so that they could be paid twice. Nowadays the music business has collapsed completely and the Practical Man is doing something else, such as delivering lectures on sustainability, or calling you up to say that the bank owes you money.

Beware of the Beautiful Stranger

The revelatory female face has been a theme for poetry since Homer raved about Helen in the *Iliad,* and not even the *Divine Comedy* would be the miracle it is if Dante had not had an eye for the girls. But in real life no woman wants to hear from a writer that he worships women, or even that he worships an abstract woman called the Muse. She wants to hear that he worships her. Nevertheless the theme, or dream, drives on. This lyric was one of my earliest statements of it. At first I thought Pete would never be able to set a stanza so four-square and regular. He did so by repeatedly, but not predictably, altering the spaces. The song was, of course, far too long to record as a single; but we were still taking pride in asking the impossible. It will be noticed that the Beautiful Stranger is not described; but then, Helen's beauty is not described by Homer, he just evokes it by describing how thousands of men react when they see her.

Have You Got a Biro I Can Borrow?

This song would have been on the all-important BBC playlist but they told us that 'Biro' was a brand name and we would have to alter it. I'm afraid I must take responsibility for an expensive digging in of the heels. Faced with a similar demand, the Rolling

Stones didn't hesitate. Listen to what Pete's melody does to my line 'So when the sun comes up tomorrow' and you see what music can do to apparently simple words. Jean Renoir in his autobiography tells us that his father, crippled with arthritis, said 'Tie the brush into my hands'.

Laughing Boy

This lyric was so clearly a personal *cri de coeur* that when we were on stage together Pete asked me to join in the singing. On tour in Britain, Australia and Hong Kong we would close the show with it, always carefully telling the audience beforehand that it was one of the first things we ever wrote together. Many years later, at the other end of my life, the landlady with the pressed flowers showed up again in my poem 'Grief Has Its Time'.

Thirty-year Man

The title I got from the novel by James Jones, *From Here to Eternity*, which I read at school before the movie came out. The book's hero Robert E. Lee Prewitt wasn't a short-time soldier, he was signed up for thirty years. When young writers ask for advice, I always try to tell them that they shouldn't dabble with this stuff, but get into it for life. Deaf ears, usually. But so had I, in the beginning. Determination emerges: it can't be instilled.

Carnations on the Roof

I got the idea for this lyric when I was working in London at a Holloway sheet-metal factory before I went up to Cambridge, but at first I thought it might be a poem, and didn't realize until later that it had to be a song lyric. At the base of the theme is the conviction that the labourer is worthy of his hire. After the war from which my father failed to return I would play with the gauges and spirit levels in his metal toolkit and imagine that my future lay in the machine shop, which is more or less how things turned out, although the things I make fold into books. My earliest Fleet Street editor and dear lost friend Nicholas Tomalin was kind enough to say, on the basis of this one song, that what we were doing was something strange, new and worth pursuing. If he had not been killed when covering the Yom Kippur War I would be still trying to impress him now.

The Hypertension Kid

In my experience, writers bent on self-destruction rarely write about self-destruction: they write about rose gardens. But there can be no doubt that I have always had within me a desire to take my place just one more time at the bar of the Early Quitter. Pete always liked this lyric more than I did: I prefer not to recognize the two speakers, but perhaps he knows them well.

Perfect Moments

Purist scholars of Charlie Parker might say that his solo on 'My Old Flame', recorded when he was near death, is a bit of a wreck: but in Cambridge I would play it over and over, close to weeping. It's a great song anyway: even Mae West can touch your heart with it.

Secret Drinker

Hart Crane used to call it 'wine talons': the grip of the grape. After I gave up drinking, by public demand, I found it easier to describe why the hooch was so glamorous for those susceptible to its embrace. But even when I was still regularly smashed I was lyrical on the subject. From the angle of civic responsibility, it surely makes more sense to evoke the attractions of a vice than to deplore its results. The obvious love poured into this lyric should be a clear warning to stay clear of the stuff. Or anyway, that's my rationale for having had such a luxurious time putting the images together. Pete, whose idea of a binge was to drink a whole half-pint in a single evening, was nevertheless inspired to a sympathetic melodic line, as if he, too, had dipped his head into liquid hell and drawn back just before the shark struck.

Tenderfoot

Before the spaghetti westerns stripped the genre of its last plausibility, the Western movies were a vast reserve of poetic *angst*, and in the cinemas of Sydney, London and Cambridge I spent a lot of time imagining myself tall in the saddle, the lone rider in search of absolution. Even today, with the last round-up entering its final phase, I still see myself riding towards the distant mountains while young Brandon deWilde cries 'Come back, Shane!'. So when I planned this lyric I had a lot of resonance to go on. Hence the operatic layout: to make room. As in all episodic lyrics, however, it's the music that supplies the shape. Ian Bostridge explains a lot about the structure of a song in his marvellous book *Schubert's Winter Journey*. Writing songs like the ones in *Winterreise*, Schubert didn't really need to write an opera. It was all happening within earshot.

Care-charmer Sleep

When the English Renaissance poet Samuel Daniel used the lovely phrase 'care-charmer sleep' to open a sonnet, it was an instant hit. Michael Drayton used the same phrase within the line instead of at the start. Dial the phrase into the Web and you can soon find a thesis devoted to Daniel by one George Keyports Brady, submitted for a PhD at the University of Illinois in 1923. Punctiliously written, the ideal introduction to the whole area of Petrarchan poetry in Europe, Brady's thesis is full of hard learning in several languages and would serve all on its own to make you wonder about those thousands of PhD theses in the humanities today, almost invariably devoted to shuffling theories about a subject that can't be theorized about, but only studied, and not even studied if it is not loved.

Canoe

When very young I was impressed by a sequence of photographs in the *National Geographic* that showed young male Polynesian canoeists studying star maps made of stones and sticks. The maps allowed them to navigate by the constellations. In performance, the song holds the audience by the way the two stories are woven together by the melody: listeners soon realize that the apparent discrepancy between the two voyages is a single tribute to human endeavour.

I Feel Like Midnight

John Garfield says the title line in the movie *Force of Evil*, which Abraham Polonsky both wrote and directed. After refusing to testify before HUAC, Polonsky was blacklisted and didn't return to directing until *Tell Them Willie Boy Is Here*. A Marxist until the end, Polonsky, when Elia Kazan was given a lifetime achievement Academy Award, said that somebody ought to shoot him on the night, so as to liven the proceedings up. Kazan had sung to the committee and Polonsky never did, so it was hard not to admire one of them more than the other. Polonsky had, on the other hand, proselytized all his life on behalf of one of the most horrible regimes in history. But he could write, and there is seldom any real substitute for that.

The Eye of the Universe

In Shelley's poem 'Hymn of Apollo' it is the narrator who says 'I am the eye with which the universe/ Beholds itself and knows it is divine.' (A variant printing is 'knows itself divine' which is the one I borrowed.) Shelley might just as well have said it of himself. With varying degrees of tact, it is a belief all poets share: why else work so hard for so little reward? From personal knowledge of the narrator, however, I know him to have been lying when he said that he had found himself 'redeemed'. High on the list of things I have never believed is the Wagnerian notion of redemption, but I still find it astonishing that Pete could give such integrated melodies to so much written evidence of inner fragmentation.

History and Geography

The lines about 'the daughters of my father's house and all the brothers too' are spoken by Viola to Orsino in *Twelfth Night*, Act II Scene 4. When we were first writing songs in Footlights, Shakespeare productions were going on all the time all around us, and some of the Footlights comedians were doubling as serious actors, thus giving themselves an enhanced opportunity to neglect the set books and come away with a ruinous degree. There were very few actors who ever got a First, but they all knew more about Shakespeare than the proper scholars did, and the proper scholars, to give them their due credit, were aware of the fact, and incorporated the thrill of the performances into their learning.

Femme Fatale

The 'weeping fields' are Virgil's *lugentes campos*. Perhaps the best translation of the phrase was by the old scholar J. W. Mackail: 'the broken-hearted fields'. While at Cambridge I taught myself quite a lot of classical poetry. The circumstances were ideal: there were undergraduates all over the place who had been through the English public schools and could tell you where the best bits of poetry were in the acres of text. In the New Hall annexe where my wife and I had our first apartment, there was a young graduate student from New Zealand who would put her finger right on the indispensable passages in Homer and get me to recite until I could make a fair fist of the metre: sometimes, I learned, the way the rhythm worked was half the point of the line. Disciplinarians might have frowned at the shortcut but we rarely enjoy seeing someone acquire, just from love, the knowledge that was imparted to us at the point of a cane. Pete's melody makes a subtle virtue of how the final lines of all three stanzas are a metrical match.

A Hill of Little Shoes

The subject matter is too sacred to permit any experimentation, but really this lyric is an exercise in the special form of the aria for the opera that cannot exist. Pete understood immediately what was required for the music: monumentality, but with a legato line. I should say, for a final note to these lyrics and a final note to the whole book, that I have always fully understood Adorno's insistence that there could be no poetry after Auschwitz. I understood it, but I didn't believe it. The question was already there when Thucydides described the first extermination camps, the quarries of Syracuse in which the Athenians were left to starve; and the answer was already there in the magisterial cadence of his prose. Poetry is a form of knowledge, not of therapy; and nothing that humans do can be beyond its reach.

Index of Titles

Index of First Lines

In the Great Rift, the wildebeest wheel and run, *385*
In the last year of her life I dined with Diana Cooper *142*
In the NHS psychiatric test *247*
Installed in my last house, I face the thought *425*
It isn't fear I feel, or lack of nerve *519*
It may not come to this, but if I should *398*
It's cold without the softness of a fall *12*

John Donne, uneasiest of apostates, *127*

Kogarah (suppress the first 'a' and it scans) *148*

Last night I drank with a practical man *479*
Last night I met the Hypertension Kid *495*
Last night the sea dreamed it was Greta Scacchi. *88*
Late summer charms the birds out of the trees *112*
Let him so keen for casting the first stone *146*
Look back and you can almost pick the minute *382*

Mask wet and snorkel dry, I'm lying loose *193*
May the Lord have mercy on all those peoples *51*
Merely a planchet waiting to be struck, *318*
More valuable than all of mine, your book *360*
Mornings now I breakfast in the tower *451*
My brother lives in fear *516*
My cataracts invest the bright spring day *409*
My latest fever clad me in cold sweat *410*
My niece is heading here to stay with us. *433*
My tears came late. I was fifty-five years old *120*

Neat name for the machine *327*
Never filmed, he was photographed only once, *108*
No moons are left to see the other side of. *38*
Nobody here yet *491*
Not gold but some base alloy, it stays good *58*

O magic wheel, draw hither to my house the man I love. *294*
Of late I try to kill my payday evenings *460*

The sky is silent. All the planes must keep *332*
The stars in their magnificent array *423*
The sun seems in control, the tide is out: *426*
The unbridled phallus of the philosopher *44*
The way his broken spirit almost healed *151*
The way my arms around you touch the centre of my being *455*
The way the bamboo leans out of the frame, *282*
The wild White Nun, rarest and loveliest *309*
They were all dying for her, *352*
Things worn out by the lapse of ages tend *131*
This afternoon the ice-cream man *446*
This is the way that winter says goodbye to spring *525*
This kind of ocean fails to reach the coast *499*
This one we didn't know we didn't know: *231*
Tired out from getting up and getting dressed *428*
To catch your eye in Paris, Tom, *178*
To Gore Vidal at – how should I commence? *190*
To stay, as Mr Larkin stays, back late *165*
Today in Castlereagh Street I *140*
Too frail to fly, I may not see again *399*
Too many of my friends are dead, and others wrecked *303*
Touch has a memory *470*
Triangular Macquarie Place, up from the Quay, *55*
Two of her little pictures grace my walls: *421*
Two winter plum trees grow beside my door. *430*

Under the jacarandas *223*

Van Wyck Brooks tells us Whitman in old age *363*

Was it twenty years ago I met that couple *314*
We never built our grand house on the edge *371*
"Were you not more than just a pretty face *325*
what time el Rouble & la Dollar spin *157*
When Kaganovich, brother-in-law of Stalin, *90*
When Mrs Taflan Gruffydd-Lewis left Dai's flat *164*
When the King of Rock and Roll sang in the desert *467*
When we were kids we fought in the mock battle *242*